PAUL SIMON

Tempo
A Rowman & Littlefield Music Series on Rock, Pop, and Culture

Series Editor: Scott Calhoun

Tempo: A Rowman & Littlefield Music Series on Rock, Pop, and Culture offers titles that explore rock and popular music through the lens of social and cultural history, revealing the dynamic relationship between musicians, music, and their milieu. Like other major art forms, rock and pop music comment on their cultural, political, and even economic situation, reflecting the technological advances, psychological concerns, religious feelings, and artistic trends of their times. Contributions to the **Tempo** series are the ideal introduction to major pop and rock artists and genres.

Bob Dylan: American Troubadour, by Donald Brown
Bon Jovi: America's Ultimate Band, by Margaret Olson
British Invasion: The Crosscurrents of Musical Influence, by Simon Philo
Bruce Springsteen: American Poet and Prophet, by Donald L. Deardorff II
Patti Smith: America's Punk Rock Rhapsodist, by Eric Wendell
Paul Simon: An American Tune, by Cornel Bonca
Ska: The Rhythm of Liberation, by Heather Augustyn

PAUL SIMON

An American Tune

Cornel Bonca

ROWMAN & LITTLEFIELD
Lanham • Boulder • New York • London

Published by Rowman & Littlefield
A wholly owned subsidiary of The Rowman & Littlefield Publishing Group,
Inc.
4501 Forbes Boulevard, Suite 200, Lanham, Maryland 20706
www.rowman.com

16 Carlisle Street, London W1D 3BT, United Kingdom

British Library Cataloguing in Publication Information Available

Library of Congress Cataloging-in-Publication Data

Bonca, Cornel, 1958–
Paul Simon : an American tune / Cornel Bonca.
pages cm. – (Tempo : a Rowman & Littlefield music series on rock, pop, and culture)
Includes bibliographical references and index.
ISBN 978-0-8108-8481-6 (cloth : alk. paper) – ISBN 978-0-8108-8482-3 (ebook)
1. Simon, Paul, 1941– –Criticism and interpretation. 2. Popular music–United States–History and
criticism. I. Title.
ML420.S563B66 2015
782.42164092–dc23
2014023319

Printed in the United States of America

This is for Angel
and
Alexey,
Nicolai, and
Annalise.

CONTENTS

SERIES EDITOR'S FOREWORD

Paul Simon: An American Tune

As a fellow English major, I'm relieved to know Paul Simon not only found work upon his graduation but also was able to use his degree to do what he liked. He's made a living in the world of words, wrangling sound, sense, and meaning from them. I feel a swell of pride, too, for his having made it. And boy, has he made it. Pop icon. Consummate lyricist. Poet. Nearly unparalleled in popular song for his voice and virtuosity as a musician, Simon is one of the few narrators to have kept pace with Bob Dylan's quality of comment on the American story. He's a hero to the bookish set, the introverts, the readers of rhythm and rhyme, who believe in figurative language, and that by speaking—by sounding—we can bring into existence beautiful questions and answers to save us all.

From modernist beginnings as the Jewish boy growing up middle class in mid-twentieth-century Queens, Simon seemingly had only his own ambition, self-awareness, and physical stature to overcome. A father's approval set him in motion and his mother's devotion gave young Paul the right stuff to become half of Simon & Garfunkel and then much more as a soloist. Witty, wry, and a quick study of pop song forms, Simon sailed through the streets of Greenwich Village in the 1960s to embark on a career as a pop-folk hero in the 1970s. Taking a turn in the 1980s to explore the African and Caribbean roots of

American pop and rock swelled him to even greater heights even before he had shown signs of sinking.

Simon's steady hand on the wheel of his professional career, though, is not all from his confidence as a navigator. There's as much the grip of trepidation in him borne out of steering into storms of personal uncertainties. Simon has the modernist's attraction to ambiguity, the mystic's search for eternity, the optimist's hope of victory, and the romantic's embrace of melancholy. Most of his songbook features all four dispositions in sublimely intricate arrangements. A standout example is "American Tune," a song in which he took both the melody and meaning of the chorale in Bach's *St. Matthew Passion*, popularly known as "O Sacred Head, Now Wounded," in order to state his own resolve to keep sailing on. Simon was thirty-two when he released the song in 1973 on his second solo album after the breakup of Simon & Garfunkel. Unbeknownst to everyone at the time, he wasn't even midway through his odyssey.

Simon's sensitivities and insecurities have been well-attuned from the start of his career. He could deliver a song full of youthful spirit and American zest, which he often did as a young songwriter and performer, particularly when working with Art Garfunkel. Yet inevitably, naturally, a song from beyond his years followed close behind, wondering if he had not, instead, lost something precious. There has always been as much Prufrock in Simon's love songs as pure pop, which speaks volumes about what we most want from the singer-songwriter in light of Simon's long and lustrous career. We may be a proud, confident nation, with an inestimable wealth of resources both raw and refined, but we often worry if we have, in fact, missed the plot of life. We too often feel alone and fear we have, indeed, been asking the wrong questions.

How encouraging it is, then, to hear Simon sing what courses through our hearts and bones, too. We are not the sole sailor on this ship. In his voice, in his exquisite tenor, still strong at the age of seventy, our humanity sounds more lovely. We are reminded there is enough mysterious beauty to encourage us for the rest of our days. Paul Simon's great gift is in making the journey for answers a more hopeful voyage.

Scott Calhoun

TIMELINE

World and Cultural Events

December 7, 1941: Japan attacks Pearl Harbor; United States enters World War II against Axis Powers.

Spring 1945: Nazi concentration camps discovered by Allied troops. Germany surrenders; Adolf Hitler dies in Berlin bunker.

August 6 and 8, 1945: United States drops atomic bombs on Hiroshima and Nagasaki.

August 14, 1945: Japan surrenders. World War II ends. Cold War begins with Soviet Union.

1950: Beginning of "McCarthy Era" or "Second Red Scare" (ends circa 1956).

Paul Simon's Life and Career

October 13, 1941: Paul Simon born in Newark, New Jersey.

1945: Simon family moves to Kew Gardens, Queens, New York.

World and Cultural Events	*Paul Simon's Life and Career*
June 1950: United States enters the Korean War.	
January 1953: Dwight D. Eisenhower assumes presidency.	
June 1953: Korean War ends.	**Summer 1953:** Paul meets Art Garfunkel during rehearsals for sixth-grade class play, *Alice in Wonderland*.
May 1954: Brown vs. Board of Education case decided by U.S. Supreme Court: segregation in public schools declared unconstitutional.	
Summer 1954: Elvis Presley records Sun Sessions in Memphis studio. Beginning of Rock Era.	
December 1955: Rosa Parks, arrested for civil disobedience, jumpstarts modern Civil Rights movement. Bill Haley's "Rock around the Clock" tops Billboard charts for eight straight weeks, certifying rock music as a powerful new commercial force.	**1955:** Simon and Art Garfunkel, now singing partners, attend Forest Hills High School together and play local gigs.
September 1956: Elvis Presley appears on *The Ed Sullivan Show*.	**1956:** Paul Simon watches Elvis Presley on The *Ed Sullivan Show*.
1957: Everly Brothers become big stars with "Bye Bye Love" and "Wake Up Little Susie."	**1957:** Simon and Garfunkel record Everly Brothers–influenced "Hey Schoolgirl" under the name Tom & Jerry. The single sells 100,000 copies and earns them a spot on *American Bandstand*.

World and Cultural Events	*Paul Simon's Life and Career*
September 1957: National Guard oversees school desegregation in Little Rock, Arkansas.	
October 1957: U.S.S.R. launches *Sputnik*.	
	1958: Simon, recording as Tom & Jerry and True Taylor, releases three more singles, all of which bomb, and a full-length album with Garfunkel, *Tom & Jerry*, which is not released in America until 1967.
1959: Newport Folk Festival vitalizes folk movement in the United States. Greenwich Village in New York City becomes folk-music mecca.	**1959:** Simon, while attending Queens College as an English major, records and releases five more failed singles under the pseudonyms Tom & Jerry, Jerry Landis, and the Mystics. Garfunkel gives up music temporarily, and the duo split up.
1960: Michelangelo Antonioni's film *L'Avventura* is released, followed in 1961 and 1962 by *La Notte* and *L'Elisse*.	**1960:** Simon, while continuing to record teeny bopper rock 'n' roll, begins to frequent Village folk clubs like Café Wha and Gerde's Folk City.
January 1961: John F. Kennedy becomes president.	
Summer 1961: "Freedom riders" intensify Civil Rights movement in the South.	
August 1961: The Berlin Wall is erected: Cold War tensions increase.	

World and Cultural Events	*Paul Simon's Life and Career*
April 1962: Bob Dylan releases debut album, *Bob Dylan*.	
October 1962: Cuban Missile Crisis brings world to brink of nuclear war.	**Fall 1962:** Simon and Garfunkel reconnect, now share a love of folk music.
May 1963: Landmark folk album, *Freewheelin' Bob Dylan*, is released, featuring "Blowin' in the Wind" and "A Hard Rain's A-Gonna Fall."	**1963:** Simon graduates from Queens College, spends summer in Paris. That fall, enrolls in Brooklyn Law School, then quits after one semester. Simon and Garfunkel start playing Village clubs. Tom Wilson, Dylan's producer, helps them get signed to Columbia Records.
August 1963: Martin Luther King, Jr. delivers "I have a dream" speech at the March on Washington.	
November 22, 1963: President Kennedy assassinated in Dallas, TX. Vice President Lyndon Johnson assumes the presidency.	
January 1964: *Meet the Beatles!* released in the United States; by spring, the Beatles hold the top five singles on Billboard Top 100.	
	March 1964: Simon & Garfunkel record their first album. Afterward, Simon travels to England, meets Kathy Chitty, and plays folk circuit in and around London.
June 1964: Goodman, Schwerner, and Chaney murdered	

World and Cultural Events	*Paul Simon's Life and Career*
during Mississippi "freedom ride," sparking national outrage.	
July 1964: The Civil Rights Act of 1964 signed into law by President Lyndon Johnson.	
August 7, 1964: The Gulf of Tonkin Resolution passes in Congress, authorizing military force in Vietnam. Massive military buildup begins.	
	October 1964: *Wednesday Morning, 3 A.M.* released. The album sells poorly.
1965: Colin Wilson's *The Outsider* published.	**January 1965:** Simon returns to England and performs as "poet and a one-man band."
March 1965: Dylan's *Bringing It All Back Home*, featuring electric instruments and rock arrangements, released. Folk rock is born.	
	May 1965: Simon records *The Paul Simon Songbook*. Released by CBS International, it also sells poorly.
	June 1965: During a break in the recording of Dylan's "Like a Rolling Stone," producer Tom Wilson overdubs electric instruments onto "The Sound of Silence." The folk-rock version is released without Simon's knowledge, and enters the charts in September. Simon returns to New York.

World and Cultural Events	Paul Simon's Life and Career
July 20, 1965: Dylan's "Like a Rolling Stone" released.	
August 1965: Dylan's *Highway 61 Revisited* released.	
	December 1965: "The Sound of Silence" tops the American singles charts. Simon & Garfunkel record their second album.
	January 1966: *Sounds of Silence* released. A #21 hit in America.
	October 1966: *Parsley, Sage, Rosemary, and Thyme* released. Reaches #4 in America.
1967: Massive demonstrations against the Vietnam War throughout the year.	**1967:** Simon & Garfunkel enter studio to work on next studio release.Simon helps organize Monterey Pop Festival.
June 1, 1967: The Beatles' *Sgt. Pepper* released.	Film director Mike Nichols asks Simon to contribute music to his next film, *The Graduate*.
June 1967: Arab-Israeli Conflict ("Six-Day War").	
June 16–18, 1967: Monterey Pop Festival.	
June–September 1967: "Summer of Love" in San Francisco.	
	December 1967: *The Graduate* (film) released. Becomes one of the biggest hits of the 1960s.
January 1968: The Tet Offensive: North Vietnam mounts massive counteroffensive, making clear the Vietnam War could last for years.	**January 1968:** Soundtrack to *The Graduate* released. Goes to #2.

World and Cultural Events	Paul Simon's Life and Career
April 4, 1968: Martin Luther King Jr. assassinated, followed by riots in D.C.	**April 1968:** *Bookends* released. Goes to #1.
April 1968: President Johnson announces he will not run for reelection.	
May 1968: Student uprisings in Paris.	
June 1968: Robert Kennedy assassinated.	
January 1969: Richard Nixon becomes President.	**January 1969:** Garfunkel goes to Mexico to film *Catch-22* for six months, occasionally returning to New York to help Simon record their fifth studio album. The sessions are extremely strained.
	March 1969: "Mrs. Robinson" wins Grammys for Record of the Year and Best Contemporary Pop Vocal Performance. *The Graduate* wins for Best Soundtrack Album.
July 1969: Apollo 11 mission successful: man walks on the moon.	
August 1969: Woodstock Festival, New York.	
	Fall 1969: Garfunkel announces he will star in *Carnal Knowledge*. Simon marries Peggy Harper.
	November 30, 1969: Simon & Garfunkel film, *Songs for America*, appears on television.

World and Cultural Events	Paul Simon's Life and Career
December 8, 1969: Disastrous Rolling Stones show at Altamont Raceway.	
	February 1970: *Bridge Over Troubled Water* released. Tops album chart, selling 5 million units in the United States. The duo tour in the United States and the U.K.
April 1970: The Beatles break up.	
May 1970: National Guard open fire on antiwar protesters at Kent State University: four students are killed.	
	August 1970: Simon appears for first time as solo artist at a benefit at Shea Stadium.
September 18, 1970: Jimi Hendrix dies.	
October 4, 1970: Janis Joplin dies.	**Fall 1970:** Simon & Garfunkel break up.
	Winter 1971: Simon begins recording first solo album.
	March 1971: Simon & Garfunkel win six Grammy awards for *Bridge Over Troubled Water*.
June 3, 1971: Jim Morrison dies.	
	January 1972: *Paul Simon* released. Reaches #4 on U.S. charts. Simon decides not to tour.
June 1972: Republican operatives break into Democratic National Headquarters at the	**June 1972:** *Simon & Garfunkel's Greatest Hits* released. Ultimately sells 14 million copies in the

World and Cultural Events	*Paul Simon's Life and Career*
Watergate hotel. "Watergate" scandal begins.	United States alone.
	September 1972: Paul and Peggy's son, Harper, born.
November 1972: Richard Nixon reelected.	**November 1972:** *Songs of Paul Simon*, a comprehensive collection of Simon's music, published in book form.
January 1973: Ceasefire announced in Vietnam War.	
May–August 1973: "Watergate" hearings are televised, riveting the nation.	**May 1973:** *There Goes Rhymin' Simon* released. Climbs to #2 on American charts, and includes "American Tune," named Song of the Year by *Rolling Stone*. Simon embarks on first major solo tour.
October 1973: Vice president Spiro Agnew charged with extortion and bribery, resigns from office. **October 1973:** 1973 Arab-Israeli War.	
1974: Disco music becomes mainstream pop.	**1974:** Paul and Peggy Simon separate.
	March 1974: *Paul Simon: Live Rhymin'* released. Tops out at #33 on charts.
August 9, 1974: Nixon resigns the presidency. Gerald Ford becomes president.	
April 1975: The fall of Saigon ends the Vietnam War.	**1975:** Paul and Peggy Simon's divorce finalized.

World and Cultural Events	*Paul Simon's Life and Career*
August 1975: Bruce Springsteen's *Born to Run* released.	
September 1975: Assassination attempts on President Ford.	
	October 1975: *Still Crazy after All These Years* released. First of Simon's solo releases to reach #1.
July 1976: U.S. celebrates Bicentennial.	**1976:** Simon takes first extended break from recording and/or touring since 1964.
	March 1976: Simon wins two Grammys for *Still Crazy after All These Years*.
January 1977: Jimmy Carter becomes president.	
	April 1977: *Annie Hall* opens, featuring Simon in a small but important role.
October 1977: Sex Pistols' *Never Mind the Bollocks*, the first breakthrough punk album, released.	
	November 1977: First solo best-of, *Greatest Hits, etc.*, released. "Slip-Sliding Away" becomes a hit single from the album.
	1978: Simon begins relationship with Carrie Fisher.
July 1979: President Carter's "malaise" speech.	**1979:** Simon works on *One-Trick Pony*. Terminates contract with Columbia Records and signs with Warner Brothers Records.

World and Cultural Events

Paul Simon's Life and Career

November 1979: Americans taken hostage by Iranians at American embassy in Tehran.

August 1980: The film and soundtrack for *One-Trick Pony* released. The film bombs, the soundtrack reaches #6 on U.S. charts. Simon tours.

December 1980: John Lennon assassinated in New York City.

January 20, 1981: Ronald Reagan inaugurated as president. American hostages held in Iran released the same day.

March 1981: Assassination attempt wounds President Reagan.

Spring 1981: Depressed and suffering writer's block, Simon goes into therapy with Rod Gorney. Begins writing music again.

July 1981: Israel bombs Beirut. Major American recession begins. Continues through end of 1982.

August 1981: MTV debuts.

September 19, 1981: Simon & Garfunkel reunite for *Concert in Central Park*. Simon & Garfunkel attempt to make a new studio album together, and fail. Simon finishes the album on his own.

February 1982: *Concert in Central Park* live album released. Goes double platinum.

July 1982: Grandmaster Flash and the Furious Five's "The

World and Cultural Events

Message," landmark of early hip hop, released.

1983: Compact discs introduced in the United States.

March 1983: Reagan calls the Soviet Union an "evil empire" in a speech; announces Strategic Defense ("Star Wars") Initiative.

1984: Michael Jackson, Madonna, Bruce Springsteen, and Prince reign as pop megastars.

November 1984: Reagan reelected in landslide.

January 1985: "We Are the World" benefit single recorded in Los Angeles. Becomes biggest-selling song in history.

Paul Simon's Life and Career

November 1982: Michael Jackson's *Thriller* released.

August 1983: Simon marries Carrie Fisher.

November 1983: *Hearts and Bones* released. First solo album not to hit top 10 in America.

Summer 1984: Simon hears Mbaqanga or "township jive" for first time. Immerses himself in South African music.

July 1984: Simon and Fisher file for divorce.

January 1985: Simon participates in recording of "We Are the World."

February 1985: Simon records with South African musicians in Johannesburg, South Africa. Returns to New York City to complete next studio album, with side trips to New Orleans, London, and Los Angeles.

World and Cultural Events	*Paul Simon's Life and Career*
October 1985: Actor Rock Hudson dies of AIDS; American awareness of AIDS increases exponentially.	
January 1986: Space Shuttle *Challenger* blows up during launch, live on TV.	
	September 1986: *Graceland* released. Becomes a worldwide hit and cultural phenomenon, selling 14 million copies. Simon is blacklisted by African National Congress for breaching the cultural boycott of South Africa.
November 1986: Iran-Contra scandal erupts.	
October 1987: Worldwide stock market crash.	**1987:** Simon begins massively successful but controversial U.S. and world tour to promote *Graceland*.
	March 1987: *Graceland* awarded Album of the Year Grammy.
	March 1988: "Graceland" awarded Song of the Year Grammy.
November 1988: George Herbert Walker Bush elected president.	
November 1989: Berlin Wall "falls." Border opens between East and West Germany. Eastern bloc begins to fall apart.	**1989:** Simon travels to Brazil to record with Brazilian and West African players in preparation for next studio album.
March 1990: Public Enemy's *Fear of a Black Planet* released.	**1990:** *The Rhythm of the Saints* released. Reaches #4 on American

World and Cultural Events	*Paul Simon's Life and Career*
Hip hop now part of the commercial mainstream.	chart, and goes double platinum. Simon meets Edie Brickell on set of Saturday Night Live. Simon & Garfunkel are inducted into the Rock 'n' Roll Hall of Fame.
August 1990: Iraq invades Kuwait; United States retaliates with Operation Desert Storm, a U.S.-led invasion of Iraq by a UN coalition. The Gulf War begins.	
February 1991: Cease-fire in the Gulf War.	**1991:** Simon goes on world tour to support *The Rhythm of the Saints*. In August, he plays Central Park (without Garfunkel) before 750,000 fans. *Paul Simon's Concert in the Park* released later that year.
March 1991: The reunification of East and West Germany.	
December 1991: U.S.S.R. dissolves. The Cold War ends: a "New World Order" begins.	
May 1992: The Serbian siege of Sarajevo begins, the most deadly European conflict since World War II.	**May 1992:** Simon and Edie Brickell are married. Their son Adrian is born near the end of the year. Begins work on *The Capeman* with poet Derek Wolcott.
November 1992: Bill Clinton elected president.	
1993: North American Free Trade Agreement signed in United States, accelerating economic globalization.	**Fall 1993:** Simon & Garfunkel go on four-month world tour.

World and Cultural Events	*Paul Simon's Life and Career*
February 1994: NATO intervention in Bosnian Civil War begins.	**1994:** Simon produces Edie Brickell's *Picture Perfect Morning*. Works on *The Capeman*.
	March 1995: Simon's daughter Lulu born. Continues work on *The Capeman*.
1996: Official end to the siege of Sarajevo. **November 1996:** Bill Clinton reelected.	**1996:** Continues work on *The Capeman*.
	November 1997: *Songs from "The Capeman"* released. Stalls at #42 on American charts. *Old Friends*, three-CD box set of Simon & Garfunkel material, released and goes gold.
1998: The Monica Lewinsky scandal unfolds, endangering Clinton's presidency.	**January 1998:** After multiple delays, *The Capeman* opens on Broadway. Closes after 68 performances. Losses amount to $11 million.
	May 1998: Simon's son Gabriel born.
February 1999: President Clinton acquitted of impeachment charges.	
	June 1999: Begins Paul/Bob 99 Tour, co-headlining with Bob Dylan.
Fall 2000: The presidential election results contested in the Supreme Court. George W. Bush declared the winner.	**October 2000:** *You're the One* released. Goes gold in United States. Simon tours.

World and Cultural Events	*Paul Simon's Life and Career*
September 11, 2001: Al Qaeda terrorists highjack commercial airliners and fly two planes into New York City's World Trade Towers. A third plane damages the Pentagon. President Bush declares a "war on terror."	**2001:** Inducted into Rock 'n' Roll Hall of Fame as a solo artist.
October 2001: The United States invades Afghanistan	
	October 2003: Simon & Garfunkel reunite again, kicking off nine-month "Old Friends" tour.
March–May 2003: The United States invades Iraq, allegedly to capture "weapons of mass destruction." None are found. War continues till 2011.	
December 2003: Iraqi dictator Saddam Hussein is captured.	
November 2004: George W. Bush reelected.	
August 2005: Hurricane Katrina devastates the gulf coast in New Orleans.	
	October 2006: *Surprise* released. Goes to #14 in America and #4 in U.K. Simon tours. Honored in *Time Magazine* as one of "100 People Who Shaped the World."
November 2006: Midterm elections return control of	

World and Cultural Events	*Paul Simon's Life and Career*
Congress to Democrats; public support of the War in Iraq sinks.	
December 2006: Saddam Hussein is executed.	
	May 2007: Simon becomes first recipient of the Gershwin Prize for Popular Song.
September 2008: Global economic crisis leads to Great Recession.	
November 2008: Barack Obama becomes first African American to be elected president.	
	May 2009: Simon tours with Garfunkel in Australia, New Zealand, and Japan.
March 2010: Patient Protection and Affordable Care Act signed into law by President Obama.	**2010:** Signs with Sony Legacy: Simon's back catalogue henceforth to be handled by Sony.
	April 2011: *So Beautiful or So What* released on Concord Music Group label. Simon tours.
May 2011: Osama Bin Laden killed by U.S. Special Forces.	
September 2011: Occupy Wall Street camps spring up all over country, protesting U.S. economic policies favorable to "the 1%."	
December 2011: Iraq War ends.	
	June 2012: Twenty-fifth-anniversary edition of *Graceland* released; includes documentary

World and Cultural Events

Paul Simon's Life and Career

film *Under African Skies* and DVD of 1987 Zimbabwe show.

September 2012: *Live in New York City* released.

November 2012: Barack Obama reelected.

2014: Sting and seventy-two-year-old Simon go on two-month tour together.

ACKNOWLEDGMENTS

First thanks goes to my colleague Stephen Mexal, who steered me toward the opportunity to write this book. Once I started writing, stimulating talks with Thom Cavalli and Dave Christian helped me focus my ideas and find the right voice to speak them. Patricia and Frank Cruz, the most generous-spirited people I've met in my life, provided tremendous support. Scott Calhoun and Bennett Graff were the best of editors, giving me the greatest possible freedom to develop my ideas and write the book the way I wanted to. And thanks to the good folks at Rowman & Littlefield for all the meticulous production work.

I wrote this book for myself because I wanted to figure out how I really felt about Paul Simon's music, but in some ways my imaginary audience were my sons, Alexey and Nicolai, whose love of music and their fascination with the ways it reflects contemporary culture is a great gratification to me. Then there's our two-year-old daughter, Annalise, whose birth was nearly simultaneous with this book's. Lots of the joy I had in writing this—and it was fun—came from the many days when I'd turn from my computer to find her behind me, her ripe brown eyes anticipating my reaction, holding in both hands a nutrition-packed kale shake that she and her mom had made to keep me going. Finally, there's her mother, my wife, Angelique, whose passion for the life we share warms, melts, and burns in equal measure. Nothing happens without her—this book's the least of it.

INTRODUCTION

As I was beginning my research for this book, I came upon a quote from an interview Paul Simon did in the early 1990s that made me wince. Here it is:

> I don't think it's very good for a serious songwriter to pay attention to [critics]. It's just too hard. And it's not informative. They don't know what they're talking about. And can't know what they're talking about, by definition. Unless you write songs and make records, you just really can't know what it's about.[1]

Not a month into my Paul Simon project, and already the man himself was telling me I may as well give up.

Now, Paul Simon can be a prickly character, and by the time he did that interview he'd been battered by a good number of brutal critics over the years; I can understand why he found music criticism uninformed and ignorant and didn't read the stuff anymore. And I had to admit that, in some ways, he's right: a lot of pop and rock criticism *is* terrible, obsessed with fame, chart success, image-mongering, the most banal kinds of enthusiasms, the most cavalier dismissals, the most lame and ignorant judgments. But not all of it is. (Lester Bangs, one of the great rock critics, once said somewhere that "95% of rock 'n' roll is a bunch of raving shit," and that probably goes for rock criticism too. But you can't forget about the 5 percent that makes it worth it.) Good pop or rock criticism does what good criticism always does: it articulates what it feels like to be on the receiving end of an art object—a poem, a painting, a film, a song. When done well, it helps other people understand their own aesthetic responses to art so that they can articulate them too. Which creates artistic discourse, which is more or less a universally good thing. Though it can't hurt, a pop music critic doesn't need to understand music theory, know how to run a guitar through a phaser, or set up a recording space to eliminate echo in order to do his or her job. Good music criticism explores the experience of what it is to be a caring listener wanting (often *needing*) to be moved, entertained, enlightened, enriched. For some of us, listening to music has given us some of our most powerful experiences in life, and pop criticism is no more and no less than the attempt to bring to life the fullness of that experience in language.

I happen to know a little about music: I play two instruments, the violin and guitar, have dabbled in recording studios, have played in orchestras and string ensembles and rock bands, even written a song or two. I can arrange three-part vocal harmonies and know how a good bridge can open out the meanings of a third verse of a song. I can hear it when a musician makes a mistake. I'm also an English professor, with years of reading and teaching poetry under my belt, not to mention experience teaching the history of rock music and culture to college students. All of this helps if you're writing a book about Paul Simon. But none of it would mean a thing if I hadn't been listening to him and the culture to which he's contributed, steadily, for four decades, going all the way back to 1972.

I was thirteen then, and living in a home where rock music didn't exist. My brothers and I all played the violin, and the records we bought and listened to were performed by Jascha Heifetz, Isaac Stern, and the New York Philharmonic, not the Beatles, Dylan, or the Stones. But I got a transistor radio for my birthday the year before, supposedly so I could listen to Dodgers baseball games, and took it up to Boy Scout camp that summer, where—what a rebel—I listened to Top 40 radio all day every day until the battery wore out. I fell in love with pop music that summer, with "American Pie" and "Brandy" and "Who's That Lady?" and "City of New Orleans" and "Alone Again, Naturally," and with a song that had a rhythm that I'd never heard before—later I learned it was reggae—and words that, for reasons I didn't understand then, made me feel like my chest was constricting in pain and expanding into bliss all at once. The song was "Mother and Child Reunion," and it was by Paul Simon.

I didn't understand the song—I'm not sure anyone does, even now—but I couldn't get certain snippets of lyrics out of my head: "I can't remember a sadder day"; "I never been laid so low / In such a mysterious way"; "The mother and child reunion / Is only a motion away." I felt myself falling into the sound of Simon's tender and understanding voice, trusting it utterly, even feeling a sort of dark love for a singer who was moving me in ways that were just as powerful as the way Heifetz could move me when I listened to the swooning melodies in the first movement of the Brahm's Violin Concerto. What I was too emotionally blocked to understand at the time was that the song meant so much to me because I was myself waiting for a mother and child reunion. My mother had left my family five years earlier on the saddest day of my life and, despite a scant letter now and again that promised that someday she would return, we hadn't heard from her since. She was gone, but the song said—just as her few letters did—that she was "only a motion away." Eighteen months later, she died, in faraway Brazil—we never did see her again—and the song has haunted me ever since.

What the song convinced me of—though I didn't understand this at the time either—was that listening to pop music could be as powerful as any artistic experience. Countless other songs have confirmed my conviction since, and made me also see that songs with that kind of power didn't necessarily have to be connected to personal trauma—they had their own formal greatness, or irresistible energy, or lyrical penetration, or musical passion, or possessed some detail that drives some songs straight into the heart. And some of these songs have been by Paul Simon: "Scarborough Fair/Canticle," "America," "The Oldest Living Boy in New York," "Peace Like a River," "American Tune," "Slip-Sliding Away," "Hearts and Bones," "The Boy in the Bubble," "Graceland," "Further to Fly," "Darling Lorraine," "Wartime Prayers," "Dazzling Blue." Listening to these songs (with the Simon & Garfunkel stuff, I had to go back into their catalogue; the others I heard almost as soon as each subsequent solo record came out) was part of an ongoing realization that Paul Simon was creating, album by album, an extraordinary American songbook studded by songs that have been aesthetic oases in my life, reliable repositories of vital memories, yearnings, happinesses. Those songs, and many others besides, are why I wrote this book.

I've titled the book *Paul Simon: An American Tune* as a kind of dodge. Yes, Simon has written—in songs like "America," several tunes from the *Paul Simon* album, "American Tune," "The Boy in the Bubble," "How Can You Live in the Northeast?," and "Wartime Prayers"— some of the most trenchant songs in the pop catalogue about America as idea and ideal. And the arc of his career has "American dream" written all over it—he's the middle-class son of Jewish immigrants who scaled the heights of superstardom not once but three times and survived so many "second acts in American [life]" that it would make F. Scott Fitzgerald blush. And then there's this New Yorker's embrace of different varieties of "world music," which might itself be called American: a generous-spirited, affirmative assimilation of other cultural traditions in the interests of creating something of universal value. (Some call this appropriation, which is just as American if not so benign.) So, I can justify the title. But I also wanted the title to sound general, one that wouldn't bind my writing too tightly to any rigid or overdetermined thesis. Pop criticism usually works best the closer it stays with individual works: with individual songs and individual albums. Mostly, the songs are the thing.

Not that an aesthetic arc in Simon's career isn't noticeable. For a while I toyed with the idea of calling this book *Paul Simon: From Waste Land to Graceland*, thinking that the through-line to the study would follow Simon as he wrestled with his early devotion to the pop-modernist Waste Land outlook (clearly evident in his early writing about alienation, Godlessness, and other existentially potent themes embodied in the work of T. S. Eliot) before finally breaking out into the more exuberant embrace of world music and the possibilities of spiritual transcendence that is evident in almost all his music since *Graceland*. But the idea was too clever, and pursuing it would have left way too much out: I wanted to investigate how Simon's songs reflect his interactions with 1960s consciousness, his competition with Bob Dylan, his own struggles with depression and love, his on-again-off-again relationship with Art Garfunkel, his periodic attempts to expand his art into film or theater, not to mention his responses to historical events like 9/11. To include this stuff while hanging on to that thesis would require the kind of critical ingenuity that's tantamount to distortion, and that would have done harm to the music.

The book proceeds chronologically, beginning with a biographical introduction, followed by chapters that each take up a phase in Simon's development as an artist. Chapter 2 takes up the years 1957–1970: it devotes a few pages to Simon's early attempts to forge a career as a teen rocker, then gives way to a lengthy discussion of his years with Simon & Garfunkel, which, in albums like *Bookends* and *Bridge Over Troubled Water*, made him a superstar. Chapter 3 concerns itself with Simon's first years as solo artist in a singer-songwriter vein, culminating in the critical and commercial triumph of *Still Crazy after All These Years*, while chapter 4 discusses the personally troubling years that gave us the album and film *One-Trick Pony* and *Hearts and Bones*. Chapter 5 deals with the third major crest of his career: the South African–influenced *Graceland*, which was followed four years later by the audacious experimentation of *The Rhythm of the Saints*, and eight years after that, the overreach of his failed Broadway musical, *The Capeman*. The final chapter brings us into the new century, with discussions of his last three solo albums, which have solidified his position as one of America's greatest songwriters. The last two chapters are unusually long, owing to the fact that Simon's songs since *Graceland* have gotten more intricate lyrically and musically: getting at "The Cool, Cool River," "Hurricane Eye," or "Love Is Eternal Sacred Light" requires a lot more explanation, and critical patience, than do relative simplicities like "The Sound of Silence" or "I Am A Rock."

A career this long, this sustained, this varied, this artistically consistent—he's made music for almost six decades, and the album he did at the age of sixty-nine, *So Beautiful or So What*, is one of his best—can't help but influence countless musicians and songwriters. Consider the variety of musicians who have recorded covers of Simon songs: in the 1960s and 1970s, Aretha Franklin did a definitive gospel cover of "Bridge Over Troubled Water," and Bob Dylan covered "The Boxer"; in the 1980s, power popsters the Bangles rocked up "A Hazy Shade of Winter"; in the 1990s, the grunge-lite band the Lemonheads broke through with "Mrs. Robinson." And in 2012, English neo-folkies Mumford & Sons added "The Boxer" as a bonus track to their album *Babel* (and brought in Simon to sing backup). Then there are the many who have acknowledged the greatness of his songwriting, a roster that includes Randy Newman, Elvis Costello, Philip Glass, Aimee Mann, and Vampire Weekend. Simon's influence threads through a large swath of the fabric of rock and modern pop history, and this book tries to get at the qualities that have made him so vital. Simon may have his reasons to pay no attention to it. I'm hoping some of the rest of us will find it helpful.

I

A KID FROM QUEENS

On a certain level, I'm still thinking, "Not bad for a kid from Queens."—Paul Simon [1]

Paul Simon is a member of the Songwriters Hall of Fame, a two-time inductee into the Rock 'N' Roll Hall of Fame, and the first recipient of the Gershwin Prize for Popular Song—an award bestowed by the Library of Congress to celebrate "the work of an artist whose career reflects lifetime achievement in promoting song as a vehicle of musical expression and cultural understanding." [2] He's won sixteen Grammy Awards, been nominated for dozens more, and is the only person who has ever been nominated for Album of the Year honors *in five consecutive decades*. The duo of which he was by far the most important partner, Simon & Garfunkel, is the only act besides the Beatles that has ever held down the top three positions on the Billboard Top 200 album chart at the same time. His worldwide record sales have been estimated at somewhere between 120,000,000 and 180,000,000 records, which, when combined with the fact that he has been a consistently large concert draw for almost forty years (and one of pop music's least foolhardy businessmen), has made him one of the richest musicians on the planet. His most famous—if hardly best—song, "Bridge Over Trouble Water," has been recorded by over two hundred artists, including skin-tingling treatments by Aretha Franklin and Elvis Presley. His pop standards are ubiquitous, heard on radios and in elevators, supermarkets, shopping malls, and hotel dinner clubs on every continent. [3] He wrote and starred in a Hollywood movie, wrote and produced a Broadway musical, and was more instrumental in bringing "world music" to mass American audiences than any other single person. In 2006, *Time* magazine cited him as one of the "100 People Who Shaped the World."

By any stretch, this is an American success story—"pure and complicated" as J. D. Salinger might have said. Not bad for a kid from Queens, indeed.

Paul Frederic Simon was born in Newark, New Jersey, on October 13, 1941, but his family moved to a house in Forest Hills, Queens (a slightly upscale part of this middle-class New York borough) in 1945, and Queens was home until he graduated from high school. His parents, Louis and Belle Simon, were Hungarian Jews who immigrated to America in the 1930s. Louis, a professional violinist when he lived in Budapest, carved out a successful career for himself in America as a stand-up bass player and bandleader for big bands, popular radio programs, and, after World War II, television shows like *The Jackie Gleason Show* or *Arthur Godfrey and His Friends*, which broadcast out of New York City. Paul remembers staying up late as a child to catch a glimpse of his dad when these shows broadcast on television, which no doubt cast his father as an even more authoritative figure than he already was to his first-born son. (One day, the elder Simon walked by Paul's bedroom as he was singing a song, stopped in the doorway and said, "That's nice, Paul. You have a nice voice." Paul remembers that tiny moment of paternal approval as a defining moment in his life—after that, his "interest in music blossomed."[4])

While Paul inherited some of his father's drive and musical talent, it was his mother who fostered Paul's confidence as a child. Giving up a school-teaching job in order to raise Paul and his brother, Eddie, she was, Simon has said, "the first nourishing person in my life. She made me feel as if I could take my needs very seriously, because she did."[5] And building Paul's confidence became vital, because the boy was not only quiet and introverted, but also unusually short: though physically aggressive when challenged, he was a target throughout his childhood of local toughs eager to brawl or shake him down for lunch money. Simon was later to cite being short—he topped out at 5'3" or 5'4"—as having "the most significant single effect on my existence, aside from my brain. In fact, it's part of an inferior-superior syndrome. I think I have a superior brain and an inferior stature, if you really want to get brutal about it."[6]

Paul met the tall and willowy Art Garfunkel at P.S. 164 when their sixth-grade classes put on a production of *Alice in Wonderland*. Paul was immensely impressed with young Artie's voice (a smooth, controlled, clarion-like soprano that listeners throughout his career have inevitably described as "angelic" and "like a choir boy's") as well as its effect on girls. "My first recollection of him was in the fourth grade," Simon recalled, "when he sang in the assembly and all the girls were talking about him. After that, I decided to try singing, too. I said, 'Hey, I want to cut in on some of this myself.'"[7] Living only three blocks apart, the two became fast though ultra-competitive friends, singing along to the doo-wop songs by the Moonglows or the Penguins that local boys were imitating on street corners during the early 1950s. As the boys reached their teens, they began hearing and sharing their growing love of the new music they heard on radio shows like Alan Freed's "Rock and Roll Jubilee"—teen pop like "Earth Angel," rhythm 'n' blues by groups like the Cadillacs and the Monotones, and the big audio dynamite of Chuck Berry's "Maybellene" and Elvis Presley's "Heartbreak Hotel." These songs, along with hits by Little Richard and Buddy Holly, blended R&B, country and western, pop, gospel, and blues into a potent multiracial admixture Freed called "rock 'n' roll" and would, in the coming years, come to transform American culture as a whole.

Paul's parents bought him an acoustic guitar in 1955, and like a lot of other boys at the time, he dreamed of becoming the next Elvis. Unlike other boys at the time, however, he had driving ambition, enviable discipline, and blooming talent as a singer, guitar player, and songwriter. He practiced the guitar incessantly, and together with Art began writing songs, some in the vein of the Everly Brothers, the California duo who hit it big with "Bye Bye Love" in 1957, and whose tight harmonies Paul and Artie found they could emulate beautifully. The two of them began performing to some local success at school dances and the like, but Paul wasn't content to be some mere neighborhood notable. When they were fifteen, the two boys began hawking their songs at the Brill Building in Manhattan, the legendary musical hothouse where dozens of producers and publishers kept their offices, and where songwriters pumped out song after song, hoping that one would become the hit that would make their fortune. No one bought their songs, but eventually Paul and Art, calling themselves Tom & Jerry, recorded a cheap demo of Simon's called "Hey Schoolgirl," an Everly Brothers rip, at a Manhattan recording studio. One of those producers, Sid Prosen, happened to hear the session, and, combining hoary cliché with pop myth, promised to make them stars.

"Hey Schoolgirl" did become a hit, a minor one, edging into the Billboard Top 50. It earned each of these high school boys about $2,000, an appearance on the popular TV music show *American Bandstand*, and a crucial if tiny taste of fame. When their follow-up singles failed to chart, however, Art, convinced that their dalliance with stardom was a lark, enrolled at Columbia University with dreams of becoming an architect. Paul, though matriculating at Queens College and taking his studies as an English major seriously, refused to give up a music career. From 1957 till 1963, he recorded a remarkable number of his own compositions—about forty songs on twenty singles, under names like Jerry Landis, Paul Kane, and Tico and the Triumphs. But only one Jerry Landis Song, a comic novelty called "Lone Teen-Ranger," made any kind of peep in the marketplace—it reached #97 on the charts; the rest of his output went nowhere.

It's a testament to Simon's tenacity, his restless desire for success, his iron will, and his belief in himself—characteristics that have stayed with him throughout his career and have led to accusations of arrogance, among other things—that all these failures did little to deter him from wanting to make it in the music business. But as the 1950s turned into the 1960s, his conception of a music career began to shift from one in which he was just trying to capitalize on whatever was hot in the marketplace to making music that actually mattered to him. Doubtless this had something to do with the poets he was reading at Queens College. T. S. Eliot, Robert Frost, Edward Arlington Robinson, Wallace Stevens, and Emily Dickenson articulated, among other things, a sense of isolation and alienation that would profoundly (if pretentiously) influence Simon's early efforts at serious songwriting. But the shift had even more to do with the music he was discovering when he took the subway downtown to Greenwich Village and visited happening folk clubs like Gerde's Folk City, Café Wha?, and the Gaslight.

In the early 1960s, folk music was the music favored by serious-minded young white liberals who worried about the Bomb, fervently supported labor and civil rights movement in the South, and found rock 'n' roll—particularly the stuff produced by the bland copycat rockers who dominated the pop charts after 1958—absurdly juvenile. The

Weavers (which featured Pete Seeger) were the folk movement's first national stars in the early 1950s, followed later in the decade by the Kingston Trio; Peter, Paul, and Mary; and Joan Baez. But the early 1960s Greenwich Village folk scene was tougher and scruffier, featuring singer-songwriters like Phil Ochs and Dave Van Ronk, who were influenced by the Beat poets, country blues, and the "hillbilly" folk sensibility of Woody Guthrie. The Village's leading light, of course, was Bob Dylan, who had made his pilgrimage from Hibbing, Minnesota, to the big city in 1961 and within two years had imprinted "Blowin' in the Wind" and "The Times They Are A-Changin'" on the social consciousness of the folk movement, if not the nation. Along with the Beatles and the Rolling Stones, who "invaded" the United States in early 1964, he would effectively inaugurate what came to be called the Counterculture of the 1960s.

Dylan's influence on this stage of Paul Simon's songwriting was profound, opening up vistas of possibility for what popular music might accomplish. It was Dylan's example that led Simon to write his first song of "social commentary"—"He Was My Brother"—a mawkish if well-intentioned song about the murder of a Southern civil rights worker. Along with Garfunkel, with whom Simon had reconnected after several years, the duo began playing in the Village in late 1963, and though their collegiate demeanor and fluffy harmonies were often scoffed at by Village hipsters—Dylan biographer Robert Shelton famously (and crushingly) called Paul "the suburban Bob Dylan"—their performance of "He Was My Brother" caught the ear of Dylan's producer, Tom Wilson, who helped get them signed to a contract with Columbia records, and produced Simon & Garfunkel's first album, *Wednesday Morning 3 A.M.*, in 1964.

The album, despite the presence of a version of "The Sound of Silence" whose sole instrumental accompaniment was Simon's acoustic guitar, sold poorly, and the pair broke up again. Simon set off for England, where he met his first serious muse/girlfriend, Kathy Chitty (who inspired "Homeward Bound," "Kathy's Song," and "America"), and played, quite successfully, the British folk circuit in and around London. Some of his demos appeared on British radio, which prompted the international arm of Columbia Records to allow Simon to record a solo album—*The Paul Simon Songbook*, recorded in a single session in early 1965. The album appeared only in England, and despite a slate of songs that would later appear, in different form, on Simon & Garfunkel albums (including "I Am a Rock" and "The Sound of Silence"), it also promptly flopped. Unfazed, Simon trudged on as a popular folk-club performer—he remembers his time in England as "by far my favorite time of my life"—until his decade of unrelenting writing, performing, recording, and hustling finally yielded one of those "breaks" that have become legendary in the music world.[8]

Unbeknownst to Simon, a few radio stations in American college towns had begun playing *Wednesday*'s version of "The Sound of Silence," his pop epic that articulated, in a simple but dramatically effective way, the sense of estrangement that many college students recognized in themselves when they read T. S. Eliot's poetry or sociological studies like *The Lonely Crowd*, *Growing Up Absurd*, or *One-Dimensional Man*, books that could be found in college dormitories all over the country. As the song was gaining airplay, Tom Wilson, the song's producer, happened to be in the studio with Bob Dylan recording "Like a Rolling Stone," that seminal six-minute blast of folk-rock beat/symbolist poetry that perhaps still stands as rock music's greatest single monument. When Dylan left for the day, Wilson asked Dylan's band to stick around to add drums, electric bass, and electric guitar to the existing acoustic version of "The Sound of Silence." They did, and Columbia released the new "folk-rock" version of the song without any input from Paul or Art. The single flew up the charts in the late fall of 1965. Simon heard about it in England, and despite initially hating Wilson's new version, hastily returned to New York City to find that by Christmastime, Simon & Garfunkel had the #1 song in America.

Simon & Garfunkel's emergence onto the national scene coincided with the emergence of the 1960s Counterculture, that amorphous group of young people—some of them anti–Vietnam War or civil rights activists, most of them middle-class college-age students—who were shocked by John F. Kennedy's assassination and found themselves eagerly experimenting with marijuana or LSD, breaking from the fiercely repressed sexuality of the 1950s, and fascinated by "Eastern" modes of thought (yoga, Zen Buddhism, meditation) and the radical social thought of Buckminster Fuller, Norman O. Brown, and Herbert Marcuse. Despite ditties like "The 59th Street Bridge Song (Feeling Groovy)" that endeared them to the hippie crowd, however, it would be a mistake to align the duo too closely with the Counterculture. The five popular albums (four studio albums and the soundtrack to that quintessential "generation gap" film, *The Graduate*) and many radio hits that the pair released over the next four years were bought by housewives, lawyers, and professors as much as they were by college radicals. It's not hard to imagine Mrs. Robinson herself—the bitter middle-aged harridan of the film who typified everything the youth generation hated at the time—enjoying Simon's "Scarborough Fair." Indeed, Simon's lyrics—more often than Bob Dylan's or John Lennon's—were taught as poetry by high school and college English teachers in the 1960s and 1970s.

Simon & Garfunkel's years of popularity—1966 through 1970—were extraordinary times for Simon, marked by levels of success that couldn't help but exert enormous psychic pressures on what was an essentially introverted, even depressive personality. There was immense pressure to write new hits (Simon was and remains a notoriously slow writer, sometimes taking months to complete a single song); pressure from Columbia to record new material (after *Sounds of Silence*, an album recorded in a few rushed sessions to cash in on the success of the single, Simon became a painstaking studio rat, spending months recording, overdubbing, and mixing *Bookends* and *Bridge Over Troubled Water*); pressure to jam dozens of tour dates into the short periods of time between recording; and finally pressure just to handle the ego trappings of fame—the growing piles of money, the fan adoration, and the power that comes to a young man on top of the pop cultural heap. Yet Simon never backed down from the challenges of his fame. He helped organize and, with Garfunkel, participated in the groundbreaking Monterey Pop Festival in 1967. (It was then that he met the Grateful Dead, which introduced him to LSD, a drug whose influence clearly shows on the album *Bookends*). Again along with Garfunkel, he produced a politically charged and ambitious TV special called "Songs of America" for CBS in 1969. Most importantly to pop history, he took up film director Mike Nichols's challenge to provide the soundtrack for one of the most explosive films of the 1960s, *The Graduate*. The success of the film and of its soundtrack—especially Simon's mischievous, lyrically inventive "Mrs. Robinson"—catapulted Simon and Garfunkel into the pop stratosphere.

All the pressures reached a climax during the recording of Simon & Garfunkel's final collaboration, *Bridge Over Troubled Water*, in 1969. By then, Simon was off drugs, had married Peggy Harper (who would inspire "Bridge Over Troubled Water," "Tenderness," "Train in the Distance," and much of *Still Crazy after All These Years*), and was trying to establish some stability after fame's whirlwind had left him feeling isolated and unhinged. As he recalls, "I wasn't involved in anything [in 1968]. I was just by myself. I was crazy most of the time, high, and relatively depressed throughout those years—quite alone."[9] Meanwhile, his musical partner was flourishing and eyeing a career in Hollywood—Mike Nichols had cast Garfunkel in his follow-up to *The Graduate*, *Catch-22*, and to Paul, Art's long months on the movie set during the making of the album showed that his priorities had shifted from the group to an independent acting career. The tensions between the partners, however, had been there since their schooldays—Art felt a deep and apparently permanent sense of betrayal when Paul made a solo single during their Tom & Jerry days—and it bears pointing out that Simon & Garfunkel would probably never have reunited at all had it not been for Tom Wilson's rockified makeover of the acoustic "The Sound of Silence."[10] In any case, Garfunkel, as willful in his own way as Simon, resented the power Paul wielded as the songwriter of the group, while Simon was always irked by the attention the tall, good-looking Garfunkel attracted when they were together. Fans seemed to believe that Garfunkel was an equal creative partner in the duo, perhaps because Art, suave and articulate before crowds, was the pair's spokesman during concerts, and was, after all, an exquisite interpreter of many of Simon's songs. All these tensions, combined with a growing difference between their musical tastes—Simon wanted their music to be slightly more funky and experimental while Garfunkel favored smooth, strings-laden "soft rock"—reached the breaking point with *Bridge*. Soon after the appearance of the album, which yielded several huge hit singles and for a short time was the biggest-selling studio album ever released, they broke up.

The cultural landscape in which Simon found himself when he went solo had by 1970 suffered some huge, tectonic shifts. By the turn of the decade, the Counterculture had reached a sort of critical mass, on the one hand celebrating the glorious advent of Charles Reich's Consciousness III (or the Age of Aquarius) at events like Woodstock, while on the other struggling with an increasingly dangerous, paranoid drug culture and the apparent impotence of the antiwar movement, which after five years had found itself unable to end the Vietnam War. At the same time, it was mourning the 1968 assassinations of Robert F. Kennedy and Martin Luther King Jr., leaders who at the time they were gunned down seemed like saviors to the young. By the early 1970s, rock music had undergone similar ground-shaking changes. Bob Dylan had withdrawn from his post as generational spokesman (1970 was the year he released the horrendous *Self-Portrait*, an album that so betrayed fans that even Dylanite Greil Marcus began his review in *Rolling Stone* by quipping: "What is this shit?"[11]). The Beatles had broken up. Four of rock's major lights—Jimi Hendrix, Janis Joplin, Jim Morrison, and the Rolling Stones' Brian Jones—died of drug- or alcohol-related causes, and the rock landscape had begun to split into "hard"—Cream, Led Zeppelin, and Black Sabbath, with their electrified blues reductions—and "soft," that is, the singer-songwriter movement, typified by guitar troubadours like James Taylor, Joni Mitchell, and Jackson Browne, who wrote contemplative confessional songs that spoke to the communal Counterculture falling apart and turning inward to more personal concerns.

Simon found himself linked, inevitably, with the singer-songwriter movement, and by 1975, with the albums *Paul Simon*, *There Goes Rhymin' Simon*, and *Still Crazy after All These Years*, had more or less dominated it. Freed from the strictures of writing for a duo, equally freed from Art's desire for lushly melodic pop productions, Simon discovered a new voice and a new sound. Though he continued to produce melodious and lyrically trenchant acoustic folk rock (e.g., "Duncan" or "American Tune"), it was his integration of new forms like reggae, calypso, Dixieland jazz, and country blues, and his continued use of gospel and South American (specifically Andean) folk music in a rock context that impressed critics and fans. *Still Crazy after All These Years* capped a five-year effort to recapture the summit of the pop world—it not only yielded three hit singles but also was given that year's Grammy award for Album of the Year—and this time he had done it on his own.

These were personally difficult years, however—*Still Crazy after All These Years* chronicled the end of Paul's union with Peggy ("the whole album was about my marriage," he's said[12]) almost as penetratingly, as Bob Dylan's *Blood on the Tracks*, released the same year, portrayed the end of his marriage to Sara Dylan. Newly single, eager to at least temporarily extricate himself from what Joni Mitchell called the "star-maker machinery behind the popular song," Simon finally took some time off. [13] Solo or with Garfunkel, Simon had released nine studio albums of original material in ten years, a level of production he would not come close to the rest of his career. (To compare: in the thirty-eight years from 1976 till the present writing in 2014, Simon has released only eight albums of new material.) Carousing with new friends like actor Charles Grodin, as well as Lorne Michaels and Chevy Chase (the producer and biggest star of the newest and hippest show on television, *Saturday Night Live*), Paul loosened up, sending up his hyper-serious image by singing "Still Crazy after All These Years" in a chicken suit on SNL, dating actress Shelley Duvall, dancing at Manhattan's disco mecca Studio 54, and beginning the tumultuous relationship with actress Carrie Fisher that would obsess him into the late 1980s.

At the age of twenty-two, Fisher, the daughter of actress Debbie Reynolds and 1950s pop crooner Eddie Fisher, had become a movie star when she played Princess Leia in *Star Wars*. Possessed of strong if not classically beautiful looks, she was charismatic, witty, talented: she supplemented her major role in the *Star Wars* trilogy with notable turns in movies such as *When Harry Met Sally* and Woody Allen's *Hannah and Her Sisters*, and would later pen two very successful *romans à clef*, one of which was made into the hit picture *Postcards from the Edge*. She was also severely manic-depressive and addled by multiple drug addictions. Simon, fifteen years her senior, found himself in the stormiest relationship of his life. At the same time, encouraged by Michaels and his acting friends, he began to dip his toe into the acting world himself, playing the memorable role of the subtly slimy music producer Tony Lacey in Woody Allen's *Annie Hall*. Gaining confidence from the positive notices he received, Paul's movie ambitions metastasized: he decided to become an auteur in his own right. He would write, direct, and star in a film of his own. After a rancorous change of record labels, from Columbia to Warner, he secured financing for a film that he would write and star in. (He eventually acquiesced to Warner's very sensible demand that they find an experienced director.) The result was the wan rock drama *One-Trick Pony*, released in 1980.

One-Trick Pony was a small, personal, melancholy film that dealt with marriage, separation, and children, as well as with the changes in the music world that were, by the late 1970s, pushing artists like Paul Simon to the margins. The most potent and original music of the second half of that decade responded aggressively, even violently, to the soft-rock meditations of the singer-songwriter movement. Bruce Springsteen exploded on the scene with *Born to Run* in 1975, and shortly afterward, punk bands like the Ramones, the Sex Pistols, and the Clash permanently shifted the musical landscape. *One-Trick Pony* notes this in a scene where Noah Levin, a faded 1960s rock star and Simon's alter ego in the film, is reduced to an opening act for the new wave band the B-52s, who share none of his musical values—or apparently any of his fans. In any case, the movie caught fire neither as a film nor as a soundtrack. It was Paul's first major career failure in fifteen years, and combined with his turbulent relationship with Carrie Fisher, it sent him into a major depression and case of writer's block.

This was a time, Simon has said, "of all kind of mistakes on top of mistakes on top of mistakes."[14] With the help of a therapist, he was able to start writing again, but the turmoil with Carrie Fisher continued unabated. Perhaps as a respite from that relationship, and certainly as a way to restore his popularity after *One-Trick Pony*'s failure, he agreed to re-team with Art for a new Simon & Garfunkel tour. Though by now the two could barely stand each other off-stage, onstage they reproduced the magic of their 1960s years. The tour was wildly successful financially, and a double LP titled *Concert in the Park* sold so well that the duo decided, despite their prickly relationship, to try to record another album together. The old tensions set in almost immediately, however, and after a few months of wrangling Paul dropped Art from the sessions and proceeded to make the album as a solo project. The result, *Hearts and Bones*, released in late 1983, is as personal an album as Simon ever made, especially about his relationship with Fisher, whom he impulsively married a few months before the album's release, and from whom he filed for divorce half a year later. The album contains some of his finest, subtlest work, but the album's original reviews were fairly tepid (since then, the album's reputation has grown steadily) and failed to garner much excitement or sales. Going into the mid-1980s, then, Paul was faced with a second failed marriage and a solo career whose star had fallen so far that Warner Brothers—the record company that had wanted his contract so badly in 1978 that it had been willing to bankroll a film by an untested screenwriter and leading man—more or less gave up on him.

For a while he drifted, existentially and musically, until a musician friend slipped him a cassette tape titled *Gumboots: Accordion Jive Hits*,

Volume II. The music, an infectiously polyrhythmic music known in South Africa as "mbaqamba" or "township jive," reignited his creative passions. With his long-time producer Roy Halee, he traveled to Johannesburg, South Africa, and played and recorded with local musicians in the hope of sparking ideas for a new album. In doing so, he put himself at the center of a mighty controversy that would have international implications.

In the mid-1980s, South Africa was still an apartheid nation. Ruled by whites, it systemically separated blacks and whites, forced blacks into black-only townships, violently suppressed blacks' attempts to end the apartheid regime, and had in 1964 sentenced its leader, Nelson Mandela, to life in prison for his political activities. At the time of Paul's visit in 1984, both the United Nations and the African National Congress had imposed a "cultural boycott" on South Africa that urged artists in the most emphatic terms not to perform in South Africa, especially in Sun City—a resort where stars were offered seven-figure paychecks to play for mostly privileged South African whites. Simon never played Sun City nor did he publically "perform" anywhere in South Africa while the boycott was in place. However, both the UN and the AFC condemned Simon for working with South African musicians at all, and Simon found himself forced to defend what he'd done. He pointed to the fact that he'd paid the South African musicians triple the rate prescribed by the American Musicians Union; he took pains to give co-writer credit to some of these musicians on five of the album's twelve cuts, and paid performer royalties to all the musicians when the album, which he called *Graceland*, finally was issued in 1986. Not only that, but he made clear that the South African musicians with whom he worked felt "that my coming would benefit them because I could help to give South African music a place in the international community of music similar to that of reggae."[15]

Graceland did in fact give a huge commercial boost to South African music, and African music generally, in the American and European market. Though "world music" ambassadors like King Sunny Adé had become increasingly popular in the United States since the early 1980s, *Graceland* turbocharged African music's infiltration of western markets, paving the way for dozens of new bands to expand their audiences. Finally heeding Simon's defense of his actions, the United Nations lifted the condemnation of Simon in 1987, soon followed by the AFC.

However, the cultural controversy surrounding a famous white musician employing and profiting off the work of black African musicians remained a potent one in an America that was, during the 1980s, deeply divided over matters of political correctness, multiculturalism, the appropriation of "exotic" musical styles by whites, and the like.

And *Graceland* was certainly profitable, selling over 14 million copies, and putting Simon in the megastar company of such 1980s acts as Madonna, Prince, Springsteen, and Michael Jackson. Simon and his band, made up primarily of South African musicians, toured the world on the album's merits for the better part of two years. *Graceland* was also an artistic peak for Paul, offering a dazzling mixture of buoyant South African rhythms and effervescent American pop melody, with a couple of joyful Mexican-American folk-rock and zydeco tunes thrown in for good measure. The album also featured a new and sly lyricism that combined conversational phrasing with a poetic density, even a transcendental yearning, that was in itself exhilarating. It was by any measure a career peak that forever quelled Paul's—or the public's— doubts about himself as a vital, important solo artist.

After the *Graceland* tour ground to a halt, Paul quickly set about to work with Brazilian musicians, who played a heavily percussive samba known as "bataque" or "batucuda." Traveling to Brazil, he worked as he did on *Graceland*, recording a series of complex rhythm tracks with these musicians, then returning to the United States to turn the tracks into Paul Simon songs. *The Rhythm of the Saints*, the result of this latest collaboration, while not as successful as *Graceland*—it's less buoyant rhythmically, significantly less melodic, and much more melancholy (though perhaps in its spiritual searching more interesting lyrically)— was a sizable hit both in the United States and abroad, and earned Simon continued respect among critics and fellow musicians.

It was on the heels of *Rhythm's* success that Simon met and fell in love with musician Edie Brickell, then the leader of the group Edie Brickell and the New Bohemians. In 1992 they married, began a family, and have apparently attained a level of stability—they're now on their third decade of marriage and have three children—that Paul had never managed to attain before. Musically, however, Paul remained as restless and ambitious as ever. He had been contemplating a Broadway musical since the late 1980s, and now had the clout to mount one. Along with Nobel Prize–winning author Derek Wolcott, with whom Paul had struck up a friendship, Paul wrote the lyrics and music for a musical based on the life of Salvador Agron, a Puerto Rican American gang member whom one writer has called "the most infamous teenage killer in New York City's history."[16] Back in the 1950s, Agron, known as the Capeman by fellow gang members, had stabbed two white college students to death with a dagger. His arrest and trial caused a media sensation, with pundits decrying him as an example of the juvenile delinquency of the time, while others pleaded for leniency for those like Agron who grew up in reform schools and in clearly racist circumstances. Though given the death penalty, Agron's sentence was commuted by governor Nelson Rockefeller after Eleanor Roosevelt herself intervened on the boy's behalf. The story was explosively dramatic, and it connected with Paul's youth—he remembers reading newspaper accounts of the trial when he was a boy. Hardly coincidentally, Agron's story allowed Paul to delve into the pop styles of the 1950s, particularly Puerto Rican street music and the doo-wop with which he himself grew up.

However powerful Simon's passions were to make *The Capeman*, a musical that put at its center a murderer—even one whose story arc involves his eventual repentance and redemption—was a long shot to succeed on a Broadway stage. Simon was, however, persistent—hubristic and controlling, many Broadway veterans said—and the production, after enduring a revolving door of directors, some major rewrites, and postponements of its opening night, finally debuted in 1997. The reviews, particularly from the *New York Times*, were devastatingly bad, and *The Capeman* closed less than two months later, losing almost its entire 11 million dollar investment, much of it Paul's own money.

Though perplexed by *The Capeman*'s quick disappearance from Broadway, and doubtless smarting from the loss of so much money, Paul was by then used to picking himself up after failure, and did so then with aplomb. Accepting an offer from Bob Dylan to co-headline a tour, Paul embarked on the very successful Paul/Bob 99 Tour, which presented each artist on an equal footing—they alternated opening and closing sets—and for a time healed old wounds between the super-competitive men. After the tour was over, Paul was stimulated enough by the experience to immediately enter the studio to record a new album.

The album, *You're the One* (2000), was the first of the three studio albums Simon has released in the new century, and in its pared-back instrumental attack, its modesty of approach, and the intimacy of its lyrics, it was his most personal album since *Hearts and Bones*. The album was a critical favorite, and spoke movingly in songs like "Old" and "Darling Lorraine" of the baby boomer generation's hopes and fears as it slip-slided into old age. *You're the One* was no great seller—he hadn't had a hit album for a decade by then, and the pop marketplace was at the time dominated by boy bands and hip hop artists—but by the turn of the century Paul seemed to have accepted that, as he entered his sixties, his days as a top-selling recording artist were over. He remained a top concert draw, however, especially when he re-teamed with Art for a Simon & Garfunkel reunion tour in 2003.

His next studio album, *Surprise* (2006), was partially inspired by the events of September 11, 2001. Paul, a lifetime New Yorker, was moved to write a number of songs that addressed the terrorist attacks on the twin towers—among them "Why Do You Live in the Northeast?" and "Wartime Prayers"—and recorded the album in collaboration with Brian Eno, producer extraordinaire and perhaps the most innovative soundscape artist of electronic avant-pop in the rock era. The album brought the by-then-expected strong reviews and good but unspectacular sales, and further developed the range of Simon's expansive, philosophically speculative lyrics. Paul's latest album, *So Beautiful or So What?*, released in 2010 when he was sixty-nine years old, is also a remarkably strong album—in the liner notes, Elvis Costello was moved to call it "one of Simon's finest achievements," and most reviewers were quick to agree. In a series of songs that in some ways constellate and apotheosize virtually all of the styles with which he has experimented over a lifetime of restlessly curious musical investigation, Paul weaves a warm and wondrous tapestry of mediations on the themes of love, the mysterious passage of time, death, and God.

Simon is now in his seventies, and perhaps because his music continues to grow—and remains consistently strong—in his sixth decade of music-making, we may expect surprising, challenging work from him as long as he remains healthy. Is there a single other performer from his generation about whom we can say the same thing? Certainly not Paul McCartney, who hasn't produced a strong pop album since the 1970s, nor the notoriously uneven Neil Young. Probably only Dylan, Simon's longtime shadow, continues to produce impressive albums into his seventies. Given Simon's competitiveness, and his ever-restless pursuit of new musical vistas, maybe that will goad him to add to the extraordinary body of work that began with the fierce imagination of that kid from Queens.

2

THE STRUGGLE FOR ORIGINALITY

1957–1970

When they were both just fifteen, Paul Simon and Art Garfunkel scored a hit (as Tom & Jerry) with "Hey Schoolgirl," a teeny-bopper Everly Brothers imitation that gave them an enticing taste of stardom. However, Simon, with and without Garfunkel—and not for want of trying—was unable to regain the ear of the pop audience, despite writing and recording some twenty singles over the next six years. Still, listening to some of Simon's product from his teens—and it is decidedly *product*: crafty and professional, to be sure, but having no reason to exist except to *sell*—reveals not only what remarkable determination and ambition he possessed from the beginning, but also what an extraordinary student of pop music Paul Simon was. He was a genuinely quick read, a marvelous imitator of pop styles, an able conduit of received wisdom. Simon didn't leave any of these qualities behind once he reached adulthood and formed Simon & Garfunkel, either. In fact, many of the qualities that account for Simon & Garfunkel's success were already apparent in those early recordings: tight, disciplined harmony vocals; crisply strummed guitar; varied, fairly interesting rhythms; hi-fidelity production (given the equipment available to him at the time); considerable melodic invention; and perhaps more than anything, an impressive command of contemporary pop idioms. While still an adolescent, Simon was arranging four-part doo-wop vocals, writing and singing syrupy teen ballads, appropriating Buddy Holly hiccups, perfecting Bo Diddley's patented rhythmic hook, imitating Elvis's coy machismo, and introducing sound effects (like chugging trains or blatting motorcycles) into his songs.

What accounts for the change in Simon's work from his teens to the stuff he did with Simon & Garfunkel can mostly be attributed to two developments. One is that Simon went to Queens College, where he majored in English and was exposed to the world of ideas. Specifically, he was drawn to the modernist poets who Simon would later namecheck (often cringingly) in some of his more pretentious compositions. He also gravitated toward a certain New York–style postwar existentialist *Weltanschauung* that was equal parts Albert Camus, Michelangelo Antonioni, T. S. Eliot, Colin Wilson (whose *The Outsider* was all the rage in the late 1950s), and God-is-dead theology, and whose bywords were *despair, alienation, anxiety,* and *absurdity.* By all appearances, the collegiate Simon was a sincere, sensitive young man who felt that his own turmoil—for example, his sense of being misunderstood, his inability to communicate his feelings, the sense of "darkness" and loneliness that he groped to express in "The Sound of Silence"—was illuminated by poets and writers for whom loneliness was less a temporary condition remedied by, say, love, than an ontological given. And it's clear that as Simon matured, he wanted to incorporate what he was learning in college into a pop song form that was being radically expanded by Greenwich Village folkies who stood as the "serious" musical vanguard ushering pop music into the 1960s.

And it's "the Sixties" itself that will have to serve as shorthand to name the second of the two developments that changed Simon's music. "The Sixties," of course, stands less for a decade than it does for a paradigm shift, most of whose radical cultural gestures were liberational. As hundreds of historians and commentators have observed—"the Sixties" by now could be its own college major—the assassination of president John F. Kennedy in November of 1963 was the first in a series of cultural and sociological shocks that forever changed American consciousness. In short order, the Beatles arrived in America and wildly expanded the scope and power of rock music and mass consumer culture generally; a free-speech movement began on the campus of UC Berkeley that ultimately convinced the young generation that their questions—about America's growing military involvement in Vietnam, about civil rights, about the relevance of higher education—would no longer be muffled by their elders; cities across the nation exploded in race riots even as Martin Luther King Jr. urged Americans to work for racial equality in peaceful ways; LSD and marijuana became the drugs of choice for a growing Counterculture of hippies, radical dissidents, and middle-class rebels who began to challenge just about every commonplace of American life, from the value of marriage or materialistic success, to our relationship to the natural world, to America's political hegemony in the world. The student protest movement against the war in Vietnam, the civil rights movement, the countercultural movement to free the individual from what were considered arbitrary or repressive social or sexual conventions: these all served as tributaries gushing into a wide cultural stream that pulled all sorts of new movements into it. By decade's end, "the Sixties" also meant the modern feminist revolution, a Chicano/a liberation movement, a gay rights movement, an ecology movement, and the first inklings of a human potential movement that would finally force the larger culture to acknowledge the importance of the inner life. That many of the energies of "the Sixties" failed to derail dearly held American values like materialism or exceptionalism—either because the Establishment culture overwhelmed those energies, or because some movements were naively idealistic, or because rebellious energies often went way too far—says little about the epoch's lasting effects, which reach into practically every corner of American life, from the way we structure our families to the way we worship to the way we relate ourselves to political authority.

Simon both reflected and played a part in creating "the Sixties"— indeed, it's difficult to imagine "the Sixties" without the indelible opening tracking shot of Benjamin Braddock's face in *The Graduate* as Simon's "The Sound of Silence" plays over it, hinting at the barely suppressed combustion ready to wreck his (and middle-class America's) quietude. It's equally difficult to imagine the end of the 1960s without "Bridge Over Troubled Water," which, amid years of turmoil, served as an oasis of spiritual calm in the same way, say, the Beatles' "Let It Be" did. But Simon's part in "the Sixties" would not likely have happened at all had it not been for Bob Dylan, who embodied both the poetic ambition Simon acquired in college and the diffuse, chaotic, liberatory energies of "the Sixties." In a case that fairly cries out for an application of Harold Bloom's theory of the anxiety of influence, Simon saw Dylan first as an example to be emulated. However, when he realized that a follower forever lies in the leader's shadow, he was forced to forge a new path artistically, to finally cease being the eager ephebe, and strive for his own kind of originality.

It was Dylan's second and third albums, *The Freewheelin' Bob Dylan* (1963) and *The Times They Are A-Changin'* (1964), that provided the template for a new generation of singer-songwriters, laying down the gauntlet with epic wind-of-change songs like "Blowin' in the Wind," "The Times They Are A-Changin'," "A Hard Rain's A-Gonna Fall," and "With God on Our Side." These songs—angry, snide, provocative—took on big ideas of history, war, violence, and power with lyrics that presented visionary landscapes specked with startling (sometimes poetic) imagery. Simon's "The Sound of Silence" can hardly be imagined without Dylan's example, just as "He Was My Brother," the song that stirred Dylan's own producer, Tom Wilson, to get Simon & Garfunkel a recording contract, is impossible to imagine without topical Dylan gems like "The Lonesome Death of Hattie Carroll." Simply put, Dylan opened the door for Simon's seriousness. The problem was that, once he'd passed through, Simon didn't have much to say that wasn't thoroughly received wisdom. And it's that struggle for originality that marks the opening years of Simon's career as a songwriter.

It should be said that the young Dylan's "ideas," as singer, social commentator, and, frankly, poet, weren't exactly original, either. In the beginning, he adopted Woody Guthrie's flat drawl, quicksilver wit, "talking blues" style, and concern for the downtrodden. But Dylan quickly broadened his palette, mixing a broad array of musical influences (everything from Jerry Reed to Blind Willie McTell) with decidedly out-of-school readings of Baudelaire, Rimbaud, and the American beat poets. Simon, in an early pique over Dylan's towering stature as rock poet, heard "Desolation Row" and dismissed it as "rehashed Ferlinghetti."[1] Though Simon wasn't entirely wrong about this, part of Dylan's genius was to incorporate high-art influences (like symbolist or beat poetry) whose rebellious spirit and dark, passional spontaneity flowed easily into a rock 'n' roll ethos. Simon's early poetic influence, on the other hand, was clearly T. S. Eliot—and a less rock 'n' roll sensibility would be difficult to find. So Simon's path to originality as a songwriter meant not only swerving away from Bob Dylan's influence but also casting off Eliot and his stodgily modernist cohorts. After a fascinating (and amusing) "Bloomian" struggle (as witnessed in Simon's "A Simple

Desultory Phillippic"), he was able to free himself from Dylan, but mainly by expanding his musical vocabulary into areas Dylan couldn't or wouldn't go. The struggle to free himself from the pretensions of college-boy modernism was equally fascinating (and amusing), and ultimately led to what I think of as his lyrical breakthrough with Simon & Garfunkel, which is "Mrs. Robinson." But the story of that struggle begins with those late 1950s and early 1960s recordings.

1957–1962 RECORDINGS

What's most striking about Simon's rock 'n' roll records from 1957 to 1962 is how not-bad they are.[2] Only "Hey Schoolgirl" made any kind of dent in the marketplace, but many of the rest of the songs easily could've been hits, given the weird alchemy of talent, luck, timing, and payola that got songs on the radio in the 1950s. Simon had no style of his own during this period: he hurled everything he was hearing on rock 'n' roll radio onto these tracks: shrill female backup singers; smoky alto sax breaks; baroquely complex doo-wop arrangements; fast shuffles and bathetic ballads; teen lyrics that obsessed on high school classrooms, dance crazes, and candy-store jukeboxes; a wide array of nonsense syllabification ("lettle lettle lettle lettle lettle yeah yeah yeah . . . let's make some noise!"); and vocal styles that stole shamelessly from Elvis, Buddy Holly, Dion, and the countless one-hit wonders who filled out the Top 40 in those days. Listening to a CD's worth of these songs today is to hear a shrewd compendium of the 1950s pop vocabulary. But while Simon was nothing but an imitator, he crafted every track with growing studio smarts and youthful enthusiasm, as if he expected every song to be a hit. "The Lone Teen Ranger," a novelty song about a boy who loses his girl when she gets obsessed with "The Lone Ranger" TV show (she kisses the screen when he's on) is fast and funny. "Wild Flower" effectively sets a Bo Diddley stomp (*Bomp Ba-Bomp Ba-Bomp—Ba-Bomp-Bomp*) against some surprisingly catchy Hawaiian background vocals. "Motorcycle" amusingly tries to capitalize on the biker movie craze (as represented by "The Wild One") of the time. "Don't Say Goodbye" is a passable Buddy Holly imitation, and "True or False" features an Elvis vocal so studied and accurate that Simon could probably have had a career as an Elvis imitator if nothing else had worked out (and had he grown, say, six or seven inches . . .). That many of these songs were written, arranged, produced, and performed by a kid who had to leave the studio early so he could finish his trigonometry homework is a testament to a burgeoning talent, certainly. However, since that talent lacked any artistic direction of its own, it could only manifest itself in proficient, dexterous pieces of pop confection celebrating the simple pleasures of a teenager being allowed to make music and hoping for a big break. That's what all those "boo-bop-a-lootchie-ba"s, "poop de waddy waddy cha cha cha"s, and "lettle lettle lettle lettle"s were really about—Simon was making himself some joyful noise. Anything more articulate would have to wait until he'd absorbed Dylan and those college poets of his.

WEDNESDAY MORNING, 3 A.M. (1964)

Listening today to *Wednesday Morning, 3 A.M.*, Simon & Garfunkel's debut album originally released in October 1964, one wonders what the two young artists—and even more, their handlers at Columbia Records—were thinking. Or maybe the thinking was all too clear. Tom Wilson, the album's producer, seemed to be trying to position the duo as a more youthful Peter, Paul, and Mary—clean-cut college folkies with the right politics (i.e., "ban the bomb" and "support civil rights in the South") whose pure-blend harmonies, conscientiously worked out as they were, suggested nothing so much as good sons eager to please their elders. While Columbia allowed Simon to sneak five of his compositions onto the twelve-song album (Simon was doubtlessly pleased; Dylan only got two of his own songs on *his* debut album), much of the rest of the album seems almost frightfully misguided: "You Can Tell the World" and "Go Tell It on the Mountain" were already campfire chestnuts by the time Simon & Garfunkel recorded them, and so treacly-earnest that a listener feels like John Belushi in *Animal House*, who violently trashes a folksinger's guitar in order to get the guy to stop singing. "Last Night I Had the Strangest Dream" and "The Sun Is Burning" are folk-political in ways that give folk-political a bad name: singsongy, simple-minded calls for world peace. The sop to Dylan, "The Times They Are A-Changin'," was by 1964 a *de rigueur* gesture by any folkie hoping to be taken seriously, and Simon & Garfunkel's version, which takes the edges off Dylan's own, did Simon no favors when the two were compared. And the decision to record "Peggy-O," an old Scottish ballad that Dylan had also covered on his debut album, only reinforced the comparisons—comparisons that Simon, at that stage of his career, was in no position to win. (It didn't help that while Dylan sang the song with throwaway ironic distance, Simon and Garfunkel sang it so prettily, their harmonies so loftily beautiful that the song's shocking ending, where a scorned lover returns to his girl's village to burn it down, is lost in the soft-focus gauze of the vocals.) Finally, the inclusion of "Benedictus," a two-part canticle sung entirely in Latin and normally only heard in Catholic high mass, was precise, pious, tastefully backed by guitar and cello—and puzzling.

The question of why a duo that proudly proclaimed its Jewishness (unlike Robert Zimmerman, who changed his name to Bob Dylan, Simon and Garfunkel didn't hide their Jewishness to suit the marketplace) would sing a song from the Catholic liturgy only called attention to other songs on the album which were explicitly Christian, namely "You Can Tell the World" and "Go Tell It on the Mountain." One answer—that like most early 1960s folkies, Simon & Garfunkel assumed a then-fashionable Christian ethic in their songs while not taking the faith literally—is superficially true but doesn't explain enough. Simon, the youthful hard-headed cynic steeped in existential angst, would take Christianity—its ethics and some of its mythology, if not Christian faith itself—very seriously his entire career. Consider "Blessed" (from *Sounds of Silence*), the sardonic invocation of Christ's beatitudes whose anger could only have come from someone who felt betrayed by a world that couldn't live up to the Christian virtues; or "Bridge Over Troubled Water," a gospel hymn lauding selfless Christian love; or *Graceland*'s pervasive desire for "a shot of redemption"; or the often-explicit New Testament vocabulary of *The Rhythm of the Saints*; or finally the concern with love, death, and God (usually Christianized) that laces the entirety of *So Beautiful or So What*. Throughout his career, Simon's music invokes Christian imagery, emotion, and ethics much more than it does the Jewish faith with which he was raised. And his regard for Christianity—particularly its values of love, sacrifice, and compassion for the poor and discarded, and its tireless struggle to approach the transcendent—will appear in his work with increasing intensity, especially in the late stages of his career.

Of the five originals on *Wednesday*, "He Was My Brother" is the most overtly Christian in spirit. The song takes up the story of a "freedom rider"—that is, one of thousands of civil rights workers who, during the early 1960s, challenged Southern states that continued to enforce local racial segregation laws despite recent Supreme Court rulings (especially 1960s Boynton vs. Virginia) that such segregation was unconstitutional. Freedom riders rode buses and cars filled with both blacks and whites through the Deep South, provoking local law enforcement into arresting them and raising the ire of Southern racists, who sometimes brutally attacked the bus riders while police looked on and did nothing. In "He Was My Brother," the freedom rider's life ends tragically but heroically—"he died so his brothers could be free." To twenty-first-century ears, the song sounds sanctimonious ("They shot my brother dead / Because he hated what was wrong"), and it is, but if we view it in historical context, we can see it as the sort of aural equivalent of King's philosophy of nonviolent resistance, indeed as a song about Jesus's command to turn the other cheek.

It's not as easy to explain away the flaws of "Sparrow" or "Wednesday Morning, 3 A.M." Lyrically, "Sparrow," an allegory about a tiny bird who can find no love or solace in a mean, cold world, reads like the product of a dutiful high school sophomore's creative writing assignment: it's structurally sound, filled out with detail, thematically unified, and—if it were not for the lovely voices singing it and the pretty Spanish guitar melody filigreed through the verses—more or less unlistenable. "Wednesday Morning, 3 A.M." may be even worse: here we have a protagonist gazing on his lover as she sleeps, but knowing that he must leave her forever because "I've committed a crime / Broken the law." His crime? Murder? A crime of passion? Nope: "I held up and robbed / A hard liquor store." That "hard" is hilarious, as if his crime would have been less serious if he'd held up a 7-11. In any case, now that he's committed his crime, his life seems "unreal"—the standard adjective preferred by early 1960s college poets who'd imbibed Eliot's "The Waste Land" and wanted to invoke a sense of confusion and isolation. The song's a gross miscalculation, and the fact that the duo decided to name the album after it an even greater one.

Which leaves us with the album's two real achievements, "Bleeker Street" and "The Sound of Silence." "Bleeker Street" is minor, a gently harmonized song that rides a long, lovely melody line. A description of one of Greenwich Village's more famous avenues, it weaves together images of homeless men sleeping in alleys, tentative lovers ("I saw a shadow touch a shadow's hand"), poets reading their verse, and church bells ringing. The song avoids the moral bluster that plagues most of the rest of the album, and rather touchingly evokes the feeling of a young poet/songwriter at the beginning of his career walking this legendary street, absorbing the atmosphere, knowing that "it's a long road to Canaan"—that is, the promised land (of artistic creation, fame and success, spiritual fulfillment). Both in its lyric and its vocal treatment, the song has a light touch—something Simon rarely achieved in his early work.

"The Sound of Silence," a "major work" according to Garfunkel's own liner notes (which bear the mark of an Ivy Leaguer steeped in stentorian modernist jargon: "Its theme is man's inability to communicate with man") is Simon's first calling card to greatness. In *Wednesday*'s version, the vocals are backed only by Simon's delicately fingered acoustic guitar, which forces our focus on the song's lyrics. Beginning with one of Simon's most famous openings, "Hello darkness, my old friend," the song presents a "vision" that the protagonist awakens to after a night of "restless dreams." Walking "lonely streets of cobblestone" lit by artificial light—the listener will hearken here to Eliot's J. Alfred Prufrock, another lonely walker of the urban landscape—the protagonist envisions "ten thousand people, maybe more" who can't connect with each other. Songs are written that no one can share. The people pray to "the neon god they made"—in the 1960s, neon was practically code for "artificial," "unnatural"—and they create a social reality that's so false that the only ones who can speak the truth are the alienated "prophets" who scrawl graffiti on tenement buildings. It's a vision of a society whose desperate truths are kept under wraps, truths we can only uncover if we listen to "the sound of silence" underneath the empty talk.

This "vision" would have been familiar to anyone exposed to early 1960s high culture. The protagonist carries on in the tradition of Baudelaire's (filtered through Eliot's) *flaneurs*, alienated night-walkers who decry/indulge the decadence of the modern city. The song also invokes the despairing visions of European moviemakers like Michelangelo Antonioni, who in films like *L'Avventura* and *La Notte* created *tableaux* of stunted communication and baffled silence that had struck a powerful chord with American art-house filmgoers in the early 1960s. Simon's song, like Dylan's "Like a Rolling Stone" or the Beatles' "Nowhere Man" and "Eleanor Rigby" (and later, of course, "A Day in the Life"), was one of rock music's opening explorations into a subject that had been roiling the minds of philosophers, poets, and filmmakers for a good half century. As a piece of pop seriousness, however, it worked because of the intimacy of its address ("Hello darkness, my old friend" is hard for a listener to resist), the dignified solemnity of its melody, the sharpness of its imagery, and the way it summed up its theme of alienation in a pop-friendly package.

As strong as the song is, however, it's been an irritant to many listeners—for its self-seriousness, first of all (unlike Dylan, Simon has rarely been able to pass off his most trenchant lines as throwaways), but perhaps even more because of the seven lines in the middle of the song, which begin, "'Fools,' said I, 'you do not know.'" These lines cast the song's speaker as the one person—beside the graffiti prophets—who's above it all, whose "words" can "teach" the noncommunicating masses if they'd only listen to the poet preaching to them. It turns the song into a scold of its own audience, and was an indication of the pretentious direction Simon's work would take in the next few years, pretentions that would turn influential rock critics like Robert Christgau, Lester Bangs, and Dave Marsh against Simon's early work.

At any rate, *Wednesday Morning, 3 A.M.* bombed commercially, selling only three thousand copies in its initial run and garnering little radio airplay. The duo promptly broke up. Garfunkel returned to his studies at Columbia, while Simon nursed his wounds by going to England, where he had a girlfriend, Kathy Chitty, and the prospect of a career as a journeyman folksinger playing the British folk circuit. In and around London he played clubs for twenty or thirty pounds a night, wrote new songs, and networked with musicians and people close to the music business. Among the latter was Judith Piepe, a well-connected friend who promoted some of his demos to BBC radio, which played them and got Simon enough exposure that he was offered a solo recording contract, this time with CBS International. In the spring of 1965, Simon recorded twelve of his own compositions that would be released as his first solo album.

THE PAUL SIMON SONGBOOK (1965)

The Paul Simon Songbook was for many years the great lost gem in the Paul Simon *oeuvre*, originally released only in England and, when it failed commercially there, quickly deleted from CBS International's catalogue. The reason for the deletion was simple: the album is mostly made up of what are essentially guitar-and-vocal demos of songs that would later be released as full-blown Simon & Garfunkel productions on *Sounds of Silence* and *Parsley, Sage, Rosemary, and Thyme*, and neither Simon nor Columbia records wanted to confuse Simon & Garfunkel's audience. (The album was finally released in America in 2004.) Listening to it now, its bare-bones unplugged quality is revelatory: simultaneously, Simon comes across as a self-conscious, sensitive, insecure poet struggling with his own pretensions[3] —the album could easily have been called *Prufrock Picks Up a Guitar*—and as a remarkably fine melodist, a creator of songs so indelibly and profligately tuneful that they mask a multitude of lyrical sins.

Two songs on the album, "The Sound of Silence" and "He Was My Brother," are solo versions of *Wednesday*'s recordings with Garfunkel. The reworking of "The Sound of Silence" is a nice surprise: he underplays the song's more portentous qualities, making it seem less an apocalyptic cultural statement than an expression of personal isolation. "He Was My Brother" is similarly shaded: more a statement of personal pain than an expression of the moral tragedy of American racism. With the latter song, he had reasons for this more personal reading. After he initially wrote "He Was My Brother" for *Wednesday*, a high school friend of Simon's, Andrew Goodman, eerily lived out the song's tragedy when he, along with two other freedom riders working to expose Southern racism, James Earl Cheney and Michael Schwerner, were murdered by the Ku Klux Klan on a Mississippi back road in June of 1964. Changing only one line to make the song specific to Goodman ("this town's gonna be your burying place" became "Mississippi's gonna be . . ."), Simon's vocal brings out the human tragedy that was somewhat buried in the earlier version's religious abstractions.

The remaining ten songs are new, and whatever the shortcomings of the lyrics, the melodies are so compulsively hummable that it's clear why eight of these songs would form the backbone of two extraordinarily popular Simon & Garfunkel albums. "Melodies are inexplicable;

they're magic," Simon once said in an interview: "Combine certain words and melodies and it all becomes very moving. Separate the words and melodies and it's not so moving."[4] Perhaps that's why one can still stomach minor efforts like "The Side of a Hill," an irritating allegory of almost Donovan-level fluff, and not program past it when one hears it on CD. Or why "A Church Is Burning," a piece of schoolmarmy earnestness about racial violence in the South, remains listenable.

The album's major statement, clearly, is "I Am a Rock," with which Simon kicks off the album. Like other "major" Simon of this period, it's melodically memorable, earnestly sensitive, exceedingly well crafted, and irritating lyrically. Playing off John Donne's "No Man Is an Island," which was taught in every English department in the land in the early 1960s (largely because of T. S. Eliot's elevation of the metaphysical poets to canonical status), the song's speaker insists that he *can* be an island and that he prefers it that way, since he wants neither to touch others nor have them touch him, and doesn't want to hear of love ("If I never loved I never would have cried") or of friendship, because "friendship causes pain." Protected by the "armor" of his books and his poetry, the singer hides in his room, proudly isolated, hard and imperturbable as stone. Certainly, the lyrics of "I Am a Rock" struck a nerve, speaking for legions of collegians (it was a #3 hit when released in a Simon & Garfunkel version a year later) who felt a little too sensitive for the buffetings of the adult world, and used the armaments of higher education to protect them from it. The boast of the lyric is meant to be ironic, of course: we're meant to realize that the speaker is deluded to think he can survive on his own, and that he's therefore on the road to tragic loneliness. But it doesn't work: irony is never effective when delivered via sledgehammer. Furthermore, Simon ends the song by trying to make us feel sorry for the speaker; singing in his supersensitive voice, he intones: "And a rock feels no pain; and an island never cries." The song curdles into sentimental self-pity just when it needs to stay garnet hard.

"Patterns," which concludes the album, is, like "Rock," melodically infectious but afflicted with some of the same sophomoric lyrical conceits. Beginning with a deft description of a pattern of shadows against a young man's bedroom wall, the speaker inflates the idea of a pattern until it becomes a symbol of the social "patterns I must follow." Seeing the pattern as a maze and himself (inevitably) as a rat, he insists, "The pattern never alters / Until the rat dies." The idea here, that the speaker fears he is about to enter a society that will force him into confining, conformist roles, will of course be central to *The Graduate* two years later, but it was already an idea of broad popular currency, familiar to viewers of Billy Wilder's *The Apartment* (1959) or readers of Paul Goodman's extremely influential sociological tract *Growing Up Absurd* (1960). To college students just familiarizing themselves with such ideas, the song would likely have had a shock of recognition—and did when it was released on Simon & Garfunkel's *Parsley, Sage, Rosemary, and Thyme* in 1967—but it's sung here with the kind of callow know-it-all fatalism that dates it as a period piece.

We needn't belabor the album's sophomoric qualities, except to note that "Flowers Never Bend with the Rainfall" and "A Most Peculiar Man" confront the listener with similarly shallow "philosophical" reflections that sound engaging the first few times, and then pale on repeated listening. "Kathy's Song" is saved from borrowed self-absorption (the singer/poet's complaint that his "words" "tear and strain to rhyme" come right out of Eliot's "Burnt Norton") by the obviously heartfelt and impressively subdued sentiments of its longing lover and by its refreshing willingness to break outside the default solipsism of Simon's usual speakers ("From the shelter of my mind / . . . I gaze *beyond* / . . . To England where my heart lies" [my italics]). "Leaves That Are Green," though hobbled by clichéd nature imagery (which suggests that the young Simon learned little from the Robert Frost he claims as his own in the later "The Dangling Conversation") has a (for once) credible innocence that supersedes its pretensions. And "April Comes She Will," with its sturdy construction, liltingly pretty melody line, and achingly sincere and sad vocal (unironized, unintellectualized) is one of the few unalloyed triumphs of the album. Its sweet, persuasive melancholy made it perfect when Simon & Garfunkel adapted it as the set piece in *The Graduate* where Benjamin Braddock grows disenchanted with his affair with Mrs. Robinson.

That leaves "A Simple Desultory Philippic," Simon's sixty-four-dollar-word-titled effort to both mimic and take a swipe at Bob Dylan. On *Songbook*, the song is still a fragment—it will be reworked and extended to greater effect on *Parsley, Sage, Rosemary, and Thyme*. I'll discuss it more in the context of that album, but for now, let me say only that the first verse, in which he wittily rattles off a series of 1960s cultural stars, from Norman Mailer to Andy Warhol to the Stones, Simon shows that he's at least a careful reader of the *Sunday New York Times*, as up-to-date as any twenty-four-year-old culture vulture might be expected to be. The verse is coffeehouse beat if not Dylanesque, simulating the way the white noise of mass media culture saturates the mind. But the second verse, in which Simon tries to imitate Dylan's vocal manner while taking potshots at youth culture for being so shallow as to know Bob Dylan better than Dylan Thomas, is not only crassly elitist but a really unfunny demonstration of sour grapes. At the time, it may have been a brave move to go at the nearly sacralized Dylan at all—Simon recorded the song before Dylan went electric and endured his first wave of real criticism—but the song stinks of jealousy: Simon's churlishness undercuts his satiric intentions.

Despite the album's impressive cache of melodies, and its ambitious if overbearing lyrical reach, *The Paul Simon Songbook* went nowhere commercially, and after its quick death by market forces, he returned to the bar and coffeehouse gigging that had sustained him for the year that he spent in England. Then one day he picked up a music trade magazine and discovered that an electrified version of "The Sound of Silence" was rocketing up the American charts. He hurried back to the States, where the real career of Simon & Garfunkel begins.

SOUNDS OF SILENCE (1966)

This album, released in January 1966, is the one most Simon & Garfunkel fans of the 1960s regarded as the "first album," and propelled by the #1 hit "The Sound of Silence" and "I Am a Rock" (which reached #3), the collection was a pop smash—it stayed on the charts for an almost unheard-of 143 weeks—in addition to being well-regarded by many (if hardly all) of the growing cadre of rock critics who had sprung up in the mid-1960s. Though credited to Bob Johnston, the production chores were mostly handled by Simon, Garfunkel, and Roy Halee, with whom Simon would establish a long-term working relationship. The album contains only three new Simon compositions (four if you include the substantially reworked version of "Wednesday Morning, 3 A.M.," redubbed "Somewhere They Can't Find Me"). However, the album successfully recasts six Simon compositions culled from the two earlier records into newly hip folk-rock contexts, and adds a short instrumental interlude called "Angie" written by an English friend of Simon's named Davy Graham. The result is an East Coast folk-rock classic rivaling anything that West Coast folk rockers like the Buffalo Springfield or the Byrds were doing at the time.

Whatever one's objections to the lyrics of "The Sound of Silence" or "I Am a Rock," which open and close the album, it's clear that electrifying the guitars, adding drums, and polishing the production gives the songs a brightness and effervescence that they simply didn't possess before. The listener is distracted from the pessimistic vision of the songs—both are about isolated, anxious urban dwellers, beset by faceless crowds and neon lights, who can communicate neither with others nor themselves—by the frankly fun shimmer and bounce of the sound. The echo of the jangly guitars in "The Sound of Silence" is so deep that one can imagine a sound of silence *behind* or *within* the sound of the record, an aural parallel to the lyrics' meaning that helps put the song over. And the catchy new guitar riff Simon wrote for the end of the chorus of "I Am a Rock" is so cheery that, together with a breezy new organ accompaniment, the speaker's self-pity is nicely swathed in hummability. Couching Simon's painfully self-conscious lyrics into a rock context partly liberated them from their seriousness: the songs are carried by melody and groove, and the lyrics, rather than seeming the main attraction, as they were on Simon's previous versions, are pushed slightly to the margins, where they seem either forgivable or—compared to 95 percent of the songs on the radio in 1966—pretty damn smart for rock songs.

Some of the other reworked material on the album is similarly improved. "A Most Peculiar Man," all ironic despair on *Songbook*, is leavened by sweet guitar arpeggios and floating organ. "Leaves That Are Green," a mild sedative on *Songbook*, is spruced up with a delightful harpsichord opening that belies the lyrics' winsome gloom. And "April Come She Will," given over to Garfunkel to sing solo, comes into its own. Garfunkel makes one significant melodic change that brings the song to a real apotheosis. In Simon's version on *Songbook*, he sings the third line of each verse the same, rising a fifth on the word "will" each time. Garfunkel holds the line steady in the two first verses, then rises surprisingly and gorgeously on "September I will *remember*," which stamps the ending with a subtle and deeply pleasurable climax.

Passing quietly over "Somewhere They Won't Find Me" (as cringe-worthy in its recalibrated rock version as it was when it was the terrible folk song "Wednesday Morning, 3 A.M.") and "We Got a Groovy Thing Goin'" (Simon's silly commercial attempt to use Counterculture lingo to connect with the hippie contingent of the rock audience), we can move on to the album's two best new songs. "Richard Cory" is Simon's interpretation of Edward Arlington Robinson's early modernist poem of the same name. Though on the album sleeve, Simon sends fulsome "apologies" to Robinson, his version isn't at all embarrassing. Filling out some of the details of the poem with reasonable conjectures, he heightens the poem's concern with class struggle: the song's speaker works in Richard Cory's factory rather than being just a representative of the town's poor. The fact, then, that the worker looks up to the man who has cursed him with poverty gives the song a sharper irony than perhaps Robinson intended, and makes the shock of Richard's suicide all the more plaintive. Paired side-by-side with "A Most Peculiar Man" on the album, making it half of what is essentially the record's suicide suite, the song is indeed heavy-handed, but it remains one of Simon's more successful literary experiments with Simon & Garfunkel.

The outlier on the album is "Blessed," a supposedly cynical reworking of the Sermon on the Mount sung by a speaker who feels so marginalized that he is sure that even Jesus's reassuring embrace of the meek and disinherited will not include him. Though marked by Simon's predictable self-pity of the period, the lyrics juxtapose two Gospel passages that give the song a plangent wit. The first is of course the iterations of the Sermon on the Mount—blessed are the meek, and so on. The second is Jesus's uncanny call to God while he's being crucified—"Why have you forsaken me?" An existentialist reading of this line, to which Simon might be expected to have been sympathetic at the time, is that Jesus feels betrayed here not only by Judas but also by God himself, so that the world becomes empty of meaning right at the moment of death. (In the Gospel of Luke, Jesus recovers, ending his life with the words, "Father, into your hands I commend my spirit." In the other three Christ narratives, the words about forsakenness are the last Jesus is credited with speaking.) By this reckoning, "Blessed" is a song about ultimate, metaphysical alienation, son abandoned by father, man by God, and in a way becomes a sort of *uber*-Simon composition. And perhaps it would be, if it weren't for the very un-Simonish musical accompaniment, which sounds like Simon had wandered into an early Velvet Underground show, walked out impressed, and wanted to rip off what he could from them. The drums on "Blessed" pound harder than anything Simon & Garfunkel had ever done; the guitars drone a-melodically; for the only time in their career, Paul and Art's twinned voices don't harmonize but simply shout the melody; and the song's bitter speaker wanders around Soho, observing the druggies and whores like some Lou Reed clone. Sonically, the song is wholly unlike anything in the Simon & Garfunkel catalogue, to me an interesting experiment that Simon never bothered to follow up on.

Sounds of Silence was Simon & Garfunkel's commercial breakthrough, their ticket to sustained stardom, and Simon's introduction to the pop world as a major songwriter. The recording and engineering of the album were completed in a matter of weeks—Columbia was eager to get the album out as the single "The Sound of Silence" was peaking—and Simon, who would soon gain a reputation as a producer every bit as painstaking as his reputation as a songwriter, was eager that the duo's next album would give him time to do his new songs justice.

PARSLEY, SAGE, ROSEMARY, AND THYME (1966)

Simon & Garfunkel's follow-up to the vastly popular Sounds of Silence was released just nine months later, in October 1966, in keeping with the extraordinary pressures record companies of the 1960s exerted on their talent rosters to capitalize as quickly as possible on any market success. The pressure came from fear and ignorance as much as from anything else, as companies like Columbia were desperately struggling to keep pace with the lightning-quick changes in 1960s popular culture that no one seemed to keep up with. Among the many changes was the pop-culture audience's shift from buying singles (45 RPM records with one song on each side) to full-length long-playing albums (LPs) that featured perhaps ten songs and allowed for thirty-plus minutes of music. As with so much else in 1960s pop music, the trailblazer was Bob Dylan, whose Bringing It All Back Home and Highway 61 Revisited (both 1965) reconceived the rock album as a fully charged work of art, a cohesive body of songs meant to be listened to together.[5] The audience was perhaps primed for this by early Beatles albums: they were stuffed

dio hits, but what listeners commonly knew and excused as "fill-
ird-rate songs thrown on an album to fill the time requirements
of an LP—were often as good as the hits, so the common Beatles
listener bought and listened to the albums, not just the singles heard on
the radio. Influenced by Dylan's seriousness, mid-period Beatles albums like *Rubber Soul* (1965) and *Revolver* (1966) possessed a sonic, if
not an attitudinal, cohesiveness that marked them as self-contained albums, as did the Beach Boys' *Pet Sounds* (1966), an album that inspired
the pinnacle of all albums-as-rock-art, the Beatles' *Sgt. Pepper's Lonely
Heart's Club Band* (1967). The point here is that when Paul Simon and
Art Garfunkel went into the studio to record a new album, the rock
audience was listening closer, demanding more from pop music than
perhaps any generation ever had: the most discerning part of the audience was beginning to sense that the walls separating high and low
culture were crashing down—that one's mind could quickly veer "from
Tolstoy to Tinkerbell" as Simon himself put it—and that one had as
much right to expect, even demand, aesthetic transcendence from Dylan—or Paul Simon—as one did from Eliot or Tolstoy.

Certainly the ever-ambitious Simon didn't shirk from the challenge.
Parsley, Sage, Rosemary, and Thyme seeks to keep company with some
of the albums mentioned above, and in places I think it succeeds. Like
the albums just mentioned, it's meant to be listened to as a whole,
consecutively, and so I will discuss it more or less in that way. Though
not a "concept album" in the way that *Sgt. Pepper*, or side 1 of Simon &
Garfunkel's *Bookends*, is, it's a statement record whose songs resonate
musically and lyrically with each other, and present a relatively complex
and coherent statement of Simon's existential and political point of view
circa 1966.

The album starts off with the gorgeous "Scarborough Fair/Canticle,"
at once a showcase for Simon & Garfunkel's elegantly airy harmonies; a
complex, inspired arrangement of a traditional British folk song (the
arrangement is Garfunkel's, underscoring his necessity to the duo's artistic success); and, lyrically, a fairly subtle condemnation of U.S. partic-
ipation in the Vietnam War. There were lots of rock groups whose
sound featured tight harmony vocals in the mid-1960s—among them
the Beatles, the Mamas and the Papas, the Byrds, and the Hollies, not
to mention pop folk groups like Peter, Paul, and Mary—but it's hard to
imagine any of these groups pulling off the creamy perfection of Simon

& Garfunkel's baroque arrangement here. The melody rides on the cushion of Garfunkel's exquisite contralto, interweaving a "Canticle"—a much-reworked and improved version of "The Side of a Hill" from *Notebook*—sung by Simon that elevates the composition to something well beyond an adaptation of a traditional folk song. (The writing was credited to Simon and Garfunkel on the record, causing a fuss among folk purists, who objected that the duo should have at least acknowledged its borrowing of traditional folk material. Though Simon & Garfunkel clearly made the song their own, the purists' charge is on target.) The "Canticle" part of the song, pitched lower in the mix so that only certain phrases clearly emerge—"And polishes a gun," "Blazing in scarlet battalions," "And to fight for a cause / They've long ago forgotten"— creates an almost subconscious discordancy in the otherwise lush context of the song: this opulent ditty about weaving shirts, true love, and herbs and spices has buried within it a critique of the war that young Americans were being asked to fight, even though most of them, too, had long forgotten what cause they were fighting for, if they'd ever known it at all. The song, which eventually reached #11 on the pop charts in 1968 when it was released as part of *The Graduate* soundtrack, is used in the film over a lyrical passage where Benjamin Braddock goes to the campus of UC Berkeley to search for Elaine Robinson. Berkeley is presented in the film as sunny and quiet, but everyone knew Berkeley was a "movement" campus highly mobilized in opposition to the Vietnam War, and the "Canticle" portion of the song deftly underscored that fact.

"Scarborough Fair/Canticle" is followed by "Patterns," Simon's reworking of his sociological critique from *Notebook*. Placed second on the album, as a sort of album thesis, it's required to carry more meaning than it can bear. Simon lays some bongo drums and a loping bass under the vocal, and throws in a biting blues guitar riff to give it some ballast, but then turns the echo way up on the crucial (and not very good) line, *"until the rat dies,"* in case the listener misses the broad message of our entrapment in the soul-killing templates of Organization Man. The mood is lightened considerably on "Cloudy," however. Simon's first obvious "drug" song, it's partly an homage to the mid-1960s California's Bay Area pot scene—"from Berkeley to Carmel"—where one hitchhikes high, and one's thoughts have "no borders, no boundaries." The mildly subversive idea here is that marijuana is one way of avoiding all those societal patterns, but the melody and arrangement sound a little too willfully whimsical—an issue Simon handles better on the LP's side 1 closer, "59th Street Bridge Song," though not by much. (Serious Simon is the wrong guy to be singing lines like "Life I love you / All is groovy.") Simon's songwriting would eventually display a sharp sense of humor—in, for example, "You're Kind," "You Can Call Me Al," "Outrageous," and "The Afterlife"—but at this point in his career either Simon forces himself to be light, or he is abrasive and caustic, as he is in *Parsley, Sage*'s "Big Bright Green Pleasure Machine," which is hitched to a theme more or less borrowed from the Rolling Stones' "Satisfaction" and a rock arrangement that would have sounded just right on a Monkees album. Luckily, humor is not an issue at all on "Homeward Bound," a song that picks up the restless traveler theme of "Cloudy" in a simple and poignant way. A top 10 hit, Simon wrote it in England during his endless solo gigging period—when he thought of himself as "a poet and a one-man band"—but did not record it till now. Though he can't help, in the song's third verse, from gnawing self-consciously on the already-gnawed theme of his self-consciousness, the song is otherwise a sweet folky paean to the idea of a musician pining for his love while on the road—one of rock's most durable themes that few songwriters have bettered, and a deserved classic.

Side 2 of the album—the programming of "sides" of an album mattered by 1966, incidentally: the first song of side 2 was a showcase song, often a single, and was nearly as important as the album opener—began with "The Dangling Conversation," perhaps the most reviled song in the Simon catalogue. Released as a single, it reached only #25 on the charts, much to Simon's disappointment, and came in for some of the nastiest criticism he ever received. Consciously arty and intellectual, the song begins by comparing an afternoon to a "still-life watercolor"; a romantically anemic couple ask if theater is dead and if psychoanalysis is effective; they read Dickenson and Frost, noting "our place with bookmarkers / That measure what we've lost," and display the kind of sighing "velleities" made current by T. S. Eliot poems like "Preludes" and "Portrait of a Lady." Ralph J. Gleason, who wrote the album's liner notes, claims the song is "straight-ahead satire" of the "cocktail conversation" of the Establishment: would that it were so. If there's satire here, it's certainly not "straight," but serves as a cover for what appears to be Simon's fantasy of his own cultural predicament at the time. The poetry-reading, theater-discussing couple in the song sound exactly like the kind of people who might write mannered Paul Simon songs about alienation, "emptiness in harmony," and being rats in the cages of social convention. And the song's super-lush string and harp (harp?!) arrangement—"beautiful" as the soundtrack to a Douglas Sirk melodrama—hardly ironizes the song's sentimental brooding; it reenforces its archness. If it weren't for its strong melody and precise lyrical details, its sense of complacency would be insufferable. Even with them, it nearly is. The only really good news about the song is that it is Simon's high-water mark of intellectual pretension. After this, he would gradually strip his songs of intellectual climbing—more precisely, of intellectual and poetic borrowing in the service of sounding smart—and grow into his own style.

The operative word of that last sentence is *gradually*. Some of the second side's five remaining tracks are afflicted with similar pretensions—particularly "Flowers Never Bend with the Rainfall," with the speaker parceling out stale existential shibboleths like "I don't know what is real / I can't touch what I feel," and so on, or "A Poem on an Underground Wall," which grandiloquently heroizes the graffiti prophets from "The Sound of Silence." This album's version of "A Simple Desultory Phillipic" adds a nice descending fuzz guitar riff to the original on *Notebook*, and concludes with Simon imitating a presumably stoned Dylan dropping his harmonica as he's performing, but the song still reeks of an unpleasant *ressentiment* toward a competitor. "For Emily, Whenever I Might Find Her," on the other hand, is probably Simon's least self-conscious song, a pure idealizing love song sung with such unbridled tenderness by Art Garfunkel that one either melts with sentiment or cringes in embarrassment. I will admit that I have no defenses against the song: having heard it hundreds of times since my teens, I reliably melt every time. To me, it's about as good as pop gets in embodying the innocent idealization of youthful love, and it's carried entirely by Garfunkel's heavenly articulation of Simon's disarmingly radiant melody. It's the kind of pop song that it does no good to argue about—melody is magic or it isn't—so I'll shut up about it now.

Parsley, Sage's album closer is "7 O'Clock News/Silent Night," which lays a news anchor's reading of the news over Simon & Garfunkel's delicate crooning of "Silent Night." Given the obviousness of the conceit—the news on this broadcast is about the death of Lenny Bruce,

a demonstration headed up by Martin Luther King Jr. called off because of threats on King's life (this a year and a half before King's
assassination), a House Un-American Activities committee meeting
about Vietnam antiwar activists, and a speech by Richard Nixon declar-
ing that "opposition to war in this country is the greatest weapon working against the U.S."—one would think the piece wouldn't work, but it
does. Perhaps it's because the news portion of the song is handled with
considerable subtlety: the news subjects were real and they're treated
with restraint and intelligence. Listening to the song gives a tiny window into the violent and chaotic nature of mid-1960s America, along
with its underlying desire for tranquility, for silent nights filled with the
possibility of redemption.

The production of *Parsley, Sage, Rosemary, and Thyme* was credited
to Bob Johnston, but Simon claims Johnston's work was altogether
nominal—it was he, Garfunkel, and engineer Roy Halee who worked
out the album's sound. The innovations in rock sound during 1966 and
1967 were happening at quantum speeds—on the West Coast, rumors
were that Brian Wilson's production of the Beach Boys' *Smile* project
would revolutionize pop music, and of course in England, the Beatles
made that revolution a reality with *Sgt. Pepper's Lonely Hearts Club
Band* in the late spring of 1967. After *Sgt. Pepper*, the top acts in rock
music—and by now Simon & Garfunkel were a top act—had to respond
to the challenge. Their response was *Bookends*.

BOOKENDS (1968), *THE GRADUATE* (FILM SOUNDTRACK) (1968), *SONGS OF AMERICA* (TV SPECIAL) (1969)

Released in April of 1968, *Bookends* was the album that, when combined with *The Graduate* soundtrack (which prominently featured their
songs) made Simon & Garfunkel superstars. At one point in 1968,
Bookends, *The Graduate* soundtrack, and *Parsley, Sage, Rosemary, and
Thyme* were #1, #2, and #3 on the Billboard album chart, something no
one except the Beatles had ever been able to accomplish. What must
have been gratifying to Simon, however, was that he and Garfunkel
were able to propel themselves to the heights of fame not by repeating
successful formulas but by extending themselves as artists. The music
on *Bookends* is more varied in style, much more confidently played and

sung, more daring and mature lyrically, and takes a great many more chances in terms of its production, which the duo and Roy Halee had now taken over completely. *Bookends'* sound, meticulously produced over the course of many months in the studio, is shoot-for-the-moon ambitious, responding with audacity to the Beatles' *Sgt. Pepper* and the raft of concept albums that had followed in its wake.

The idea of a "concept album"—an album unified by one musical or lyrical idea, or by a certain cohesive narrative structure, had been bubbling beneath the surface of pop culture since Dylan made rockers take the album form seriously in 1965, but *Sgt. Pepper's* explosive appearance on the scene in the spring of 1967 had upped the ante. Unified less by any literary or philosophical "concept"—though ingenious rock critics often tried to impose one on it—than by its delirious, clearly psychedelic musical experimentation designed to break the boundaries of what was then called popular music, *Sgt. Pepper* was *of a piece*, the songs flowing one into the other, incorporating modernist symphonic arrangements and odd sound effects, the songs building and reflecting on each other sonically and occasionally lyrically. The idea was to make the album a single listening experience, a pop version of a symphony or opera. Other rock acts immediately seized on the idea—the Stones with *Their Satanic Majesties Request*, the Kinks with a string of concept albums from 1968 into the mid-1970s, the Who with *The Who Sell Out* and later the "rock opera" *Tommy*—and Simon was caught up in the excitement. Simon's concept was to try to encompass in a single song suite the journey from one "bookend"—youth—to another—old age and death. (The suite only takes up one side of the album: Simon has never been a prolific songwriter, and he didn't stoop to write filler just to balloon the concept to an album's length requirements. Thus, side 2 of the record consists of some singles that the duo released during 1967, along with the definitive version of "Mrs. Robinson.")

The bookends concept turned out to be much too broad and unwieldy to unify the seven tracks on side 1 in any cohesive and resonant way, but it does introduce an idea that has come to obsess Simon's work: the idea of the strangeness and mystery of time's passage: how we inhabit time, "pass through" it, change and get older in it, feel it slip away into memory that's harder and harder to grasp, and can feel trapped in it as it relentlessly marches us toward death. "Time it was, and what a time it was" goes the plaintive opening of the reprise of

"Bookends," and that plaintiveness one can see scattered throughout his work: it's in the concert version of "The Boxer" where Simon wryly laments how "I'm older than I was once, but younger than I'll be, but that's not unusual"; it's in the saxophone and string section break of "Still Crazy after All These Years"; it's in the melancholy admission of "Slip-Sliding Away" that "the nearer your destination the more you're slip-sliding away"; it's in the moving narrative of "Darling Lorraine" as it describes a long and sad relationship ending in death, and in *So Beautiful or So What*'s "Love and Hard Times." It's even on side 2 of *Bookends*, on "A Hazy Shade of Winter," in which the speaker wonders, "Time time time, what's become of me?" Simon had on previous albums dealt with the theme, of course—on "Leaves That Are Green," "April Come She Will," and "The Dangling Conversation"—but on *Bookends*, he begins to let the subject breathe, lets the theme resonate as an idea to be lived with rather than a question that must be answered in some bookish and definitive way. *Bookends*, in fact, is where we might say *the primacy of the book ends for Simon*, where he begins to trust experience as a source for his ideas, and therefore where he genuinely starts to grow up artistically.

The suite opens with the "Bookends Theme," a quiet, short, pretty instrumental guitar figure that lulls the listener, making her unprepared for the crash of drums and the blast of Moog synthesizer that opens "Save the Life of My Child." (The Moog, a first-generation analog synthesizer with an eerie "spacey" sound, was introduced to an astonished pop audience at the Monterey Pop Festival in 1967. Simon & Garfunkel helped organize the festival, and performed there, and presumably this is where Simon first got excited about the Moog's possibilities as a pop instrument.) "Save the Life" is a tautly told narrative about how a community deals with a boy who gets up on a rooftop and threatens to hurl himself off. (The scenario in some ways recalls Philip Roth's story "The Conversion of the Jews," published in 1959, which Simon, an avid reader of contemporary fiction, might be presumed to have read.) A man, looking up at the boy on the ledge, faints; the boy's mother screams; neighbors run for the police; a newspaper shrieks a headline: "Save the Life of My Child!" Hours pass, it gets dark, and "an atmosphere of freaky holiday" envelops the crowd when the police put a spotlight on the boy. Spotting the boy, the crowd bizarrely cheers—and then "He flew away": that is, he jumps, thinking as he falls, "Oh my grace, I got no hiding place." The musical accompaniment invokes the hysteria of the crowd: besides the edgy Moog, there is a huge echoey multi-tracked female choir sounding like they're rehearsing a Wagner opera; there is a short interlude of studio-created, studio-mangled "noise." In the context of the suite, the song is about "youth"—about the despairs of a generation that are so acute that they lead to suicide. ("Save the Life" is, incidentally, Simon's third song about suicide in two years.) But it also about the older generation's confusion: the line "What's becoming of the children?," which the crowd keeps asking itself, is possibly the song's key line. It's a "generation gap" song, though it also demonstrates an interest in how the media converts private experience into spectacle (which Simon will pick up again in "Me and Julio Down by the Schoolyard" and later works). True, the song's grandiose and shrill, and hasn't survived the Simon & Garfunkel years—Simon never plays it solo, and in reunion tours Simon & Garfunkel haven't included it in their set lists—but it's an interesting experiment, like "Blessed," and a more than honorable failure.

The next track is "America," one of Simon's best early songs. Pulling back from the elaborate production of "Save the Life," the sound is more like the popular folk rock of the time, though its simplicity is only apparent: every rock instrument—guitar, bass, drums, organ—at some point in the song acts as the lead instrument, and a muted clarinet slithers through the song, changing its mood at key moments to reinforce the song's drama. It's also Simon's first explicit song about America, a theme he will return to in the TV documentary *Songs of America* and in compositions like "American Tune" (1974), "The Boy in the Bubble" (1986), and "Why Do You Live in the Northeast?" (2004). This "America" describes an America of 1960s youth, a country of young lovers infatuated with travel, adventure, wanderlust. In the song, which has the structure and detail of a good short story, two young people meet and decide to go on a trip together. The boy has hitchhiked from Michigan with "some real estate here in my bag" (perhaps some marijuana he can sell to finance the trip); after buying cigarettes and "Mrs. Wagner's pies"—great detail, that—they "walked off to look for America." The song clearly taps into the emerging Counterculture's desire for freedom, for free love (the couple become lovers only during the voyage, not before), for the gifts of the open road. They climb on a Greyhound bus in Pittsburgh and head north. The song's second verse shows the couple on the bus, laughing and pretending the bus's passengers are spies, which at once acknowledges and makes light of the Counterculture's paranoia during the mid-to-late 1960s. The clarinet intercedes at this point, pulling the song down from the lovers' laughter to a more subdued place: the girl starts to read a magazine and the boy looks out the bus's window. The instrumental passage perfectly evokes the exciting but also embarrassing moment when new lovers realize something vital is happening to them, and they each turn inward to absorb the changes. In a beautiful moment, the boy, while looking out the window, notices the moon rising over a field. Though by now he knows the girl is asleep, he says to her, "Kathy, I'm lost. . . . I'm eighteen and aching and *I don't know why*"—with the duo singing those last four words with an ingenuous longing that is altogether convincing. That one line says more about Simon's themes of alienation and confused purpose and the desire to live life fully than any song he's written so far, and the reason it works is because it dramatizes (with the quiet restraint of a confident artist) rather than explains, because it evokes the spirited desires and confusion of youth with a sense of wonder and tenderness, rather than intellectualizing about it. To my mind, it's Simon's first unreservedly great and original song.

The remaining tracks that complete the suite slip up for a couple of numbers before recovering. "Overs" is Simon's first attempt at what is essentially a jazz composition, light on hummable melody and heavy on minor-key chord changes and self-serious atmospherics (the song begins with someone striking a match, then lighting and inhaling a cigarette, *thoughtfully*). If "America" is about the beginning of love, "Overs" is about it being "over." Time has done its bit (good times, bad times) to this relationship, and now "there's no times at all / Just the New York Times"—that is, just the dailiness of a relationship without laughter, without excitement or sex. Now "time is tapping on my forehead," reminding the singer that he's wasting time in a relationship that's become merely "habit, like saccharine." But when he thinks it "over"—the double meaning is supposed to be clever—he stops, too fearful to imagine being alone. The song is the suite's first explicit evocation of the time theme, but it's too affected to put it across effectively.

"Voices" is comprised of an edited tape of elderly people talking about their lives into a microphone that Art Garfunkel brought to an old folks home. Presumably, Garfunkel wanted the old people to speak for themselves, and they do, though nothing startling or very interesting emerges. This is followed by the stronger "Old Friends," perhaps Simon's answer to the Beatles "When I'm 64," Paul McCartney's bouncy music hall tune about old age. Simon, more serious, avers, "How terribly strange / To be seventy," and this attempt to touch on the mystery of time's passage hits the mark. The song is about two old men sitting on a park bench "like bookends . . . lost in their overcoats," equally lost in memory that the music evokes with considerable melancholic power. The suite's final song, "Bookends," reiterates the feeling of time slipping through one's fingers. The song, this one presumably spoken by one of the old friends, recalls a past filled with confidence and innocence, then suggests that that time was "long ago / *It must be*" (my italics), as if he can't even grasp that the past was ever real at all; he can only capture it in the simulacrum of a photograph. The side closes with a pensive reprise of the "Bookends theme."

As concept albums go (or, in this case, as concept suites go), this is more successful than most, boasting one sure-fire classic in "America" and a number of moving meditations on time. Simon's literary training keeps him focused thematically, which is something most rock writers have trouble with (Pete Townsend's lyrics on the Who's *Tommy* go notoriously off-task, for example), and helped push the rock music audience—already being pushed by the Beatles and Dylan—into a more complex, mature phase.

Side 2 of *Bookends*, as I've noted, sweeps up a number of singles (the A and B sides) that Simon & Garfunkel released in 1967, during the eighteen-month span (an eternity in 1960s-record-company years) between the releases of *Parsley, Sage* and *Bookends*. Two of the tracks, "At the Zoo" and "Punky's Dilemma," are more Simonish whimsy— obvious attempts of a natural depressive to capture what he hopes is caprice—while "A Hazy Shade of Winter" is the album's most direct address of the theme of time's slippery passage, and properly belongs in the *Bookends* suite. (Had it replaced "Voices," it would have made the suite much stronger.) With a long, beguiling melody line that involves a number of rhythmic shifts and a solid vocal performance by the duo, the song doesn't transcend the lyrical clichés of "Leaves That Are Green," but the music is far more taut and energetic, conveying an anxiety about time's passage—and the necessity to make the present *count*—that the too-sedate arrangement of "Leaves" can't approach.

"Fakin' It," a #23 hit in the summer of 1967 that has become lost in the Simon *oeuvre* (it wasn't included in Simon & Garfunkel's *Greatest Hits*) seems, in retrospect, an important signpost in Simon's development as a writer, if only because Simon seems to be calling his own bluff as a pretentious poet. Though the song's ostensibly about a guy who fakes it through a love affair, it's easy to see Simon peeking through his persona (e.g., the seen-it-all poet posing in a black turtleneck and cape [a cape? really?] and holding a cigarette on the back cover of *Sounds of Silence*) and 'fessing up to the fact that much of his writing since *Sounds of Silence* has been fake: derivative, therefore fundamentally unfelt, therefore false. He even admits, "This feelin' of fakin' it / I still haven't shaken it," which sounds like an honest addendum to the confessions of a recovering *poseur*. What makes this reading of the song plausible is that, after *Bookends*, the poseur in Paul Simon does begin to disappear, and in his place appears a new and confident *songwriter— as opposed to poet*—who is witty, subtly ironic, shrewdly intelligent, unbeholden to modern poets or to Bob Dylan, and able to explore the manifold possibilities of popular song with all the freedom of an unfettered artist.

That artist appears on "America," as I've suggested, but he appears even more so on "Mrs. Robinson," Simon's true breakthrough composition. Driven by a propulsive rhythm track, a wiry and indelible guitar figure, and slyly silly vocal fills—the "deet-ditty-deet-deet-deet-deet-deet-deet-deet-ditty-dee" of the opening, the "woo-woo-woos," and the John Lennon–borrowed "goo-goo-goo-joob"—the song grabs hold of the listener the way the best pop songs do: with charmingly insistent hooks that keep on coming. But it's the lyrics that make it a breakthrough. Whereas Simon has in the past been almost anally insistent on clarity, "Mrs. Robinson" thrives on its fuzziness, and even more so on its free-floating ironies. We can try to piece the song together if we like: in the first verse the singer tells us about a woman who has gone to what appears to be a kind of Christian rehab facility, where she is interviewed, proselytized to, and asked to "stroll around the grounds / Until you feel at home." In the second, she is back at home—evidently the rehab didn't take—and is now stealing away something in "the pantry with your cupcakes"—possibly the addictive substances she went into the facility to kick in the first place—and hiding it from her children. In the third and fourth verse, the singer contemplates going to a candidate's debate, though it's a waste of time since "ev'ry way you look at it you lose," a sentiment that makes the singer, and Mrs. Robinson, consider the loss of heroes like Yankees slugger Joe DiMaggio: "Our nation turns its lonely eyes to you." The song touches on all sorts of social issues that pressed the Counterculture's buttons: the "mother's little helper" prescription drug addiction of the middle class, the hypocrisy of the Establishment, paranoia, the hiding of the self, the lure of salvational answers, political cynicism, and the values drift that was occurring all over the country. To 1960s ears, the song felt undeniably *relevant* but playfully un-pin-downable. Not only are the verses fragments that don't quite connect, but also the position of the song's speaker is unclear: this is satire without a moral center, and evidently without the need for one. (Simon's previous songs, when they were satirical, were grounded in deep moral disapproval.) The singer expresses a kind of cheerful absurdity that one finds in the contemporaneous fiction of Joseph Heller or Donald Barthelme, though the song's unanchored irony, its acquaintance with the dark, guilt-ridden corners of American life, don't feel influenced by anyone—they feel altogether original. What's more, the song doesn't end with the closure we're used to in Simon songs: it trails off, lyrically and musically, as if it were a bizarre little piece of 1960s flotsam that happened to catch on to the American airwaves. What's strongest about the song, in the end, is that it doesn't feel like a Paul Simon song at all: released from self-seriousness, he writes his most trenchant song to date. "Mrs. Robinson" is a song in which Simon erases traces of his own personality, and, in a final irony, emerges with a composition that will come to typify the future Paul Simon song.[6]

"Mrs. Robinson" became Simon & Garfunkel's second #1 hit when it was released in April 1968, but the pump was primed by the release, just four months earlier, of the movie and Simon & Garfunkel's soundtrack of *The Graduate*. Director Mike Nichols shrewdly employed some of the fashionably self-conscious aspects of the European art film (shock edits, freeze frames, wide-angle shots that swooped quickly into close-up, a thoroughly ambiguous ending) into a film that became not only a huge and very hip hit, but also something of a cultural landmark. Its anti-hero, Benjamin Braddock, who comes home after graduating from college to find himself aimlessly pursuing an affair with the much-older Mrs. Robinson before falling in love with her daughter, captured in a pop (and 1960s West Coast) way some of the bewilderment, restless anxiety, (self-)disgust, and social estrangement of Holden Caulfield of *The Catcher in the Rye,* which by the mid-1960s was a bible to a large segment of educated American youth. Nichols, who recognized that Benjamin's story was ready-made for Simon's themes of alienated middle-class young people, asked Simon to write the soundtrack. Simon agreed, but struggled mightily to come up with new material. In the end, the soundtrack consisted of older Simon & Garfunkel material ("The Sound of Silence," "April Come She Will," "Scarborough Fair/Canticle"), an early version of "Big Bright Green Pleasure Machine," two fragments of the at-the-time-incomplete "Mrs. Robinson," a new version of "The Sound of Silence" (featuring Art Garfunkel rather beautifully double-tracking his own harmony vocals), and some short guitar fragments. The material didn't add up to a complete soundtrack, so Columbia records executive Clive Davis, sure that he had a major moneymaker on his hands, interspersed, among Simon's material, some of the film score composed by Dave Grusin. The result was not only a souvenir of the movie (which is why most people bought soundtracks in the 1960s) but also a fascinating time capsule that demonstrates quite succinctly the musical gap that separated the young from the Establishment generation. Grusin's score consists of cocktail jazz, foxtrots, jaunty cha-cha-chas, fat horns blaring striptease music; juxtaposed to Simon's contributions, it sounds greasy, boozy, superficial—chemical- and alcohol-enhanced cheeriness. Next to Grusin's music, "The Sound of Silence" sounds like, well, true voice-of-a-generation stuff, with "April Comes She Will" and "Scarborough Fair/Canticle" coming off in this new context as more touchingly vulnerable and youthfully sensitive than ever. As a marketing move, *The Graduate* soundtrack was genius—Clive Davis's—selling millions of copies of mostly already-released material along with teases of new songs that would later appear on *Bookends.* Simon originally objected to the soundtrack, thinking that it would compete with *Bookends*, but the sales of one ended up reinforcing sales of the other, and by late 1968, Simon & Garfunkel were selling more records than the Beatles. They were the biggest act in the record business.

So big that, in 1969, the CBS television network offered them a prime-time one-hour special, to be sponsored by AT&T, which the pair seized on as one more way to broaden their by-now vast audience. Working with actor Charles Grodin, with whom Simon had struck up a friendship, they envisioned the show as a documentary that not only would show Simon & Garfunkel in the studio and in concert working out material from the album that would become *Bridge Over Troubled Water*, but also would allow the duo to comment on the vast social changes of the 1960s. The three budding filmmakers were given free rein to make the documentary they wanted—AT&T had no idea, apparently, that Simon & Garfunkel, who looked as well-behaved as their music sounded, had countercultural political convictions. Once AT&T executives saw the finished product, however, they balked. The antiwar, anti-Establishment material was, to them, incendiary. In the end, it seemed to come down to their objection to Simon uttering the words, "We shouldn't be in Vietnam." When AT&T asked the artists to edit the comments, Simon & Garfunkel pointedly refused: "Fuck you," they informed the company. "This is the show we made. This is what we believe in."[7] At this point, AT&T pulled the plug on the sponsorship and sold the rights to Alberto Culver, who agreed to sponsor the show. The show ended up airing in its original form on November 30, 1969.

In any case, *Songs of America* is an impressive filmic debut, and no doubt further kindled Simon's interest in movies as a form. Keyed to the "Kathy, I'm lost. . . . I'm eighteen and aching and I don't know why" line from "America," the documentary was altogether fitting for an evaluation of a country that, by 1969, was enduring its greatest period of chaos since the Civil War.[8] Mainstream liberal (but hardly radical) in its politics, vaguely countercultural in its appreciation of the younger generation's search for solidarity in the face of problems (entrenched racism, the burgeoning war in Vietnam) that seemed insurmountable, touching in its attempts to express youthful confusions about identity and purpose that by 1969 had become pandemic, *Songs of America* is unusually measured and thoughtful for a film "conceived and executed" (as the credits put it) by a twenty-something actor and two young pop singers.

The film, a little over fifty minutes in length, begins with the song "America" playing over footage of sublime mountain ranges—purple mountains' majesty stuff that evokes idealisms that are bred in the American bone—before the singers intone, "They've all come to look for America," whereby the film plunges into grittier images of 1960s turmoil: impoverished blacks in blighted urban areas, trash dumps, bloody demonstrations against the war, and so on. The too-simplistic contrast between the ideal and the actual continues throughout the film: over "Scarborough Fair/Canticle," for instance, we get loving and bucolic images of Woodstock hippies contrasted with footage of wounded soldiers and napalm bombings in Vietnam, while over the absurdist "Punky's Dilemma" ("Wish I was a Kellogg's corn flake") we get images of old-man politicians dithering in committee meetings while war and racism rage on. But there is no real acknowledgment that by 1969, the Counterculture's ideals were in tatters: Martin Luther King's peaceful campaign for racial equality had exploded in urban violence after his 1968 assassination, and the ideals of the hippie community were being shattered by stories of deadly drug abuse in Haight-Ashbury, not to mention the inconceivably brutal Manson murders. Still, the contrast is more subtly executed than most left-liberal documentaries of the era, and some of the commentary, particularly by the soft-spoken but articulate Garfunkel, is searchingly wistful. The songs the film introduces for the first time—among them "Bridge Over Troubled Water"—must have been stunning to any TV viewer, and the overall sense the film conveys is of thoughtful young people fairly and gamefully grappling with immense societal confusion.

What the film doesn't grapple with—except in brief moments that one might not spot unless one were looking for it—is the rising tension between the principals. Though close since childhood and now as phenomenally successful as they could have dreamed, Simon and Garfunkel rankled each other, and their close proximity over the past four years exacerbated their annoyances. Simon was jealous of Garfunkel's stature, good looks, and glorious voice; of the assumption fans often made that Garfunkel was his equal as a creative partner; and of Garfunkel's budding film career, which Garfunkel seemed to put ahead of Simon when he headed off to make *Catch-22* during the *Bridge Over Troubled Water* sessions. They were also, crucially, battling over musical direction: Garfunkel was content to make "beautiful" but vapid pop music—the kind he would indeed make as a solo artist in the 1970s—while Simon was eager to branch out in riskier directions. There's a brief scene at the beginning of the film that captures a flare of tension. The two are talking in a taxi: Garfunkel insists that certain kinds of harmony just aren't done; Simon rebuts him with the rather pretentious tale of Beethoven disregarding the rules of music to pursue his muse; Garfunkel steadies his gaze at Simon and says, "He was a fool, Beethoven." Other than that, it's impossible to imagine that these two mega-stars of popular music would, within a year, decide to call off the partnership.

BRIDGE OVER TROUBLED WATER (1970)

Bridge Over Troubled Water, released in January 1970, is a triumph of pop in the rock era. It was a commercial juggernaut, selling 5 million copies upon its initial release, and since then another 20 million units worldwide. The album stayed at #1 for ten consecutive weeks in America (thirty-three weeks in Britain) and spun off three top 10 U.S. hits and another one that went to #18. It won five Grammy awards, including Best Album and Best Song (for "Bridge Over Troubled Water"), which put the official industry imprimatur on the duo's music. It was an extraordinary way for Simon & Garfunkel to go out—at the top of their game not just commercially but aesthetically as well. *Bridge* is the duo's best, most tuneful, most rhythmically interesting, most musically diverse, most consistent album—there's not a single dud on the record—and features Simon songs so liberated from his old concerns of seriousness that he's able not only to be convincingly loose and silly ("Why Don't You Write Me?," "Cecilia," "Baby Driver") and acknowledge his fluffy rock 'n' roll roots (the cover of "Bye Bye Love"), but also to write songs of a new and original seriousness that are miles away from the constricted, pretentious poetics of "I Am a Rock" or "The Dangling Conversation." Recorded at a time when the pair could often barely stand to be in the same room, the album nonetheless sounds not only unrushed and meticulously polished, but also high-spirited and—of all things Simonish—joyful.

It begins, of course, with the title tune, a slow-building piano-based gospel ballad with a soaring and tender vocal by Art Garfunkel. The words are elegantly simple and soothing: the title metaphor is so spot-on apt that it's a wonder no one had thought to use it before: the song, like many that become standards of the pop tradition, feels at once instantly familiar and captivatingly new. Recorded by over two hundred artists over the years, "Bridge" obviously speaks to a more or less universal yearning for comfort and friendship "when evening falls so hard . . . [and] when darkness comes / And pain is all around," and

Garfunkel's rendering of the stately melody—gentle, vulnerable, sung so high in the register that he sounds almost like an innocent child reassuring a troubled parent (which is partly why it's heartbreaking)—uncannily puts across that yearning, but the song's impact on first release in January 1970 is something else again, and deserves discussion.

1969 was a terrible year for the United States. The country was still reeling from 1968, when the country witnessed two major assassinations (of Martin Luther King Jr. and of Senator and presidential candidate Robert F. Kennedy) that had not only shocked the country but also unraveled a growing momentum in the country for racial equality and an end to the Vietnam War. By the end of 1968, Richard Nixon had been elected president, and despite a promise to wind down the war, he actually expanded it, bulking total troop strength to 550,000 and secretly planning to widen operations into Laos and Cambodia. And far from addressing the widespread poverty and inequality of inner-city blacks who were left leaderless in the wake of MLK Jr.'s death, Nixon, elected on a "law and order" platform, cracked down on the increasingly despairing attempts by blacks to be heard, and reduced support for Lyndon Johnson's Great Society programs that promised poor black Americans a way out of blighted economic conditions. By 1970, riots by blacks had burned out the urban core of scores of American cities, and black activism—which before MLK Jr.'s death was largely principled and nonviolent—had becoming increasingly radical, violent, and anarchic. Similarly, by the beginning of the same year, the Counterculture's belief in "peace and love"—the naïve belief that major political and cultural change could be effected not by conflict or violence but by peacefully projecting a loving attitude toward one's antagonists—was a joke, with the peace movement impotent in the face of Nixon's intransigence, and with some of the movement's leaders increasingly turning to violent—even terrorist—methods, to try to effect some change. The country was brutally split: between blacks and whites, the Counterculture and the Establishment, liberal and conservative. Even man's first landing on the moon in July 1969—which caused a brief flurry of hope and optimism about the future—did little to brighten the dark mood.

It was into this cultural milieu of exhausted hopes that "Bridge Over Troubled Water" landed when the single was released. Though it would be nonsense to claim that the song changed anything culturally, it certainly was a balm to millions of listeners, even a kind of "bridge" across the generation gap, since Simon & Garfunkel's audience encompassed teenagers and thirty- and forty-somethings alike. Like the Beatles' "Let It Be," released two months later, the song was infused with a soothing but evidently much-needed spirituality that was largely missing from popular culture at the time. That spirituality isn't in the lyrics—which are secular, technically a promise of devotion from one "friend" to another—but the gospel trappings are unmistakable, and the song's production, which builds from Garfunkel's sweet whisper to the swirl of a huge orchestra punctuated by a final cannon-like boom, is clearly spine-tingling, and to many achieves a rare kind of pop transcendence.[9]

"The Boxer," the album's second major composition, is written in the tradition of "Homeward Bound" and "America," songs about characters who embark on earnest journeys, confronting loneliness on their way to discovering themselves and the world around them. ("Duncan" and "American Tune," from Simon's early 1970s solo career, are part of this tradition as well.) Released as a single in March 1969, the song was a top 10 hit in the spring of 1969, and many at the time thought the song, with its lyrics about a bloodied fighter who keeps shouting, "I am leaving; I am leaving," but remains in the ring anyway, was a reference to America's by-then endless entanglement in the Vietnam War—an interpretation buttressed by the explosive percussion sounds that detonate like bombs during the chorus. But that says more about the country's (justifiable) obsession with the war—and about Counterculture listeners' tendencies to search for social relevance in everything they heard—than it did about the song itself. The song itself is about a boy who has left his home and family in search of "promises"—presumably the American promise—which he realizes, early in the song, are "lies and jest," "mumbles" whose seductive power wore down his "resistance" when he was young. Hanging out in railroad stations, journeying to "where the ragged people go," looking for work in the city and finding only the offers of prostitutes, he longs for home, but finds that even though he says he is leaving, he "remains," a boxer and a fighter who won't give up his search, even though he doesn't know why. Musically, the song starts out as simple folk-rock, and builds into what is essentially a power ballad, filled with strings, multi-tracked harmony vocals, and those percussive explosions. The song's vision is as dark as anything Simon had written during the self-serious days of "I Am a Rock," only now Simon has learned to deflect his emotions onto a character, and thus avoid the temptation to self-pity. In the end, it's a song about the bewilderment of the American searcher who, even in the current dispirited environment, can't give up the search, still yearns for the promise whose allure he, as an American, has no resistance to.

None of the songs that follow are quite as imposing as "Bridge" or "The Boxer," but that gives Simon license to explore an impressively wide spectrum of pop styles and moods. In "El Condor Pasa (If I Could)," Simon takes a melancholy folk melody by the Peruvian group Los Incas that he had originally heard in Paris in 1965 and adds lyrics that, in their folky imagery ("I'd rather be a sparrow than a snail"), has the air both of a wise children's tale and an ambiguous allegory readable in countless ways. What Simon learned in "Mrs. Robinson"—that it's better to *evoke* intelligently than to *declare* assuredly, that listeners love to sink into the mystery of a lyric as long as it isn't obscurantist—he applies here, and with such a light touch that when he does lower the boom into a bit of straightforward seriousness ("A man gets tied up to the ground / He gives the world its saddest sound"), the listener is apt to attend to the lyric as the *bon mot* that it is. Too, the song's braiding of a non-American song tradition with Simon's lyrics is also a precursor of things to come: *Graceland* and *Rhythm of the Saints* will build on what Simon is doing here.

Four songs on the album show off a songwriter freed from the need to be smart, who has discovered how to use his sense of humor, who appears to be having fun making music for the first time since his teenybopper days. These songs don't try to mean anything and are the better for it. "Keep the Customer Satisfied" was interpreted in wise-guy dorm-room conversations in the 1970s as a song about a drug dealer, but who cares? The words seem like wry placeholders for the drivingly infectious rhythm and melody, which together generate an all-out horn assault in the last third of the song that is deliriously overdone, and all the more fun for it. "Cecilia," which began in the studio with Simon, Garfunkel, and Roy Halee experimenting with dense hyperactive rhythms (handclaps, hand slaps over thighs, the dropping of drum sticks on the studio floor, etc.), is even funnier, while presaging the way Simon would, in *Graceland* and *The Rhythm of the Saints*, record complex rhythm tracks *before* he had a song to attach them to. The rhythm track to "Cecilia" is crazily kinetic, and mirrors the nuttiness of the lyric, which is about a guy who after making love to his girl gets up to go the bathroom only to find "someone's taken my place" when he gets back. Yet the poor fool's undaunted: he ends up making love to her again (if there's any doubt about this, listen to the singers' "get it up; get it up" during an instrumental passage), after which the guy is jubilant: "She loves me again! / I fall on the floor and I laughing." The "I laughing" is perfect: dumb ecstasy has made him really lose it, grammar included. "Baby Driver," with its intentionally nonsensical lyrics about a guy whose solution for everything is "to hit the road and I'm gone," and with its motorcycle-engine noises laid over the end of the track, is frankly reminiscent of "Motorcycle," a pre–Simon & Garfunkel song Simon recorded in 1961 when he was still trying to be a teen idol. The song is all absurd propulsion, the singing as sunny and fun as early 1960s Beach Boys. "Bye Bye Love," recorded live during a 1969 tour, looks back to Simon's beginnings as well: it's a belated homage to the Everly Brothers, a loving tribute to the duo that pioneered the kind of clean precise harmonies Simon & Garfunkel learned so much from when they first sung together as school boys.

Then there are the group of four songs that refer, sometimes obliquely, to the relationship between Simon and Garfunkel. "Why Don't You Write Me?," as loopy as the songs just discussed, sounds a hilariously desperate note. Written when Simon was alone in the studio and Garfunkel was off in Mexico filming *Catch-22* with Mike Nichols, it could have been a song about mopey abandonment, or even about betrayal—certainly those feelings were paramount in Simon's mind during much of the making of the album—but instead Simon turns these feelings into a funny caricature about his own lonesomeness. (Simon, to this point, hasn't had much ability to make fun of himself.) At the end of the song, the singer is wailing, "Why don't you write me?," and is contemplating killing himself, but the bouncy rhythm and infectious pop touches (the basso "why don't you write" or the parodic "la la la"s) ensure this is just one big aural cartoon. In "The Only Living Boy in New York," Simon stakes out the same emotional territory—his sense of abandonment and loneliness at Garfunkel's privileging of his film career over Simon & Garfunkel—but here turns it into a generous-spirited *envoi* to his long-time partner. Addressing Garfunkel as "Tom"—Art's moniker when they were Tom & Jerry—he sends him off to Mexico with the assurance that Garfunkel's "part will go fine" and urges him to "let your honesty shine shine shine . . . like it shines on me." This optimistic spirit is dampened, however, by the singer's acknowledgment that he's alone now. Simon's "Da-n-da-da-n-da-da-n-da-n and here I am" is genuinely wistful, a tone Simon hasn't been able to capture successfully before, and the deeply echoed and lushly layered harmonies that end the song are simply some of the most beautiful of Simon & Garfunkel's career. "Song for the Asking," a near-fragment that ends the album, is written in the same generous spirit. Simon's voice—melancholic but controlled, such that it never veers into self-pity—offers songs for (I think it's fair to say) Garfunkel's asking, pleading with him: "Don't turn away." Then "thinking it over," he offers to "change my way of thinking" if Garfunkel will continue to sing with him. It's one of the most unguarded songs Simon has sung to this point in his career—surely it's one of the most affectingly vulnerable. The quartet of Garfunkel songs is rounded out by "So Long, Frank Lloyd Wright." Garfunkel, who had studied architecture for a time at Columbia, had asked Simon to write a song about his hero, but when Simon emerged with the composition, which appropriates some of the elements of the Brazilian *bossa nova*, Wright has become a stand-in for Garfunkel himself, the singing partner with whom he "harmonize[d] till dawn" so long ago. Like "Only Living Boy," it's a song that takes leave of Garfunkel, seemingly offering his blessing as they part.

That Simon & Garfunkel broke up just as *Bridge Over Troubled Water* was amassing critical hosannas, immense sales, and eventually multiple Grammys was nearly as shocking to listeners as the Beatles breakup that same year. But it helps to recall that the only reason the duo came together again in 1965 was because of the fluke success of a single that was re-recorded without their input. Having worked since 1957 to become a star, Simon was not about to overlook the opportunity that the folk-rock version of "The Sound of Silence" provided, and as success built on success, it was easy, for a while, to overlook the fundamental differences between Simon and Garfunkel as personalities and artists, and to let slide some of the basic antagonisms that preyed on their partnership. By the time those differences and antagonisms could no longer be overlooked—during the *Bridge* sessions—the duo were so rich, so famous, so lauded, that they both possessed the confidence to strike out on their own. In any case, it was the end of the 1960s, a fairly apocalyptic moment, and no one at the time thought that rock acts could endure for long. For Simon, it was time to start over as a solo act.

3

IN THE AGE'S MOST UNCERTAIN HOURS

1970–1977

The Paul Simon who ventured out into the world as a solo artist in early 1970 was a different man from the young song hustler who had banged around the folk pub circuit in England as a "poet and a one-man band" in 1964 and 1965. Back in his salad days, he was making twenty or thirty pounds a night, sleeping on friends' couches, exploring his first real romantic relationship with a girlfriend, mastering his craft, and dreaming of a big break. When the break came—with the release of the rock version of "The Sound of Silence" in America—his life changed all at once, and for the next five years he and Garfunkel rode a path to success that exceeded any expectations he could have possibly envisioned. By the time the duo broke up in 1970, Simon was a household name whose songs were sung, hummed, and pondered by millions. Simon & Garfunkel's record sales rivaled and sometimes exceeded that of the Beatles. They were a huge concert attraction. Simon's reputation with critics rose with each new album, and he had gained much-justified confidence as a songwriter, performer, record producer, and arranger. He was also, at the age of twenty-eight, extraordinarily rich, able to build a sprawling mansion on Long Island and dedicate himself generously to any number of charitable causes. After an unhappy period of experimentation with marijuana and LSD, he had stopped taking drugs. And he had even gone domestic, marrying the former wife of his manager, Peggy Harper, in 1969 and settling into an apartment on New

York City's Upper East Side. In some ways, it would be hard to imagine firmer ground on which to build a solo career.

On the other hand, the year 1970 could hardly be considered firm ground for any pop artist. The cultural landscape was changing much too fast. The 1960s as we know it were ending not just chronologically but in spirit as well. Todd Gitlin subtitled his superb chronicle of the decade (called *The Sixties*) "Years of Hope, Days of Rage." By his reckoning, the years of hope lasted at least through 1967, when Martin Luther King Jr.'s campaign for racial equality was still making headway, when peaceful antiwar demonstrators were still changing American hearts and minds about the morality of the Vietnam War, and when the Counterculture's ingenuous dreams of peace, love, and social transformation briefly flowered into a Summer of Love—all accompanied by millions of car radios and living-room stereos blasting songs from the Beatles' *Sgt. Pepper's Lonely Heart's Club Band*. And though tendrils of that hopeful period reached into 1969—the three-day music festival at Woodstock, as rain-sodden and horribly administered as it was, still stands out in a generation's mind as the apotheosis of good vibes and peaceful cooperation—clearly 1968 was the year that the rage began.

As the year of King Jr.'s assassination, 1968 also saw the rise of apoplectic urban riots and threats of race war. It was the year of the Tet Offensive, when the North Vietnamese military mounted sustained and for a time successful attacks on American and South Vietnamese fortifications, and made it clear that the United States wasn't close to "winning" the Vietnam War, as President Johnson and his generals had been claiming since 1965. It was an election year in which the Counterculture's choice for the presidency—Robert F. Kennedy—was gunned down in June, and the only viable Democratic candidate—Hubert H. Humphrey—was vice president in the very administration that had ratcheted up the war to such a disastrous degree. And the year was capped off by the election of Richard Nixon, liberal America's nemesis since 1948, and the Counterculture's poster boy for all that horrified them about the Establishment.

In 1969 and 1970, the rage only worsened. Woodstock's celebratory energy was countered by the very bad vibes of the Rolling Stones concert at Altamont, where an audience member was murdered by members of the Hells Angels, whom the Stones, in a triumph of idiocy, had hired for $500 worth of beer to keep security for the show. And by May of 1970, it was revealed that President Nixon, despite his stated policy that the United States would turn battle operations over to the South Vietnamese and slowly exit the war, had secretly expanded the war into Laos and Cambodia, a revelation that brought hundreds of thousands of demonstrators back into the streets and onto college campuses, and led to the killing of four college students at Kent State University by National Guardsmen. After Kent State, the prevailing feeling among the Counterculture was that the movement—the peaceful attempt to effect major social and political change in the United States—had failed.

The tempests of history hardly abated during the years addressed in this chapter—the first half of the 1970s. Thanks to iconic texts like Simone de Beauvoir's *The Second Sex*, Betty Friedan's *The Feminist Mystique*, and Germaine's Greer's *The Female Eunuch*, as well as the speedy development of grassroots consciousness-raising groups around the country, the feminist movement began to engage the minds of millions of women, and soon overshadowed the civil rights movement in the scope of its ambitions and, ultimately, in its success in changing social relations in the country. Meanwhile, the Vietnam War dragged on, with hundreds of Americans continuing to come home in body bags week after week, even as President Nixon promised "Vietnamization" of the war and a gradual American withdrawal. By 1972, leftist political activity had degenerated into farce or violence, and a tattered youth Counterculture, in one final exhausted effort, united with what remained of the liberal establishment to nominate George McGovern for the presidency, only to see their candidate suffer an absolute rout at the polls at the hands of Richard Nixon. Years of hope had degenerated into days of rage, and after rage there seemed only perplexity, paralysis, and paranoia. After Nixon's reinauguration in January 1973, earlier newspaper reports of his campaign's involvement in the criminal break-in of Democratic headquarters at the Watergate Hotel in Washington, DC— and, worse, of his personal involvement in obstructing justice by covering up an investigation of the break-in—metastasized into investigations into multiple impeachable offenses by the president that ultimately led to Nixon's complete loss of support in his own party, and finally to his resignation in August 1974—the first by any sitting American president. On top of all this, 1973 and 1974 witnessed the nation's first major oil crisis, which precipitously ended the twenty-five-year-long post–World War II economic boom, plunged the country into a prolonged and severe recession, and drove the nation to policies that flat-lined economic progress for the middle and working class for the next forty years. By 1978, a new president, Jimmy Carter, would make his infamous "malaise" speech, in which he suggested that the country was suffering from "a crisis of confidence. It is a crisis that strikes at the very heart and soul and spirit of our national will. We can see this crisis in the growing doubt about the meaning of our own lives and in the loss of a unity of purpose for our nation."[1] If that "crisis" could be said to have an origin, it was in the collapse of 1960s optimism in the face of endless war and Watergate's massive political corruption.

Musical artists who tried to enter these treacherous political waters usually came off as callow—Country Joe and the Fish's "I Feel Like I'm Fixin' to Die Rag"—or confused—see the Beatles' two different versions of "Revolution." Even the Rolling Stones, never a band to back down from a challenge from authority, threw up its hands in "Street Fighting Man," with Mick Jagger abjuring political rebellion and singing, "What can a poor boy do but sing in a rock 'n' roll band?" By 1970, rock artists, who had surfed a powerful cultural wave of intense social and political involvement for half a decade, began to abandon the political and turn inward.

As with so many other cultural pivot points during this period, this turn inward was presaged by Bob Dylan, who after the turbulent creative peak of *Blonde on Blonde*, suffered a motorcycle accident in late 1966, which led him to retreat to a farm in Woodstock, New York. There he recovered and reemerged, in 1968, with a string of albums (including *John Wesley Harding*, *Nashville Skyline*, and *New Morning*), which pulled back from social engagement and embraced old folk idioms—traditional values of home and family—as well as, to the rock audience, the corniest and most conservative of musical forms—country music. Following Dylan's lead were a group of what came to be called "singer-songwriters"—mostly acoustic guitar-wielding balladeers who wrote introspective, often confessional (and self-absorbed) songs in a "mellow" folk-rock vein about their own efforts to overcome the confusions of growing up into the wider world. By the end of 1970, a number of these artists—James Taylor, Carole King, Jackson Browne, Joni Mitchell, Van Morrison, and Neil Young chief among them—had achieved enough commercial success that record companies across the country were convinced they'd uncovered a new (and more domesticatible) form of countercultural music, thereby opening the floodgates to the dozens of singer-songwriters who would dominate much of radio airplay and record sales until the mid-1970s. (The roll call of 1970s singer-songwriters is large if not always artistically impressive. It includes, in addition to the ones I've already cited, Eric Anderson, David Blue, Jimmy Buffet, Jim Croce, John Denver, Dan Fogelberg, Arlo Guthrie, Dave Mason, Elliot Murphy, Randy Newman, Laura Nyro, John Prine, Cat Stevens, Loudon Wainwright III, and countless one- or two-shot artists like Lobo or Michael Murphey. And one mustn't forget that Bruce Springsteen, when he first arrived on the scene in 1972, was pigeon-holed as a "New Dylan"–style singer-songwriter.) It was with these singer-songwriters, in fact, that Simon found himself grouped as the ever-shifting pop marketplace tumbled into the 1970s.

Simon set forth on his solo career with understandable trepidation: it would be no easy thing to follow up the mega-success of *Bridge Over Troubled Water*; nor would it be easy to walk onto a stage and perform alone, after sharing it with the more glamorous Garfunkel for five years. At the same time, he was now his own boss and could make the kind of music he wanted, free of the compromises he was forced to make with his headstrong partner. Perhaps most important of all, he had used the five years of writing for Simon & Garfunkel to flush out his early poetic pretensions and work through his Dylan issues to emerge as a versatile, intelligent songwriter eager to explore his newfound lyrical voice as well as explore a wide world of pop music forms. It no doubt helped that Simon was discovering his own songwriting voice just as Dylan was going through his first major dry spell—1969 through 1973 were lean years for Dylan fans. In any case, Simon began, on his first solo album, experimenting with Peruvian folk music, reggae, Latin, a touch of cocktail lounge jazz, and most of all, acoustic blues. And except for "Duncan," a delicate folk-rock tale that in mood and sound updated "Homeward Bound" or "America," or "The Boxer" for the early 1970s, none of it sounded like Simon & Garfunkel. It was his declaration of independence.

PAUL SIMON (1972)

Simon's solo debut was such a surprise in the depressed atmosphere of 1960s hangover that characterized early 1972 that it prompted Robert Christgau, the highly influential *Village Voice* rock critic, to reverse his long-standing contempt for Simon's music with S & G and declare: "I've been saying nasty things about Simon since 1967, but this is the only thing in the universe to make me positively happy in the first two weeks of February 1972." He went on to call it "a professional tour of Manhattan for youth culture grads," and later named it his second-best album of the year, right after the Stones' monumental *Exile on Main Street*.[2] What gave the record its freshness wasn't just Simon's obvious delight in exercising his newfound musical freedom, or the wry touch of its comedy, or even the confident way Simon appropriated the confessional mode of the singer-songwriter for his own ironic purposes: it was the way Simon managed to evoke—with verve, nerve, sharp wit, and penetrating brevity (the album is less than thirty-four minutes long)—a whole culture where, as one lyric goes, "everything put together sooner or later falls apart." High-spirited about his own and the country's depressive fatigue, it's an album that conflates Simon's personal demons with national ones, and stands as the middle section of a state-of-the-union triptych, with "America" on one (hopeful) side and the (despairing) "American Tune" on the other. *Paul Simon* begins his exploration of America's most "uncertain hours."

The opening track, the #4 pop hit "Mother and Child Reunion," is one of the high points of the Simon canon. Set to authentic reggae rhythms that hadn't been heard on American commercial radio before—he recorded it in Kingston with Jamaican reggae artists—the syncopated chug of its beat and the melancholy of its melody beautifully invoke the mystery of its theme, which has to do with the desire to reunite with a deceased loved one. In a 1972 interview, Simon explained that the idea for the song began when he and his wife Peggy lost a beloved dog—his first personal brush with real death—and it reminded him that the loss might have been Peggy herself.[3] This set him off on a rumination about mortality that evidently transformed the object of loss into the archetypal mother figure. The song seems to have two speakers—one who feels he "can't . . . remember a sadder day . . . [and has] never been laid so low / In such a mysterious way" as by the death of his mother; the other appears to be a confidante who keeps telling him that "the mother and child reunion / Is only a motion away." That "motion away" contains the song's essential mystery. What does "motion" mean, and how is it supposed to reunite him with his mother? Is he suggesting suicide as a way to bring him together with his mother? Or some less extreme, more spiritual "motion" toward her? The song's lyrical force depends on our reading of the word, but Simon hovers gingerly over it, refusing to commit to a single meaning. The song's insistence on sticking with ambiguity and mystery, on evocation rather than determined meaning, is something Simon learned from "Mrs. Robinson," and it lends the song a delicate lingering mystique about our longing for the departed that hasn't paled with the years.

"Mother" is followed by "Duncan," the latest of Simon story songs about lonely searchers going on the road. Set in a familiar folk-rock structure but embellished by a group of Peruvian musicians known as Los Incas whose music Simon had first encountered in Paris in 1965 (and with whom he reunited in Paris to record the track), "Duncan" begins with a young man in a cheap motel room listening to lovers in the next room, "bound to win a prize" for having sex all night. Searching for some answer for how he's found himself in this lonesome predicament, he thinks back on his history. Raised in a dull fishing town, he struck out on his own, but soon discovered what it meant to be destitute and desperate. It's during an encounter with a born-again Christian girl—with whom he was so impressed that he saw "that girl as the road to my survival"—that we get the song's twist. That night the girl took him into the woods and seduced him—"and just like a dog I was befriended." Nonetheless, by the end of the night, he was basking in finally losing his virginity, playing his guitar, and "thanking the Lord for my fingers." The song is cross-hatched with mixed messages—is he grateful for what his fingers can do musically, or sexually? Is he really thanking a Lord he believes in, or is he just using a conventional phrase? And if he's happy at the end of the song, why the comparison to a dog? Finally, what about the song's frame, where the adult Duncan finds himself alone and longing for companionship in that motel room? The song's ironies are playful, gentle, rueful—a delicate portrayal of vulnerable American (the hero's name is *Lincoln* Duncan) search that skews darker than, say, "Homeward Bound," "America," or "The Boxer"—in keeping with the shadier hues of early 1970s America.

The album then expands its exploration of death, loss, and confusion with a plunge into American entropy circa the early 1970s. The title of the next song, "Everything Put Together Falls Apart," makes the theme plain enough. The lyric begins with the word *paraphernalia*, which must be the most unpromising word anyone has ever started a song with, and a joke (as well as a songwriting challenge for Simon) in its own right. Another joke—this one also in the album's rueful mood—is that the song's wandering melody is sung in the languorous style of a cocktail lounge crooner, though there's no languor in the words, which insists with Beckett-like flatness that things just break down, and there's no point in taking drugs to overcome it, or crying or lying—or even dying with grief—over the breakdown. The song is saved from lugubriousness by Simon's sly vocal, which ends on a choice bit of falsetto so charmingly absurd that he evokes an old grandmother shaking a finger at a naughty boy: when "they lay you down for dead," he sings, "just remember what I said." The ironic balance of the last lines is worthy of Randy Newman at his best, if not Beckett himself. "Run That Body Down," which follows hard on this song, reinforces the entropy theme, though with a more conventional melody and a clear narrative telling the story of "Paul" and "Peg," who must ask themselves how long they can abuse their bodies (with sex, drugs, partying): "How long you think you can do what you been doin'? / Now, who you foolin'?" Paul hauls out the falsetto again on these lines, which tease the listener with similar warnings about the sexual and drug-taking excesses that dogged a Counterculture generation now moving inevitably into the abodes of adulthood.

Side 1 of the LP ends with the first of two songs that address the Vietnam War, which by 1972 Americans had been fighting for seven exhausting years. Both "Armistice Day" and "Peace Like a River" begin with the (pipe) dream of the war finally ending: "Armistice Day" opens with Simon singing "On Armistice Day / The Philharmonic will play" over hard twangy blues picking. A digressive second verse expanding the meaning of *armistice* to include a truce between two lovers dilutes the song's effectiveness and focus, but the last half of the song throws a blanket of dissonant horns over the hard blues, and has the singer lamenting that "I'm weary from waiting / In Washington, DC" to meet a congressman who is "avoiding" his pleas to stop the war. The song generates (and I think reflects) the uneasy and pervasive feeling in 1972 that legitimate political activity to stop the war had become altogether impotent. "Peace Like a River" counterbalances this sense of impotence, however, and stands out as one of the buried treasures of Simon's entire catalogue. Beginning with a sedate vocal voiced over another blues guitar riff, the singer speaks of dreaming that the war was over, and that "peace like a river ran through the city"—no doubt a common fantasy of millions of Americans driven to despair by the conflict, and by their own helplessness in the face of the lies of a U.S. government implacably dedicated to continuing the war whatever the costs. However, in the dream the singer discovers that the wrong information has been circulating, and that the war isn't over at all. What follows in the second verse is one of the most moving passages in Simon's work. Over multiply tracked backing vocals (all Simon's), the speaker sings in a calm but defiant voice:

> You can beat us with wires
> You can beat us with chains
> You can run out your rules
> But you know you can't outrun the history train
> I've seen a glorious day

The idea that history was on the side of those against the Vietnam War had been in the air during the halcyon days of the mid-1960s, but in the burned-out atmosphere of 1972 it was an inspiring balm to the spirit to hear it again. Especially inspiring is the falsetto Simon again employs after the words "glorious day": rather than serving an ironic purpose as it does in two previous songs on the album, this time the sweet, high lilt of his voice reinforces the glorious day he foresees into a moment of genuine hope. And not only that: for the song's speaker, the dream helps him rededicate himself to the struggle for peace. After some rest, he concludes, "I'm going to be up for a while." In other words, the countercultural dream of transformation is dead; the struggle for piecemeal political change continues, which of course has become the post-1960s attitude of American liberals ever since.

Side 2 of the LP begins with "Me and Julio Down by the School-yard," a boisterous burst of Latin-tinged rhythmic urgency, the single for which reached #22 and sustained the commercial momentum of the album through the spring of 1972. (The album went top 5 and sold a little less than a million copies upon first release, a strong showing for a solo debut, though disappointing to Simon, who was used to mega-sales with S & G.) "Me and Julio" is another story song, but unlike "Duncan," the narrative of "Me and Julio" seems propelled by the serendipity of its rhymes rather than by a sober and controlled effort to play out a sensible storyline. The song is "about" the narrator getting caught with a "Julio" in what appears to be a gay sexual tryst, but the lyrical progress of the song suggests Simon had no idea where the song was going when he started it, and went where the rhythms and the accidents of rhyme led him. Thus, the father says, "Oy"—does that make him Jewish?—because that rhymes with "get that boy"; he wants to stick him "in a house of detention" because his mother spits every time "my name gets mentioned." When the narrator is taken away, the "press let the story leak," which allows Simon to introduce a "radical priest" who gets the boy "released," and gets the narrator and the clergyman on "the cover of Newsweek." As with "Mrs. Robinson," we can make the song make sense if we must, but beyond a certain zeitgeisty plangency—gays were in the news in 1972 in the aftermath of the Stonewall riots, and the idea of reality being distorted by mass media coverage was gaining currency among "society of the spectacle" theorists—the story is a bit of witty silliness driven under our skin by the crisp guitar strumming, the comic embellishments of background "boops" and moans, and the airheaded whimsy of a whistling solo.

"Me and Julio" is followed by "Peace Like a River"; the side then concludes with four tracks that reinforce the depleted and fatigued mood of side 1. "Papa Hobo" is another road song, and like many of the album's songs, this one's melody meanders: it picks up a familiar strain, then stutters trying to maintain momentum before withering away to a worn-out nonconclusion. (Simon, usually fecund with melodic ideas, includes only four songs on the album that are structured around conventional, hummable pop melodies. Fragments of compelling melody lines are strewn about the rest of the songs, but it's as if Simon left them intentionally undeveloped—as if he wanted to avoid the trap of prettiness that he felt plagued S & G.) The singer's road journey also never really takes off. Stuck in Detroit, breathing its poisonous air, he's naively planning a getaway, but can't quite break himself free of the city's "automotive dream"—of, one assumes, the promise of a union job with a car company, even if that means staying in (and participating in the industry of) a town whose carbon and monoxide "lay you down by noon." By song's end, he's standing in a road, asking someone he calls Papa Hobo to "slip me a ride" since he's enervated and directionless.

The fiddle-and-guitar instrumental fragment that follows, "Hobo's Blues," briefly lifts the mood, and sends us into the absurdist comedy of "Paranoia Blues." Dominated by the incisive bottleneck slide of blues guitarist Stefan Grossman and of Simon's deadpan vocals, the song explores the pervasive paranoid mood of the early 1970s—a mood created by countless press stories of government lying as well as snooping on private citizens, novels of all-encompassing suspicion like *Catch-22* and *The Crying of Lot 49*, and doubtless by a culture that had taken up as its drug of choice marijuana, infamous for its paranoia-inducing qualities. The song's a funny and evocative period piece.

The album concludes with "Congratulations," which would have fit in perfectly on Simon's 1975 marital breakup album, *Still Crazy after All These Years*, though this one was written when his marriage to Peggy Harper was only two years old. The song is like a melancholic answer to Simon's unabashed paean to romantic love, "For Emily, Wherever I Might Find Her," which by 1972 Simon found embarrassingly trite. Again employing a wavering melody line that follows the lyric rather than having the lyric fit into a preconceived melodic structure, "Congratulations" bemoans the many couples he sees "slipping away" into divorce—the phrase will find its way into his superb song of depression, "Slip Sliding Away," five years later—and declares that "love's no romance / Love will do you in," before concluding with the pleading question, "Can a man and a woman / Live together in peace?" If much of the rest of the album portrays the end of a generation's hope for "peace," this song does the same thing for "love"—a song inspired, one can hardly doubt, by personal experience but speaking for many who entered the 1970s wondering what in the world adult love really meant.

The question at the end of the song will hang like L.A. smog over Simon's next four studio albums. *There Goes Rhymin' Simon* (1973), *Still Crazy after All These Years* (1975), *One-Trick Pony* (1980), and *Hearts and Bones* (1983)—though each occasionally takes up public material (the state of the nation in "American Tune," the music business in *One-Trick Pony*)—form a quartet of Simon's most personal music, taking him through the end of his marriage to Peggy Harper and into his stormy relationship with, marriage to, and quick divorce from Carrie Fisher. Though rarely openly confessional in the sense that, say, Joni Mitchell or Jackson Browne were during these years, Simon's next albums explore his personal travails through a variety of musical and lyrical filters and led to some of his most affecting and resilient music.

THERE GOES RHYMIN' SIMON (1973)

The title seems to go for comic uplift, but a single listen to Simon's second solo album gives the lie to any idea that we're in for "Me and Julio"–like lightheartedness. Simon is always rhymin', and he's up to his usual musical explorations—this time his palette includes dixieland jazz, black Southern gospel, torch songs, calypso, R&B, and more blues— but the prevailing mood of the record's major songs is dark, brooding, even despondent. "Tenderness" isn't a celebration of tenderness, but the plea of a man whose relationship lacks it; "Something So Right" is about a guy who can't recognize that his relationship is going well even when it is. "Learn How to Fall" is steeped in regret; "One Man's Ceiling Is Another Man's Floor" in an obscure shame. The catchy hooks of "Kodachrome" leading into the lines about "how all the world's a sunny day" are entirely ironic. That the album was a bigger commercial hit than *Paul Simon* underscores Simon's superb pop instincts, his ability to corral his darker moods into deeply pleasurable pop artifacts.

The album's centerpiece clearly is "American Tune," one of the most nakedly melancholic songs Simon's ever written, and a deeply affecting and concise framing of the bewildered, weary American mood in 1973. It is one of the greatest songs anyone has written about the fallout of failed 1960s idealism—Jackson Browne's moving 1960s elegy "Before the Deluge" is one of the few songs that can fairly be compared to it. (It's interesting to speculate what would have happened if Bob Dylan had written and put out "American Tune" in 1973. My guess is that he would instantly have regained his messiah status; Dylanologists would have been turning cartwheels, calling for a Nobel Prize.) Though the single barely broke into the top 40 (cresting at #35), the editors at *Rolling Stone* understood what Simon had offered up to the rock 'n' roll world, and voted it Song of the Year.

It begins as a simple guitar-and-voice folk song, with Simon's sincere tenor mirroring the sad, searching lyrics, which speak of a weary man who admits to confusion and mistakes, who feels "forsaken" and "misused." He doesn't "know a soul who's not been battered . . . a dream that's not been shattered." And when he "thinks of the road we're traveling on, I wonder what went wrong / I can't help it; I wonder what went wrong." The references could hardly have been clearer to any listener in 1973. The road is the path America took in the 1960s that began with extraordinary hope and ended in bitter disillusionment. And what went wrong was . . . seemingly everything: a war that still wasn't over, multiple assassinations of heroic figures, a Counterculture that had overreached, and a nation opening its eyes to the jaw-dropping corruptions of Watergate. In the song's third stanza, the speaker dreams that he's dying, and that he is rising above, detached from the earth and all its cares, to look down on himself and the country that was his. And what he sees is this: "The Statue of Liberty / Sailing away to sea." It's a beautiful, sad image that encapsulates the failure of national ideals, and cogently enough evokes what makes this "the age's most uncertain hours." Nonetheless, as in "Peace Like a River," the song's speaker doesn't give up—"Still, tomorrow's going to be another working day," the speaker concludes, even in this land where "You can't be forever blessed." "American Tune" is a perfectly pitched and poetically charged death-of-the-American-dream song—filled with pained, dignified grief—that completes the arc of songs about America that began with "America," continued through the state of the union messages on *Paul Simon*, and concludes here. Aside from the minor "Learn How to Fall" on this album, and the satire "Have a Good Time" from *Still Crazy*, "American Tune" will be Simon's temporary goodbye to social commentary—on the rest of this album and the three that succeed it, he will, like much of his generation, turn inward.

The most personal songs on *Rhymin' Simon*, "Tenderness" and "Something So Right," are clearly about his marriage to Peggy Harper. "Something So Right," which reads almost like an apology to her, portrays the speaker as a solitary depressive: he "is the last to know / When something goes right," a man who's got "a wall around me / That you can't even see," and is unable even to say "I love you" to the woman who calmed him down when he "was in crazy motion." The speaker's virtually the same self-protecting isolate who sang "I Am a Rock"—only now there is no ironic boastfulness, only a pained recognition of inadequacy. If the song casts blame for their relationship problems on Simon himself, "Tenderness" finds fault in Peggy as well.[4] In an intimate light-jazz arrangement that calls up a torch singer in a smoky cocktail lounge, the speaker comes to the point almost immediately: "I know you see through me / But there's no tenderness / Beneath your honesty." The other undisguisedly personal song on the album is the touching go-to-sleep song for his young son, Harper, called "St. Judy's Comet."

This leaves us with the five remaining tracks, all of which are basically genre pieces that impressively exploit one musical style or another, with two of them, "Kodachrome" and "Loves Me Like a Rock," becoming huge radio hits that solidified Simon's position as a major solo star. "Kodachrome" was the album's first breakout hit, climbing all the way to #2 on the merits of a string of undeniable melodic hooks, a rollicking piano, the expert rhythm-and-blues backup of the legendary Muscle Shoals Rhythm Section, and the fortuitous dustup caused by its being the first song on top 40 radio ever to feature the word *crap*. (Many radio stations cut or bleeped it, but since the word was in the song's first line, it was impossible to miss.) Like "Me and Julio," the lyric's meaning seems secondary to the way the words fit into the melody line. When Simon was first composing the song, he used the words "going home" as syllabic placeholders till the word "Kodachrome" came to him. As such, the song's no great shakes lyrically: it's about a snide little narrator who, despite his "lack of education . . . can read the writing on the wall." For him, the world's an ugly place, and it helps to have something like a Nikon camera loaded with Kodachrome film that, when it's developed, "Makes you think all the world's a sunny day." That self-assured "crap" in the first line gives way, later in the song, to a spoiled punk who can't give up his illusions, and is hilariously/desperately whining, "Everything looks worse in black and white," and begging, "Mama don't take my Kodachrome away." But it's unclear that Simon meant much by it—in the 1981 *The Concert in Central Park*, he'd sing this key line as "Everything looks *better* in black and white," which pretty much obscures any critique he may originally have had for the song.

The other hit single, "Loves Me Like a Rock," was almost as big a success as "Kodachrome" (it reached #4), and is an expert grafting of gospel idioms onto an undeniably catchy strand of pop melody. Like "Kodachrome," there's little to it lyrically: the speaker is basically an incorruptible soul whose mama "loves me like the rock of ages"; the song is a joyous, if ironically rendered, celebration of righteousness. The background vocals are supplied by the Dixie Hummingbirds, and the song seems like Simon's excuse to work with the legendary gospel quartet. As nicely executed as the song is, however, it isn't gospel: it's "gospel," that is, an appreciative appropriation of a style that's distant from Simon's own (white, Jewish, Queens) roots. There's not a moment during the song when the listener thinks Simon *means* any of what the speaker's saying: he's using Christian tropes and black gospel trappings simply as a formal gesture—something that he finds musically interesting and fun. (At this point in Simon's life, religious or spiritual motifs were musical motifs and no more. This will begin to change on *Still Crazy*.) For gospel purists, for whom gospel music is an actual form of prayer, "Love Me Like a Rock" is soulless cultural borrowing at best, offensive at worst. In 1973, however, such critiques were muted; it was not until 1986—when he released *Graceland*—at the height of the cultural discourse about white musicians stealing and profiting from black styles, that Simon was forced to defend his use of borrowed musical idioms.

The other genre pieces here—the Dixieland jazz of "Take Me to the Mardi Gras," the urban blues of "One Man's Ceiling Is Another Man's Floor," and the breezy calypso of "Was a Sunny Day"—are similarly proficient adaptations of non- or pre-rock styles to a pop-rock context. In one sense, they're evidence of Simon spreading his wings, of the joy he was taking in exploring the wide world of pop styles, and of his need to declare his difference not only from Dylan but also from other singer-songwriters, most of whom in the early 1970s were still sticking to folk- and "soft"-rock contexts. (Randy Newman and Joni Mitchell are the compelling exceptions here, writers as interested in musical discovery as lyrical expressiveness.) In another sense, the songs also seem like genre exercises, shallow excursions into new musical territory as a way to avoid the personal. There's a moment at the end of "One Man's Ceiling," for instance, a pleasant and fairly witty blues about the need for tolerance—that is, a song about a moral cliché that barely seems to engage Simon's sensibility—when we get a description of an alley where "some people congregate in shame," and the speaker hears one of them "call my name." It's a rather startling moment—promising an opening into self-revelatory material—but Simon drops it as soon as he introduces it. It's a frustrating example of how Simon can use his increasing mastery of musical styles to avoid personal expression as much as he uses it to explore it.

There Goes Rhymin' Simon is divided evenly, then, between the five songs in which clear, earnest lyrical (and usually personal) expression is paramount, and five songs where the lyrics seems more or less incidental, secondary to musical ideas. This is not a new dichotomy in Simon's music—*Bridge Over Troubled Water* was similarly split—but *Bridge*'s genre exercises were, well, superb ("Baby Driver" is a masterful update of 1950s pop fluff, "Keep the Customer Satisfied" an irrepressible engine of rock energy), while *Rhymin*'s exercises *sound* like exercises, the dutiful work of a talented musician/composer searching for something to say through style, and not always succeeding. This won't be an issue with the next album. He won't have to search for something to say in *Still Crazy after All These Years*, musically or lyrically. When his marriage to Peggy Harper broke up, his theme was right in front of him.

PAUL SIMON IN CONCERT: LIVE RHYMIN' (1974), STILL CRAZY AFTER ALL THESE YEARS (1975), GREATEST HITS, ETC. (1977)

The live album Simon released in 1974 was a stopgap gesture in some ways: unprolific songwriter that he was (and remains), he hadn't assembled enough material to release the one album per year that Columbia records (and the public at large) still expected in the early seventies, and a live album gave him the opportunity to show not only how Simon & Garfunkel songs could work solo, but also how well his new solo material stood up side-by-side with the duo's stuff. It also gave this endlessly restless artist the chance to transform some of his best material: to give "The Sound of Silence" a gospel turn, for instance, or to give "The Boxer" the Peruvian folk treatment. The album is broken into four mini-sets: an acoustic solo opener of three songs, highlighted by a delicate and vulnerable rendition of "Homeward Bound" that includes a verse excluded from the original studio version, and that seems more personal to Simon in 1974 than it did when he first wrote it. The second section begins with Simon bringing on Urubamba, the renamed Los Incas band he had used on studio versions of "El Condor Pasa" and "Duncan." The clear highlight of their live collaboration is the new "Boxer." In the studio version, a trumpet plays the beautiful interlude melody; here, Simon moves the interlude to song's end, and has Urubamba's wooden flute player perform it. The flute solo is not just gorgeous but also tender and almost childlike, the performance of the player shy but determined to do justice to the melody's beauty. The solo is an analogue, in a way, to Simon's stage presence on the whole album: excited to be presenting songs he feels great confidence in, but clearly tentative at being the center of attention. For the next five songs, Simon brings on a gospel group, the Jessy Dixon Singers. One of the songs is "Jesus Is the Answer," in which Simon doesn't appear at all, which is a generous gesture on Simon's part since the gospel group was able to reap royalties from the song's presence on the record. The fourth section is a coda in which Simon returns solo with "America." The recording includes a moment before the song begins when an audience member shouts out, "Say a few words!" Simon immediately takes the bait, and begins to talk to the hushed crowd: "Well, let's hope . . . let's hope that we learn to live . . . ," he begins, and then stops, not knowing, apparently, where to go with this. Then he apparently decides that what he's said is enough, whereupon the crowd erupts in applause. Whether the applause expresses delight—or relief that Simon got out of an awkward moment with a lucky pause—is debatable. That Simon decided to leave the exchange on the album is curious: the audience member's request casts Simon as a modern-day oracle, a role that one had assumed Simon had grown out of by now. The generous way to think of his response—which, in any case, seems rather lame to me—is that he's making fun of himself, but I worry that at the time he thought he was, serendipitously, saying something profound, in which case he was still "fakin' it" a little bit in the 1970s. In any case, the album hit only #33 on the national album charts, and barely whet the appetite of fans waiting for new Simon music.

On first or second listen, it's difficult to understand why, forty years on, *Still Crazy after All These Years* was such a commercial sensation and Grammy magnet in 1975. (It was his first solo #1, and won awards for Best Album of the Year and Best Male Pop Vocal Performance.) Yes, it contained Simon's first collaboration with Garfunkel in five years, "My Little Town," a fine song that certainly spurred sales as well as speculation about a more permanent reunion. And, yes it contained a fluke #1 single, "50 Ways to Leave Your Lover," which had a chorus so compulsively singable that it was easy for any casual radio listener to miss the verses' considerable wit. But the album is by no means "crazy"—far from letting it all hang out (as those hippies used to say), it's the most tight-fisted, serious, and depressed of Simon's career to that point, devoted in large part to the sad dissolution of his marriage and its painful aftermath. (Bob Dylan released *his* end-of-marriage album, *Blood on the Tracks*, the same year, a coincidence hardly lost on those who follow the Dylan/Simon rivalry. That Simon got the sales and the industry plaudits for an album that wasn't quite as strong as Dylan's has caused no small amount of resentment among Dylanites.) What's more, *Still Crazy* contains the two LP side-enders "Night Game" and "Silent Eyes," one of which comes off as a puzzling fragment and the other as a highly self-conscious art song about God and the state of Israel. The album is, finally, slight in terms of length—like his other two solo albums, this one clocks in at less than thirty-five minutes—and gives the impression of an artist squeezing his reserves to fill out the ten-song album requirement.

On the other hand, *Still Crazy after All These Years* exemplifies mature, post-1960s pop, grown-up music for Counterculture veterans. The album is by no means rock (the melodies and arrangements are more Sinatra than Stones), but it's infused with a humor, intelligence, and a sharpened sense of irony—not to mention a sense of existential weightlessness—that was forged by the youth generation of the 1960s, and shows him heading into his thirties with the experiences and instincts of a weary and wary survivor. As personal as the album is, and as much as it's about that prevailing question from "Congratulations" ("Can a man and a woman / Live together in peace") the album speaks more broadly of (and very much to) that generation he portrayed in "American Tune":

> I don't know a soul that's not been battered
> I don't have a friend who feels at ease
> I don't know a dream that's not been shattered
> Or driven to its knees

The quiet opening notes of a moody electric piano on the title track tip us off to the album's atmosphere, and the lyric fills out the feeling: "Still Crazy after All These Years" is about a guy who's up in the middle of the night, "crapped out, yawning / Longing my life away." Writing from a Manhattan hotel room after he broke up with Peggy, Simon gives us a character who is already nostalgic for a past (and a marriage) that's barely behind him, and reconciled to solitude and a life that's destined to "fade." Perhaps because he's simultaneously longing and despairing—meaning he hopes and can't hope at the same time—he stares out a window and fears "I'll do some damage / One fine day." It's a song about emotional paralysis, in other words, which is a very odd emotion with which to begin an album of commercial pop songs. Musically, this paralysis is reinforced by the string and woodwind arrangement on the bridge that follows "it's all gonna fade." The arrangement starts off with prickly anxious strings that aurally underscore the singer's angst and confusion, then briefly breaks out into what appears to be a liberating saxophone solo. Only the liberation is short-lived, and after the solo spends itself, the arrangement returns to the broken moodiness of the song's beginning. If that solo promises the speaker release from paralysis, the song's ending says, "Not so fast there. You've barely begun dealing with your problems." Simon's insistence on beginning with "Still Crazy"—rather than the obvious commercial choice, the jazz-gospel "Gone at Last," which is the only real "up" song on the record—suggests how confident Simon was in his craft, the melancholy subject matter of the songs, and the ability of his audience to appreciate them.

"My Little Town," a brief detour from the album's portrait of marital woes, follows. Vintage Simon & Garfunkel, it sounds very much as if the two had never parted—the harmonies are intact, the melody is vivid and soaring, there's a blustery horn arrangement right out of "Keep the Customer Satisfied," and the lyrics are, as in the best S & G, darker and more penetrating than the pretty voices imply. "My Little Town" is about a speaker who looks back on an innocent youth riding his bicycle past the factories of a small town where the values of God and country prevailed. But all's not well here: the line "my mom doing the laundry," which the pair sing with childlike sprightliness, is immediately followed by the dour detail that she hangs out the clothes "in the dirty breeze." Furthermore, the rainbows that come after the rains in this town "are black / It's not that the colors aren't there / It's just imagination they lack." Which is the song's key line: this conformist little town stifles individuality and imagination, which makes it a place of "nothing but the dead and dying." Simon appends an epigraph to the song from the opening poem of Ted Hughes's now-canonical book, *Crow*, one of the harshest visions of post–World War II British poetry. The song borrows from the poem the idea of some life force (in the poem, the bird Crow, in the song, the bike-riding boy) that manages to fly above the emptiness surrounding him, and so, as bitter as the song is, it's about transcending limitations. But perhaps a silent and more salient influence over the song is Wallace Stevens, the American poet whom Simon had begun to mention more and more in interviews during these years. In early (and more easily accessible) poems like "Domination of Black," "Disillusionment of Ten O'Clock," "The Snow Man," and "A High-Toned Old Christian Woman," Stevens made his primary theme the necessity to transcend the mundanity of contemporary reality through the use of the poetic imagination. The colorlessness of the rainbow in "My Little Town" is akin to the colorlessness of the white-gowned women in "Disillusionment of Ten O'Clock" or the morally rigid character in "A High-Toned Old Christian Woman." In both Stevens's poems and Simon's song, the imagination—free, even gaudy, "squiggling like saxophones" in Stevens, blaring like the horns in "My Little Town"—is what's needed to counteract the arid rigidity of contemporary life, to literally give color and life to "the dead and dying." Among other things, "My Little Town" is an indication of how far he'd left T. S. Eliot behind—here he'd embraced some of the poetic views of Eliot's main modernist rival.

"I Do It for Your Love," a wan jazz-tinged ballad, the wan-ness of which turns out to be its very strength, returns us to the theme of marriage and its discontents. It chronicles, with impressively concise domestic detail, the story of a doomed couple who marry "on a rainy day," and who touchingly drink orange juice all through their first winter to ward off the cold they share. One day the man buys an old rug for his wife, but on the way home "the colors ran / The orange bled the blue," which sums up both his efforts to "do it for [her] love" and the odd, unforeseeable obstacles that keep their love from succeeding. The marriage then falls apart, with the couple in the final verse as far apart as "the northern and southern / Hemispheres." The man, saddened and confused, can only conclude that "love emerges / And it disappears." The music, touched with affection toward the hapless couple, is almost purposefully enervated, as if it, too, shares the couple's winter cold and their emotional entropy: the song will serve as a prototype for the longer, more developed marital drama of "Darling Lorraine" later in his career.

"50 Ways to Leave Your Lover," Simon's first solo #1 record, goes at marital discontent from a wryer angle. It begins with a famously catchy drum riff, something that studio drummer Steve Gadd was fooling around with in the studio and Simon seized on as something he could use to hook radio listeners. There is a second hook as well, the equally famous and equally catchy "slip out the back, jack" faux-gospel chorus, whose lyrics Simon has said came from a rhyming game he used to play with his son. The hook of the chorus is, one ought to note, wearying, especially on top 40 AM radio, where it played in the heaviest of rotations during the winter of 1975–1976. But what gives the song ballast is the sly irony of the verse lyrics, which tell the story of a man who wants to leave his lover, and is asking a female friend for advice. Simon's conversational vocal is expert here, shading the character's dialogue with the nuance necessary to get across their two-faced intentions, which are (1) to pretend that they're both merely helpful friends while (2) moving in for the romantic kill. When the female friend purrs to him that "it grieves me so / To see you in such pain," and that she wishes she could do something to help him, the man smugly replies, "I appreciate that" with a cheater's best game face on. Of course, the two end up in bed, consummating the charade. Despite the calculated silliness of the chorus, the song ended up being one of the wittiest and most sophisticated singles of that year.

"Night Game" ends the side on an obscure note. Reducing the instrumentals to nothing but a very quietly strummed electric guitar, a bass, and Toots Thielmans's disconsolate harmonica, Simon opens this dreamlike composition with the image of a baseball pitcher who dies on the mound in the middle of the eighth inning. After his teammates leave his spikes and uniform on the ground as some sort of ritualistic homage, "the night turned cold," and the point of view pans out to take in the old stadium, the frigid moon, and stars as "white as bones." With the baseball and summer "season[s] lost," Simon concludes with the image of a tarpaulin rolled over the field's winter frost. I have listened to this song perhaps three hundred times over the years and still have no idea what Simon is trying to get at. It aims, I think, to be "haunting," to throw the seemingly dissonant ideas of death and baseball together in a disconcerting way, but I find it simply inert, whatever meaning it might have for Simon still locked up in his head.

"Gone at Last" launches side 2 of the LP with a galloping piano riff that propels Simon and his duet partner here, Phoebe Snow, into an energetic gospel rocker that deservedly spent a good while on the Billboard singles charts, topping off at #23. Bursting with kinetic energy, sleekly professional yet filled with spontaneity in the vocals (particularly from the charming Snow), it's the album's single affirmative bright spot, with the song's prayer that the speaker's "bad luck . . . is gone at last" answered when Simon sings near the end, "Once in a while from out of nowhere . . . somebody will come and lift you higher." After that, the side is filled out with a trio of infectiously melodic songs whose subtle emotional and tonal ranges don't just summon up Simon negotiating a post-marital life but also comprise a canny picture of American desperation circa the mid-1970s. The album then concludes with "Silent Eyes."

The title, "Some Folks' Lives Roll Easy," is deceptive: the key line is, "Most folks' lives, they stumble / Lord they fall," and the song is about a man whose soul has been so battered by circumstance that he finds himself—to his own chagrin—looking to God for help. The vocal is transparently (and thus touchingly) desperate, adolescent in its frightened need for succor. "But you said," he complains like a schoolboy reminding a parent of a promise, "If I ever got so low / I was busted / You could be trusted." It's the first Simon lyric that openly longs for God, even if here the longing is safely couched in a character, not Simon himself. (That longing will bloom with the decades.) The desperation of the song is echoed ironically in the next track, "Have a Good Time," a droll satire on a creature who had not yet been named in the culture—the thirty-something Me Generation baby boomer who would, in the late 1970s, participate in EST personal trainings, read books like *Looking Out for #1*, wholeheartedly adopt the hedonism of the sexual revolution, and embrace guiltlessly the careerist, materialistic ethos that would soon turn them into that hoary 1980s archetype, the Reaganite Yuppie. Dedicated to the Gospel of Self, the song's speaker is "exhausted from loving so well" and utterly cynical about the "paranoid" world, but genuflects just enough to finer sensibilities to admit that "Maybe I'm blind / To the fate of mankind," before throwing his hands in the air and stating the Gospel outright:

> So God bless the goods we was given
> And God bless the U.S. of A.
> And God bless our standard of livin'
> Let's keep it that way
> And we'll all have a good time

With its sly, slippery vocal caressing a fine waggish melody, and a sexy chorus featuring Valerie Simpson, the song was released as the album's fifth single (the first four had all gone top 40, two top 5), but for whatever reason—Simon burnout on the radio, perhaps, though just as likely the audience's awareness that the song's sarcasm cut a little too close to the bone—the single stiffed. Perhaps Columbia records ought to have released the album's next track, "You're Kind," instead, a funnier, more tender-hearted if just as ironically charged composition. Blessed with a simple melody and an even simpler sentiment—thank you, the speaker tells a lover, for being so kind—the speaker does a 180 in the final two verses, when he lets on that he's "agitated" to think that his lover will stay with him forever, whereupon he leaves her, his sole excuse being "I like to sleep with the window open / And you keep the window closed." It's a dexterous portrait of the commitment-phobic male that would become so recognizable as the late 1970s unfolded.

The album's coda, "Silent Eyes," is different from anything Simon had yet done. The words read less like song lyrics than a genuine attempt at a modernist poem—there are only two rhymes in its nineteen lines, and the imagery hearkens back to Eliot's desert imagery in "The Waste Land" or "The Hollow Men"—though we should reiterate that by now Simon has tamed the Eliot influence, and is able to use it for his own original purposes. His purpose here is to meditate on the city of Jerusalem, the epicenter of the religion of Simon's Jewish forefathers. When Simon wrote the song, Israel had recently fought and won two quick but bloody wars—in 1967 and again in 1973—in order to preserve their security, and the song is about a presumably American outsider—presumably Simon himself—who watches silently as "Jerusalem / Weeps alone." The song expresses a solidarity with Israel and with Judaism that has been wholly absent in Simon's work so far—Jerusalem "calls my name," says the speaker—and concludes with the speaker singing over a surging gospel choir that everyone will be "called before the eyes of God" to stand as witnesses to Jerusalem's vulnerability. (In 1975, it was perhaps easier for a liberal like Simon to stand wholly behind Israel than it might have been in future decades, when Israel's occupation of Palestine had made American liberal support of Israel much more fraught.) In any case, for the second time on the album, the word *God* is invoked, this time with no ironic inflection whatsoever, and further suggests Simon's ginger grappling with the religious issues that would later occupy a much larger part of his imagination.

Still Crazy was followed, in 1977, by *Greatest Hits, Etc.*, a profit-taking move on the part of Columbia Records, with whom Simon had parted on highly fractious terms. (Columbia's president, Clive Davis, with whom Simon had a strong relationship, had been forced out and was replaced by Walter Yetnikoff, whose relationship with Simon quickly soured, and who at one point ordered his security guards to forcibly remove Simon if he so much as entered Columbia's headquarters in New York!) Simon moved on to Warner Brothers records, but not before recording two new songs that were appended to this best-of compilation. "Stranded in a Limousine," a fast-paced and crisply percussive tune that tells the inconclusive story of a "mean individual" in a limousine who stops at a traffic light, attracts a crowd, then mysteriously vanishes, is of little consequence. But "Slip Sliding Away," which Simon felt so strong about that he opened an album of his best solo work with it, is one of the highlights of his solo career, and remains a staple of his concert repertoire. A ballad of aching melancholy delivered in a voice so open to the pain of love's disappointments as to be naked, it gives us vignettes of three people whose lives are slip-sliding away—that is, whose grasp of a secure, loving, meaningful life is so tenuous that they live in constant fear that they will lose it. The first verse presents a portrait of a man "who wore his passion for his woman like a thorny crown," and who tells her that "my love for you's so overpowering / I'm afraid I will disappear." This extraordinarily concise and vivid characterization of desperate love is followed by a second verse in which a severely depressed wife (perhaps the woman from the first verse) can barely imagine a "good day" as anything better than one in which it doesn't rain, while "a bad day" is one where she stays in bed and "think[s] of things that might have been." The third verse gives us a father—this one doubtless autobiographically informed—who has been separated from his young son and "longs to tell him the reasons for the things he'd done"—presumably why he'd left him when he divorced his wife. But when he arrives at the sleeping boy's bed, he finds himself unable to explain himself, so he merely kisses the boy and leaves. For all these characters, life and time slip through their fingers, *even as they watch it slipping away*: before their very eyes, love overwhelms them, depression smothers the will, and shame and guilt forbid connection. In a final verse, the speaker informs us that while God has made his plans, "the information's unavailable to the mortal man" (that Simon is able to smoothly sing this marble-mouthed line is a testament to his genius for finding "the right combination of words to a melody line," as he'll put it later in "Everything about It Is a Love Song"). While we go about our business, we can never tell whether the lives we're creating are meaningful or not. God's appearance in the song is a surprise—though at best He is a distant, bemused diety watching His creation—but this is nonetheless Simon's best song to date about existential alienation: honest, felt in the bone, totally unencumbered by pretension.

Still Crazy after All These Years and *Greatest Hits, Etc.* constitute a mid-career culmination. *Still Crazy* came at the end of an eleven-year period of feverish songwriting, record-making, and live performance that began with *Wednesday Morning, 3 A.M.* and produced, in all, nine studio albums of mostly original material (five S & G albums plus four solo albums, including *The Paul Simon Songbook*), along with the soundtrack for *The Graduate*, a live solo album, the TV documentary *Songs of America*, and *Simon & Garfunkel's Greatest Hits*, which includes some previously unreleased live material. Simon would never again put out so many records in such a short period of time. *Still Crazy*, both in its abundant sales and in its critical reception, confirmed his status as an elite solo artist, and left him with nothing more to prove. Moreover, the music he was creating—a brilliant amalgam of folk rock, traditional American pop, light jazz, gospel, and other forms—was in the absolute mainstream of 1970s pop. Little did he know that popular music was about to undergo a tectonic shift, with three new and hugely influential styles of music—disco, punk, and hip-hop—beginning to filter into American consciousness in the mid- to late 1970s. These developments would leave Paul Simon, for the first time in his career, outside the mainstream, and along with changes in his personal life, would lead to his first major career crisis.

4

MISTAKES ON TOP OF MISTAKES ON TOP OF MISTAKES

1978–1983

It was a difficult time for me. . . . What was I thinking? . . . All kinds of mistakes on top of mistakes on top of mistakes. So now I had a personal blow, a career setback, and the combination of the two put me in a tailspin.[1]

After the major success of *Still Crazy after All These Years*—an album that spun off three hit singles, amassed platinum sales, and earned two Grammys, including Album of the Year—Paul Simon had, again, hit the pinnacle of the pop music world, only now he'd done it as a solo artist. He had walked away from being part of the most successful rock duo in history—walked away from the riches, fame, and security it provided—taken up the challenge of a solo career, and floated to the top of the singer-songwriter pantheon in less than five years. Not only had he already written a flurry of pop standards, but he had helped expand the palette of modern pop music, incorporating more diverse styles (and with more professional panache) onto his records than any other song-writer of his time (his only rival here was Paul McCartney). Finally, and most importantly from an artistic point of view, he had shed his early influences and, in songs like "Mrs. Robinson," "The Boxer," "Peace Like a River," "American Tune," and "Still Crazy after All These Years," had found his own voice—discerning, wry, rueful, melancholy, vulnerable.

But by 1975, Paul Simon was also alone, his marriage to Peggy having disintegrated as the count of his career successes mounted. He had moved out of one apartment and into another, still on New York's fashionable Upper East Side and—fortuitously, it turned out—close to those of two new friends, Lorne Michaels and Chevy Chase. These two were the producer and star, respectively, of a new late-night television show called *Saturday Night Live* that, with its super-hip satire, theatrical experimentation (including its willingness to break the fourth wall), and its ability to express the comic sensibility of the Boomer generation that had survived the 1960s Counterculture, was beginning to transform broadcast television. Michaels made Simon one of the show's first musical guests; he sang "My Little Town" with guest Art Garfunkel and other songs from *Still Crazy*—including the title track, which he performed in a chicken suit, Simon's attempt to shed the ultra-serious artist image that had dogged him long after he had ceased cultivating it. That chicken suit was indicative of Simon's attempt to loosen up generally: newly single, he had begun carousing around Manhattan with his new TV buddies, dating Hollywood starlets like Shelley Duvall and eventually Carrie Fisher, even dancing at New York's Studio 54. In a way, he might have been trying to de-ironize "Have a Good Time"— that is, really trying to put his conscience, his work, and his penchant for brooding aside for once in his life in favor of a lighthearted pleasure principle. By 1977, in fact, he had bagged a key small role as a sybaritic music producer in Woody Allen's breakout film, *Annie Hall*, which would put him on the Hollywood map as an actor.

These tentative feelers he was putting out into the worlds of TV and film were also a way of finding a new place for himself in a pop world that was moving quickly away from him. In 1975, Bruce Springsteen released *Born to Run*, an adrenaline shot of hard-rock traditionalism that galvanized critics and the most discriminating element of the rock audience and suddenly made Simon's form of soft rock seem tepid. On the top 40 front, the singer-songwriter movement that had provided the bedrock of audience support for Simon's own music through the first half of the 1970s had been superseded by disco, a slick, lush dance-friendly form of R&B that Simon was totally unsuited for. And then in 1976 and 1977, punk rock emerged—first the Ramones in New York, followed by the Sex Pistols and the Clash, among many others, in Britain—an explosion of rebellious anger and musical primitivism whose sensibility was miles away from Simon's. By the late 1970s, the punk, post-punk, and New Wave movements—not to mention the first green shoots of hip hop—were not only getting the lion's share of ink from the rock press but also forcing rock's "dinosaur" old guard to radically reassess what rock was supposed to be all about. Simon, at the center of pop rock's mainstream since 1965, found himself, for the first time, shunted to the margins, dallying with irrelevance.

Though Simon had always avidly experimented with pop styles, the styles that were hot during the late 1970s and early 1980s—disco, punk, New Wave, and hip hop—were so far outside his interests and abilities that it would have been foolish for him to pursue them. The Stones could ably mimic disco in "Miss You," and white rockers like Blondie could absorb hip hop in "Rapture," but Simon knew he had no business dabbling in these forms. As fascinated as he was with rhythm, his songs had never been exactly *danceable*; and despite an agile voice that lent his speakers character and genuine nuance, Simon's voice didn't and couldn't *rock*: he couldn't yell or scream or bellow; he couldn't persuasively deliver rage or sexual passion. In his first three solo albums, he had forged an intelligently quiet, often jazz-tinged musical environment, and had mastered it. But as the horizon of a new decade neared, it was unclear if that style had much mileage left in it.

One other context of late 1970s pop music is worth mentioning here, and that is its unprecedented commercial expansion. Just as *Jaws* and *Star Wars* had ushered in the era of the mega-blockbuster in the world of Hollywood film, acts like Peter Frampton, Fleetwood Mac, and the Bee Gees (especially the *Saturday Night Fever* soundtrack) began selling records that were not merely earning platinum status (meaning selling 1 million copies, which in the 1960s and early 1970s certified a big hit) but were going eight, ten, or even fifteen times platinum. In some ways, this made sense: the rock audience had been expanding since the mid-1950s, and there were now three generations of consumers who were listening to pop radio, buying albums, and paying good money to go to rock concerts. A few savvy (or in the case of Frampton, lucky) hitmakers were bound to find the right formula to appeal to nearly all of them. But the phenomenon of the mega-hit also reflected the music industry's growing ability to saturate markets with advertising, using ever-more sophisticated means to exploit their audiences. Too, the up-and-coming bands had shed the distaste for overt capitalist display that their 1960s counterparts affected: make no bones about it, Boston, Foreigner, and REO Speedwagon were in it for the money (and, of course, the girls). Meanwhile, the singer-songwriters of the early 1970s found themselves grasping for some new purchase on the pop audience: in albums like *Don Juan's Reckless Daughter*, Joni Mitchell went the West Coast jazz route, to disappointing (and pretentious) results; Jackson Browne tried to rock (which worked in "Running on Empty," and didn't on "Boulevard" or "For America"); James Taylor and Van Morrison drifted into a decade-long decline; and Bob Dylan, after 1978's compellingly strange *Street Legal*, began putting out his three born-again Christian albums, which led into a long slide of mostly terrible albums that didn't halt until 1989's *Oh Mercy*! Only Neil Young, whose status as a 1970s singer-songwriter was the fluky result of 1970's folk-rock smash *After the Gold Rush*, managed to embrace the new aesthetic: he jumped on punk's noise and rebellion, turned his amps up to eleven, and emerged with the searingly brilliant *Rust Never Sleeps*. Simon, perhaps the most marketplace-savvy of all the singer-songwriters, had the luxury, after *Still Crazy*, of having time on his side. He didn't rush back into the game, and when he did, he decided to go the ambitious route: he would write the screenplay, star, and write and perform the music for a major Hollywood release. It would be the first of his many "mistakes" of the period.

ONE-TRICK PONY (1980)

One-Trick Pony isn't a good movie: it's got a threadbare, deeply unoriginal plot featuring an inexperienced male lead (Simon) who can't carry a film; Robert Young's direction is leaden, barely serviceable; and a good third of the film (the "band on the road" sequences) features not only an inexpressive Simon but also four members of Simon's band who had never been in a movie before and apparently didn't learn much from being in this one. Even old pros—character actors like Rip Torn and Allen Garfield—look lost. That the movie got made at all, given the savage environment of late-1970s Hollywood deal-making, only makes sense if we see it as an inside job—essentially a vanity production.

When Simon's relationship with Columbia Records soured in the wake of the Clive Davis firing, Simon found a new home with Warner Brothers Records, which happened to be partners with the Warner Brothers film studio. WB Records was able to use its influence to get WB studios to finance a Paul Simon vehicle. Not that, on the surface, the bet on Simon didn't have its appeal. Here was a talented, intelligent, ambitious, and confident artist with a great sales history, even experience making a documentary film. Here was a man who had shown some acting chops in *Annie Hall*. The promise of a huge-selling soundtrack full of Paul Simon songs called up giddy memories of *The Graduate*. And Simon, in his mid-thirties, had even grown into his looks: no longer the awkward pseudo-intellectual nerd pictured on the back of early Simon & Garfunkel records, Simon had gotten himself a flattering haircut, peeled off fifteen pounds so as to show off a leading-man's jawline, and taken enough acting lessons to trust that his brown eyes—large, sad, soulful—would do a lot of the work for him. Warner Brothers argued him out of the idea of directing the film, but it finally gave him the green light.

One-Trick Pony is about a journeyman musician named Jonah Levin who had one big hit during the 1960s with an antiwar folk song called "Soft Parachutes" and has been living off that fame ever since. (The song, curiously not included on the original soundtrack, perhaps because Simon considered it too naïve, is sweetly sung and a fine example of the "sensitive" protest song that probably would have been a hit in the 1960s. It wouldn't have been a detriment to an early Simon & Garfunkel album. It was finally added to the "remastered" CD more than a decade later.) Jonah's playing clubs anywhere he can with his band—they're touring Cleveland and the drearier parts of the Midwest as the film opens—traveling in a van and sleeping in dive motels. He has recently separated from his wife Marion (played by the solidly professional Blair Brown, who unfortunately highlights Simon's amateurishness in their scenes together), with whom they have a son, Matty. The tension in the film arises on two fronts. The first is the marriage, which is falling apart because Jonah is on the road so much and because Marion, trying valiantly to hold the family together in Manhattan, has lost sympathy with his dreams of making it again. During their first big scene together, Marion tells him, "Rock 'n' roll, when you get to be a certain age . . . it's kind of . . . it's pathetic." Jonah, angry and defensive, responds by looking her in the eye and saying, "You are so fucking *boring*"—their *contretemps* here essentially setting up the lines of their conflict.[2] It's not, to be sure, particularly original: morally grounded movie wives have been trying to get their artistically flighty movie husbands off the road for decades. And it doesn't help that Jonah is painfully adolescent in the film: his dialogue with Marion mostly consists of a slew of ironic one-liners that, while showcasing his wit, evade rather than face his problems. Soulful eyes notwithstanding, Jonah isn't a character that an audience can easily warm to.

The plot's other major tension is also fairly clichéd. Jonah is offered a deal to make a record that may make him relevant again, but the path toward success is littered by the need to compromise his art. First, he learns that he's only getting the chance to make the record because he slept with a woman—the wife of a record company executive—who convinced her husband to offer him a contract. Secondly, when he does make his record, the company insists that he work with a top 40 producer (played by Lou Reed, looking distressingly under-directed) who insists on using shrill female back-up vocals and a string section to up the pop-hit quotient on the prospective single, "Ace in the Hole." At the end of the movie, Jonah decides compromise is not for him: he sneaks into the studio, steals the master tape, takes it onto a Manhattan side street, and unreels the tape onto the wet pavement, ruining it.

Except for a couple of sweet scenes between Jonah and Matty—which are reminiscent of the father-son scenes in *Kramer vs. Kramer* and *Manhattan*, two New York City–based domestic dramas from 1979 to which *Pony* was often compared—and two strong performances by Mare Winningham and Joan Hackett, the film is surprisingly lifeless. Most of the scenes of Jonah's band performing in clubs are not only downbeat but also weirdly sweaty: Simon's face and body have been sprayed with more movie-sweat than the slow, depressing ballads he's singing could possibly inspire. Our concern for Jonah's marriage is undercut by his willingness to sleep with a young woman on the road (Winningham) as well as with the record executive's wife (Hackett). (Yes, he's separated, but while he's in Manhattan, sleeping with the Hackett character, he's still sleeping with Marion.) The top 40 production touches that the Reed character adds to "Ace in the Hole" are supposed to be horrifying to an artist like Jonah, but they actually don't sound that different from effects Simon had himself used on his own previous records. Finally, Jonah's decision to break up the band and return to his wife not only is unmotivated but also doesn't resolve the film's conflicts in any credible way: at the end we're left wondering what Jonah's going to do in Manhattan without a band or a record to make. When Jonah ruins the master tape, it's a defiant but empty gesture.

And then there's the music. Though at times it's supposed to, it doesn't rock—"Ace in the Hole" stirs up a bit of a rhythmic stew but never boils over, as the film expects it to—and some of it, particularly "Nobody" and "Long, Long Day," falls short of Simon's typically tough-minded, melancholy self-analysis and drifts into frankly maudlin territory. Still—though it's not saying that much—it's a lot more interesting and subtle than the movie it soundtracks. "That's Why God Made the Movies" has little to do with the film's themes, but its quiet wit and flowing melodic line would have made the song a worthy addition to *There Goes Rhymin' Simon* or *Still Crazy*. Jonah's road blues is much more effectively put across in "How the Heart Approaches What It Yearns" than in those dreary scenes of the band bus crawling through rust-belt cityscapes, or in Jonah's lonesome calls home. The lyric of "Oh, Marion" about how "the boy's got a voice / But the voice is his natural disguise" does more to characterize Jonah's evasions of familial responsibility than any of his fights with Marion. "Jonah," with its lyric about how "Jonah / Was swallowed by a song"—that is, is obsessed with music to the point where it distorts the rest of his life—also characterizes Jonah better than the screenplay does. "One-Trick Pony" succinctly lays out Jonah's initial situation in the film, and "God Bless the Absentee" is practically a plot summary set to music. This is decent stuff, but it's essentially program music. Only "Late in the Evening," the album's one hit single (it ended up in the top 10) stands out on its own, and is the only song from the album that has made it into Simon's long-term concert repertoire. Like "Stranded in a Limousine," it's driven by a skeletal but propulsive bass line and Simon's lively vocal, which narrates an endearingly nostalgic tale of a boy growing up singing in *a cappella* groups "on the stoops" of his neighborhood. Soon the boy learns to play guitar, and before long is blowing away audiences at his shows. It's a professionally deft, catchy celebration of the musician's vocation, and Simon's band digs into the song's groove for all it's worth.

Still, with all the anticipatory build-up—it had been five years be-tween major projects—*One-Trick Pony* as film and soundtrack were both underwhelming. The music—moody and slightly inert, depressed without being illuminating about its depression, and really springing to life only on band workouts like "Ace in the Hole," "Late in the Eve-ning," and the title cut—gives the listener little sense of the *joie de vivre* that presumably makes Jonah so avid and committed a musician. The draggy mood surely comes from the movie's themes. Simon's screen-play was attempting to confront, in some ways, the failure of his mar-riage to Peggy Harper, but he wasn't able to translate the autobiograph-ical material into something that was dramatically clear, vivid, or widely accessible. But the problem was also musical. The band arrangements, while taut and professional, are surprisingly colorless: where are the reggae arrangements, the gospel borrowings, the South American touches that animated his first three solo albums? *One-Trick Pony* seems like a dead-end, musically—it neither builds on the stylistic ex-periments of his previous records nor adapts itself to any of the new music that was captivating listeners in the late 1970s. There's an early scene where Jonah's band opens for the B-52s, hot at the time, who perform their first big hit, "Rock Lobster." The film presents the band as shallow, one-trick ponies of the New Wave that have pushed serious musicians like Jonah to the margins. Only "Rock Lobster" has more energy, humor, and simple rock 'n' roll joy in it than anything that Jonah's band performs, and so makes Simon's portrayal of Jonah as an artist ignored by his times seem more self-pitying than justified.

The film tanked at the box office; the soundtrack did well initially, due to the single's success, then sank into the lower reaches of the top 100. *One-Trick Pony* was Simon's first failure since *Wednesday Morn-ing, 3 A.M.*, ending a fifteen-year run of wild success. What made things worse is that failure came at a time of immense romantic turmoil: his relationship with the twenty-two-year-old Carrie Fisher, who had rock-eted to stardom as Princess Leia in *Star Wars*, was a tumultuous mess, filled with fights, infidelities, and her drug-taking. And Simon's attempt to ingratiate himself with Hollywood—he actually hosted the 1981 Grammy Awards, doing smarmy bits of comedy between the announce-ments of the award winners—seemed way out of character. To top it all off, he hurt his hand in an accident and for months couldn't pick up—

not to mention play—his guitar. The "mistakes" began piling up now, mistakes that would plummet him to the nadir of his career.

SIMON & GARFUNKEL: THE CONCERT IN CENTRAL PARK (1982), HEARTS AND BONES (1983)

"In 1980," Simon once said in an interview, "when *One-Trick Pony* came out to mixed reviews and the soundtrack album didn't do nearly as well as I'd hoped, it was a period of great depression for me. I was immobilized. And it was about that time that I came under the influence of a man named Rod Gorney, who's a teacher and a psychiatrist in Los Angeles."[3] Simon was right to point to the film's failure as one cause of his depression, but his new psychiatrist helped him see that the sources of his immobilization—by which he meant, among other things, that he had a terrible case of writer's block—went well beyond that. He was still hurt by the way he had been treated by the new CBS Records president Walter Yetnikoff. He was undergoing a fundamental crisis about his role as a songwriter and performer: "I felt that what I did was of absolutely no importance."[4] And then there was probably the greatest source of his unhappiness: his on-again, off-again relationship with Carrie Fisher. Fisher, very young, very talented, a bipolar movie star who drank heavily and was an indiscriminate drug-taker (including, reportedly, LSD, Ecstasy, and MDA, as well as the prescription painkiller Percodan, to which she was addicted), couldn't be faithful to Simon: she had an affair with *Saturday Night Live* and *Blues Brothers* star Dan Aykroyd while Simon was making *One-Trick Pony*.[5] She was wholly unlike any woman Simon had ever taken up with before: in her, the careful, measured, thoughtful Simon had met his wild opposite— Carl Jung would call it his shadow self—and it caused a maelstrom in Simon's psyche that, when combined with the movie's failure, paralyzed him.

In a number of intense sessions, Gorney was able to help Simon— that is, Gorney was able to help him overcome his writer's block, though his destructive relationship with Fisher was to continue for several frenzied years and would become a central focus of *Hearts and Bones*. Meantime, a call came from promoter Ron Delsener asking Simon if he and Garfunkel would consider getting back together to stage a huge free concert in New York's Central Park. The concert would be free to the audience, but lucrative arrangements were made with HBO to broadcast the show on its cable channel (and subsequently put it out on video) and with Warner Records to release a double-album of the show. Garfunkel was eager to participate. His career had nose-dived since the mid-1970s—his film *Bad Timing: A Sensual Obsession*, which was (curiously) released the same day as *One-Trick Pony*, had bombed, and the sales of his solo albums *Fate for Breakfast* and *Scissors Cut* were disappointing—and he was recovering from the shock of his wife, Laurie Bird, committing suicide in 1979. The Central Park concert promised to revive Simon and Garfunkel's careers as well as their spirits.

Despite the usual wrangling between the two men—Paul insisted on performing with a full band and orchestra, while Art wanted to perform as they always had done: just their voices, a guitar, and maybe a piano—the show, performed to Simon's specifications on September 19, 1981, was a huge success, drawing a crowd of a half-million fans. Of the nineteen songs on the album release, six were Simon solo compositions, one was a song from Garfunkel's latest solo release (a love song to Manhattan, "A Heart in New York"), and the remaining twelve were songs from the S & G repertoire. That Simon insisted that a third of the songs come from his solo career affirmed that the concert was, for Simon at least, not merely an exercise in nostalgia, but a statement about the continuity (and sustained quality) of his work through the years. It was a gamble but it paid off: the performances of "Slip Slidin' Away," "American Tune," and "Me and Julio" hold up beautifully next to the hand-in-glove reiterations of "Mrs. Robinson" or "April Come She Will," and the audience's reaction to the solo material was appreciative, if not up to their enthusiasm to the S & G material.

The HBO presentation of the show was a ratings hit; the album went double-platinum—a relief for two stars of the 1960s and 1970s whose careers needed a boost in the new decade. The show went so well, in fact, that the duo succumbed to the temptation to go on an extensive European and North American tour, and finally agreed to Warner's high-pressure suggestions that they reunite for a new studio album. Simon had a batch of very personal songs that he had been working on since his breakthrough with Gorney—songs like "Allergies," "Think Too Much," and "Hearts and Bones," which issued from meditations on his relationships with Fisher—and at first he managed to convince himself that the magic of the partnership could be rekindled, that the new material was amenable to the duo's vocal style and arrangements. He was dead wrong about this—he and Garfunkel fought for months, and during a break in recording Simon told Garfunkel he was off the project. Simon ended up making the album solo.

The album sold poorly on its release: it didn't even make the Billboard top 30, and Warner Bros. chalked it up as Simon's second studio failure in a row. Though *Hearts and Bones* contains, to me, some of the best songwriting of Simon's career till that point, divining reasons for its commercial failure isn't hard to do. The album came out in 1983, the same year that Michael Jackson, Madonna, and Prince emerged not just as superstars but as megastars: their burgeoning success coincided with the resurgence of the American economy after the deep recession of 1981–1982 as well as with the emergence of MTV, which rewrote the rules for pop stardom by making image, spectacle, and sexuality vastly more important than they'd ever been to a pop act. Needless to say, MTV was not kind to a cerebral 5'3" thirty-something who'd never projected sexuality in his whole career. The album does try to update its sound: there are lots of synthesizers on this record—sometimes oppressively so (as in "Cars Are Cars")—and Simon managed to induce Nile Rodgers, the leader of the disco band Chic and the production mastermind behind a number of huge 1980s hits (like David Bowie's *Let's Dance*, Madonna's *Like a Virgin*, and Duran Duran's "The Reflex") to play bass on a couple of cuts on the record, but Rodgers's magic didn't rub off. *Hearts and Bones'* sound is studio-fussy, its effects sounding massaged in a lab: the instrumentation tends toward the super-clean, the filtered, the synthetic. The album sounds like it's playing catch-up to 1980s production values—which of course it is—and as a result sounds forced, unnatural, a little desperate for acceptance by a 1980s audience that had lost interest in the more organic production sounds of the 1970s. Even the album cover—a pixilated still of a video shot of a wary Simon, clad in loose skinny tie and bright red and blue shirt (standard cool attire in the early 1980s), standing outside a neon-bright store of some kind—plays catch-up: it exudes the discomfort of a star who's trying to find a place for himself in a new pop landscape.

Thank goodness, then, for the songwriting, which is the most psychologically acute and penetrating, the most melodically inventive and beautiful, and the most emotionally expressive of his solo career to date. It features confident vocals that are conversational, open-hearted, nimble, able to express earnest vulnerability one moment and curl into sly irony or naïve humor the next. It's also the most thematically unified album Simon ever wrote. *Hearts and Bones* is, with few exceptions, about the inner struggle that comes from the confusions of love: it's about the war between the "left" and "right" brains—that is, between the rational/moralistic and emotional/intuitive sides of consciousness— and between the demands of the mind and those of the body. It's a striking portrait of a man who "thinks too much" (*Think Too Much* was the album's original title, which Warner Bros. nixed) coming to terms with emotional issues that mere "thinking" can't address, not to mention solve.

The album kicks off with "Allergies," a song whose irresistible rhythm section and razor-sharp guitar solo by Al DiMeola more than make up for the production gloss that otherwise mars the track. "Allergies" was the first song Simon wrote after seeing Dr. Gorney, and it lays out the fundamental problem the album will deal with. "Maladies / Melodies" are the first two lines, and it's if Simon were admitting how he's always dealt with problems ("maladies") before: by turning to music ("melodies"). He images the problems as "allergies" ("my heart is allergic to the women I love") but also asks himself, in a superb play on words, "Where do allergies go / When it's after the show / And they want to get something to eat?" Which is to say, after Simon writes or plays music, the allergies stick around, and in fact feast on the host, Simon himself: the melodies don't remedy the malady. "Doctor, please / Open up, it's me again," he pleads. Something in his life has to change.

The other song on the album that addresses the malady/melody issue is the side-1-ending "Song about the Moon," also written in the first months after Simon unblocked his songwriting paralysis. The warm, easy-tempered voice follows a memorable melody and delivers a lyric that accommodates a full range of tonalities—charmingly poetic intelligence, wistful nostalgia, deft irony, and by the end full-out elation (*"Then do it!* Write a song about the moon"). Simon's speaker is talking to himself here ("Hey Songwriter") and asks what he ought to do if he wants to write a song about the moon, a symbol that, of course, among other things, stands for woman and for the mystery of love. His advice? "Walk along the craters of the afternoon." That is, enter the life of your subject: feel the moon's specific gravity, experience its deep shadows and alien light. Do that, and "Presto / Song about the moon." The advice is at once light-hearted, poetically charged, and of course ironic: there's nothing "presto" about dwelling in love's shadows and alien light, and there's certainly nothing quick or easy about writing a song (especially if you're Paul Simon). But the song's advice is just beginning. To write a song about the moon—about love and about women—turns out to be so grand an undertaking that it encompasses "the heart," "the face," the whole "human race." Unlock the mystery of the moon in song, the speaker suggests, and you've uncovered the secret of all songs. To listen to "Song about the Moon" is to hear Simon overcoming his own writer's block, from the initial challenge to himself to write a love song to the final elation at his own success. It's one of the album's strongest songs, one of Simon's first to reference his own songwriting in a way that evades the self-conscious pretentions of his S & G years, and opens up a subject (songwriting) that will be a rich source of inspiration for him in the future.

The album's centerpiece is one of Simon's greatest songs about the moon, going deep into its dark craters filled with alien light. It is "Hearts and Bones," a plaintive, elegiac track driven by acoustic guitars (no synthesizers here) that traces "the arc of a love affair"—Simon's with Fisher—from its apex to its nadir. (Incidentally, in the song, the couple is married and then breaks up, which has been a source of confusion to listeners. Simon had not married Fisher when he recorded the song. He did not marry her until August 1983, long after the album had been delivered to Warner Brothers, and did not break up with her until mid-1984, months after the album's release.) The "one and one-half wandering Jews" are, of course, Simon and Fisher—Fisher is half-Jewish. The allusion to the figure of the wandering Jew is telling: the wandering Jew, in Christian mythology, is basically a doomed sinner, fated to travel endlessly, homelessly, until Christ's second coming. Simon doesn't press the allusion, but behind the song's narrative are characters who, unable to find love together, become spiritually homeless souls waiting on some kind of salvation. While traveling together, the speaker remembers, their love was once "like lightning / Shaking till it moans," but since then the relationship has disintegrated into "negotiations" (to use the term from "Train in the Distance") about what love means to each of them. For the (naïve) woman, it means unconditional acceptance ("Why don't you love me for who I am?") while he refuses to go along with this. "That's not how the world is, baby," he insists, which the music underlines by going quiet when the speaker says, and then repeats, "*This* is how I love you, baby." It's a rare moment in pop music when a song marks the end of a relationship not with tears or rage or acting out, but with a clear, mature, understated recognition that two people have no business being together: they aren't compatible. It is, to me, one of the high moments in Simon's music.

The incompatibility, in any case, creates a split that's as big as the Continental Divide (the song, not me, suggests the simile: Simon situates the first half of the song in New Mexico's Sangre de Cristo mountains), and soon enough, the lovers split up and "return to their natural coasts" (alluding to Simon's return to New York, Fisher's to California) where they "speculate who has been damaged the most" and wait and hope for their love to somehow be "restored." The song's mood is, throughout, clear-eyed, mournful, and filled with regret, and hints that the problem between the two lovers is pride, and that the solution might be self-sacrifice (after all, the song begins in the "Blood of Christ" mountains)—a theme that will become stronger and stronger in Simon's love songs from here on out.

The song that follows, "When Numbers Get Serious," is a misstep: though melodically pleasant enough, and the singing often humorous ("I will love you innumerably" is hilarious), the song sounds a little bloodless, due to the too-pristine use of the synclavier, and in any case is a tepid complaint about the extent to which the world's tendency to quantify everything pushes aside the emotional. The album's theme of the struggle between left and right brains, or head vs. heart, is too stark here, isn't in fact a struggle at all. The song's speaker simply longs for release from all the rational number-mongering into the heart's embrace ("the shelter of your arms") and ends with the predictable and clichéd desire for "two [to become] a one." In any case, the theme of numbers taking over our lives was much more effectively exploited by Depeche Mode's song of the same season, "Everything Counts in Large Amounts."

But "Think Too Much [b]" snaps us back to attention, beginning with lines that would have amused one of Simon's idols, the West Coast–averse Woody Allen:

> The smartest people in the world
> Had gathered in Los Angeles

To analyze our love affair

The synthesizer effects on the song—a baby's cry filtered through some kind of phaser—are uncharacteristically effective, and lead into the lyrics' main point, that the left brain (as least Simon's left brain) "dominates the right," to the detriment of his relationship with Fisher, and that he must allow the right brain to "labor through the long and speechless night" in order to balance the psyche. This is to say that the rational, "thinking" self must give way to emotive dream states in which the psyche's unconscious is free to express itself. What is interesting, however, is the precise dream the speaker enters when the rational side lets up on him: he dreams of his father coming to his side, holding him, and telling him that he should accept things as they are and to "go on and get some rest." This is a mirror image of the scene from "Slip Slidin' Away," in which the speaker goes to his son's side but is then *unable* to talk to him in any soothing, loving way. What the father in "Think Too Much" is counseling is "letting go" of rational control, of lovingly embracing the flow of life as it presents itself. The speaker ends with at least a temporary acceptance of this advice: "And I said yeah / Maybe I think too much."

The album's second side begins with "Think Too Much [a]," a cheerful reprise of the first side's song of the same name. The ultraclean production—and the synclavier—gives the track a sterile sound that's contrary to the lively spirit of the music and the lyrics—but if the listener can imagine a different, more organic sonic setting (perhaps one more dominated by Bernard Edwards's rubbery bass), the song is quite strong. Again, the theme is the need for the right brain's emotional, intuitive, dreamy side to assert itself against the left brain's rational, hyper-controlling side. The speaker recalls that his left brain's dominance goes back to early adolescence, when "in a state of [religious] disbelief," he and some Catholic school girls talked about God "up in the mezzanine." The sly implication is that maybe he ought to have been doing something else in the mezzanine with these schoolgirls, and that his tendency to "think too much" was hardly the expression of mature theological inclinations but a way to evade the danger of intense emotion and sexuality—that is, thinking as a defense against fear. In the third stanza, the speaker recalls moments when he "experienced a period of grace / When your brain takes a seat behind your face"—that is, when the brain took a back seat and allowed wonder in. In such a state, it's like "an Elephant Dance," time slowed to a crawl that allows for appreciation for all that's "funny" and "sunny." That is what the speaker's missing, he realizes, which suggests to him that he ought to approach his lover differently: "I ought to just hold her / Stop trying to mold her." It's the album's most credible moment of light-heartedness (and made more poignant by the fact that whatever efforts Simon may have made to follow his own song's advice failed with Fisher).

The last four songs of the album are, each in their own way, explorations of how nostalgic emotion might help balance the left and right brains. They attempt to grapple with the failures of the present by reaching back to a past that seemed to have held some promise of love or beauty that might have some instructive power now. "Train in the Distance" looks back on Simon's marriage to Peggy Harper—a fitting coda to *Still Crazy after All These Years*. Autobiographically accurate (Peggy *was* married when they met; their marriage did begin to fall apart after the birth of their son) but tempered by the passage of time, the song caresses its details with the soft glove of honeyed memory, suggesting that despite the failure of the marriage, Simon still "makes her laugh," and she occasionally "cooks a meal or two" for them, details that give their past together a golden glow. Yet the song is also a warning: the speaker keeps reiterating, "Everybody loves the sound of the train in the distance / Everybody thinks it's true," reminding himself that, just as the sound of a train in the distance calls up nostalgic yearnings, so do our memories of past (fragile) happiness. And nostalgia is by no mean a trustworthy way of discovering what's "true."

"René and Georgette Magritte with Their Dog after the War" is an almost perfect musical fantasy featuring the surrealist painter and his wife (and of course, their dog). Based on a real photograph that showed the couple and their pooch—a black and white picture that is reproduced on the lyric sheet—Simon doubtlessly was inspired by the rueful/comic possibilities of the photograph's official caption. The sound is airy, ethereal, featuring a realistically detailed but deliciously fanciful narrative, and showcasing woozily romantic orchestration by the legendary film composer George Delerue (who first achieved fame composing scores for French New Wave directors like Resnais, Truffaut, and Godard) as well as background vocals by the Harptones, who evoke the pre-rock vocal ensembles mentioned in the song—the Penguins, the Moonglows, and the Five Satins—in a way that sweetly and expertly calls up nostalgia for a time when Frenchmen (and Americans, too, of course) were filled with the fragile hopes for a return to normality in the period following World War II's end. The idea of a French surrealist painter and his wife dancing naked "by the light of the moon" to the sound of American songs that Simon himself revered is itself mildly surreal. And the detail about the dog gives the song a fine painterly touch: it's one of Simon's most successful compositions: so light it floats, but with exquisite grace.

"Cars Are Cars" is the album's most skip-able song, confounding in its lulling repetition of its opaque, tautological title, its clinical-sounding synthesizer chirps, and in the fact that in order to make the song at all comprehensible, Simon is forced to explain himself in the song's last verse. "If some of my cars / Were more like my home / I probably wouldn't have / Traveled this far." Three minutes of dull music for a platitude. Luckily, the album ends on a high note, the ambitious "The Late Great Johnny Ace," which brings together Simon's boyhood memories of the death (by accidental gunshot wound) of 1950s R&B star Johnny Ace with the recent shock (1980) of John Lennon's assassination, linking the 1950s star to the Beatles icon with an evocative passage about Simon's halcyon days in England in 1964: "We were staying up all night / And giving the days away." The last part of the song presents us with the narrative of the speaker hearing of Lennon's murder, going to a bar to drink, and concluding: "And every song we played / Was for the Late Great Johnny Ace." This time, of course, it's Lennon who's the Ace: the name deftly absorbs into itself the whole history of rock 'n' roll sadness and tragedy. But the song's surprises aren't over yet: Simon appends to the song's conclusion a one-minute coda, a short Philip Glass–written arrangement for violin, viola, cello, flute, and bass clarinet that functions as an austere, tender elegy for Lennon's death. The song as a whole, in fact, is one of the best songs about Lennon—far surpassing the slickly maudlin tribute of Elton John's "Empty Garden," the scatterbrained sentimentality of Paul McCartney's "Here Today," or Bob Dylan's surprisingly awkward late entry, "Roll on John."

Whatever the remarkable quality of most of the songwriting in *Hearts and Bones*, the album's production probably doomed it at the time to minor sales and half-hearted reviews. Throw in the failure of his second marriage—he and Fisher divorced in 1984—and it was clear that Simon had scraped a new bottom, both professionally and personally. But one of the salient features of Simon's career is his obstinent faith in himself: surely, that was what helped him weather the failure of a dozen singles and two albums between 1957 and 1965. As depressed as the failure of *One-Trick Pony* and *Hearts and Bones* made him, his resilience remained with him, and helped him endure until the fateful day in 1984 when a friend gave him a second-hand cassette tape with the words "Gumboots: Accordian Jive Hits, Volume II" scribbled on the side. It was a tape that would change the course of his career and lead to the greatest music he ever made.

5

DAYS OF MIRACLE AND WONDER

1984–1998

The story of Paul Simon's mid-1980s re-ascendance into pop's world empyrean, not to mention his renaissance as an artist, has become such a perfect piece of pop mythology that the idea that it all actually happened tends to get lost in the folklore. But all the plot points that make for good legend began to line up in 1984, when Simon actually *was* at the lowest point in his life, perplexed and saddened by his divorce from Carrie Fisher (his second divorce in nine years). He actually *was* in a deep trough professionally, having failed to connect to his audience with his last two studio albums, one a bafflingly dispirited soundtrack to his own tepid film, the other a set of mostly strong songs undone by poor production and Simon's wavering sense of who his audience even was anymore. Further, he was so disheartened and paralyzed by his divorce that, in 1984, he did almost no music-making, instead busying himself with supervising the building of a new house on Long Island: "I wasn't doing anything. I was sitting looking at the sea," he explained.[1] And it's true that the catalyst for his resurgence was something that happened more or less by chance (or if you believe such things, fate): while driving, he happened to play a cassette tape given to him by his friend Heidi Berg with the words "Gumboots: Accordion Jive Hits, Volume II" written on its label. The tape contained a South African music style called *mbaqanga* (or "township jive") and he quickly became obsessed with it. Within a few months he booked a trip to South

Africa, where he met and recorded with South African musicians, despite a United Nations–imposed cultural boycott on South Africa (much more on this shortly). And to top it all off, Simon used the rhythm tracks of these recordings as the basis for the album *Graceland*, a record that would bust the charts worldwide and become a global sensation—selling more than 14 million copies and placing the stubby, aging Simon (he was now forty-five and, well, still only 5'4") back in the pop music stratosphere alongside youthful, sexy megastars like Michael Jackson, Prince, Madonna, and Springsteen. It brought him a new audience that didn't know or particularly care that he'd been a 1960s superstar, and embodied an exciting musical hybrid that defined "world music" for white Western audiences. The album did all this while embroiling Simon in a messy political controversy from which he ultimately emerged with his artistic and political reputation unblemished. Sounds almost too good to be true, but for once in the life of this melancholy music master, true it was. These are his days of miracle and wonder.

If we ply the story away from its legendary moorings, of course, it gets more complex—also more interesting. It helps to remember that one of the things that freed Simon up to experiment with something as foreign to him as African music was precisely that his career was in the dumps. No one at Warner Brothers records was breathing down his neck about a new album, since his last two with the company had been money losers. The lack of pressure from his label—pressure Simon had been extremely sensitive to in the past—liberated him from the need to calibrate or strategize about a pop market that, by the mid-1980s, had grown so broad and diverse that Simon's share of it—the middle-class boomers who had survived the 1960s and were now, many of them, embracing Reaganite yuppiedom—was something he could no longer reliably connect to. Simon's embrace of South African music was a wild swing at the fences, but it was personally, artistically motivated; commercial calculation had nothing to do with it. African-influenced music by white Western musicians—the Talking Heads' *Remain In Light*, Brian Eno and David Byrne's *My Life in the Bush of Ghosts*, and Peter Gabriel's *III* and *Security*—were respectable sellers but hardly models for launching a comeback, and the world-beat music of African musicians like Sunny Adé and Fela Kuti served only a boutique American market. No, *Graceland* was music—and the album makes this clear from its opening moments to its close—that came from love: love for "the roots of rhythm" (as he puts it on "Under African Skies") that unite and cross-pollinate American pop music with African, and for the sheer joy of creative experimentation: uniting rhythm, melody, harmony, and language from various traditions into new and exhilarating combinations.

Another major complicating factor in this story, of course, is Simon's working with South African musicians *in* South Africa, a skirting of the cultural ban imposed by both the United Nations Anti-Apartheid Committee and the African National Congress in 1980. When Simon traveled to Johannesburg in February of 1985 (along with his producer Roy Halee) to play with some of South Africa's best and most famous black musicians, South African blacks had been subject to the degrading conditions of apartheid for nearly forty years: apartheid (Africaaner for "apart-hood," or the state of living apart) had been the law of the land since 1948. Millions of blacks had been relocated from their homes into all-black zones whose public services—schools, hospitals, roads, all forms of infrastructure—were vastly inferior to those in white areas. All blacks were stripped of citizenship and therefore of equal rights, not to mention equal education or economic opportunity. Intermarriage was outlawed; even sexual congress outside of marriage between those of different races was prohibited. Black opposition groups hoping to improve their lot were violently put down, their ranks routinely brutalized and often murdered, and their leaders imprisoned—including, of course, Nelson Mandela, who at the time of Simon's arrival had been in jail for twenty-three years. By the 1980s, some Western democracies (though not the Reagan administration in the United States) and some international corporations had begun to impose sanctions or trade bans on the South African government as a means of pressuring them to abandon apartheid—the UN cultural boycott was only one of many means of pressure that were being applied. The sanctions and boycotts were having some effect—South Africa was feeling increasingly isolated and deprived economically and culturally, and many white South Africans were beginning to acknowledge that the days of apartheid were numbered. Still, prime minister P. M. Botha's government rigidly resisted change.

The UN and African National Congress (ANC) boycotts asked that foreign musicians not *perform* in South Africa, an ambiguity that made it unclear whether the ban prohibited foreign musicians from playing in

South Africa at all (that is, playing and recording in a South African studio, for instance) or whether the ban referred only to *playing in public for money*. A major target of the boycott, after all, was Sun City, a huge and rather garish vacation resort complex in Bophuthatswana that was frequented by South Africans and foreign tourists, and was used by the South African regime to advertise itself deceptively as an integrated society (since some blacks also attended performances). A slew of pop acts, including Tina Turner, Elton John, and Linda Ronstadt, were lured to play Sun City with promises of outlandish paydays (sometimes a million dollars for a single appearance), and many musicians succumbed to the temptation. Simon had previously been offered the chance to play Sun City twice but had turned it down—being a long-time liberal, he was fully aware of, and supported, the boycott. Before he flew to South Africa, in fact, he took counsel from *uber*producer Quincy Jones, who served as a kind of paterfamilias to black musicians in America, as well as Harry Belafonte, the singer and activist with many ties to South African black musicians. Both men listened to his plan to merely *play and record with black musicians, but not to perform publically with them*—or to profit from them. (In fact, Simon ended up paying his South African session players three times the going American Musician's Union rates, paid them performing royalties when *Graceland* came out, and shared songwriting credit—and therefore royalties—on five of the eleven songs on the album.) Both Jones and Belafonte gave their blessings, though Belafonte strongly suggested that Simon contact the African National Congress and obtain their OK before he went. Simon chose not to contact the ANC—he didn't believe an artist had an obligation to get any political body's approval to make music—a decision that, while highly principled, was maybe a tactical mistake. Had he consulted the ANC, they may have not only restrained themselves from the shower of brutal criticism that followed but also advised him how not to allow his presence in South Africa to be used by the government propaganda machine. Much of the controversy might have been avoided.

In any case, he arrived with Roy Halee in February of 1985, and quickly booked studio time at Ovation Studios in Johannesburg with some of South Africa's most prominent black musicians, including Tao Ea Matsekha, General M. D. Shirinda and the Gaza Sisters, the Boyoyo Boys Band, and Roy Phiri's band Stimela. For seventeen days, Simon and his cohorts jammed, eventually laying down rhythm tracks for six of the album's eleven songs. Returning to New York, Simon began writing material around and on top of these rhythm tracks: he and Halee painstakingly stitched together the South African recordings with music that Simon and New York session musicians came up with. To complete the album, he went down to New Orleans to record "That Was Your Mother" with a group of crack zydeco musicians. He invited the South African *a cappella* group Ladysmith Black Mambazo to record two songs, one in New York City and the other in London; finally, he flew to Los Angeles to record "All Around the World, or the Myth of Fingerprints" with the Mexican American rock band Los Lobos, and "Under African Skies" with band Stimela and Linda Ronstadt. The result was a tantalizing gumbo of world music that mingled several traditions into a rhythmically stirring, aurally lustrous, melodically tuneful, and lyrically arresting album.

(During this period, Simon also found the time to write a set of lyrics for Philip Glass's album *Song for Liquid Days*, his avant-gardist collaboration with pop musicians. Simon's contribution turned into the opening track, "Changing Opinion," a strange little meditation about a man who gets obsessed with a "hum in the room"; it feels like a cross between Francis Coppola's film *The Conversation* and Don DeLillo's *White Noise*, a song touching on the odd sensitivities and paranoias of modern consciousness. It's a strong if idiosyncratic lyric, but the melody Glass came up with to carry it is weak, and makes a listener wonder, given Simon's superb melodic gift, what he could have come up with if he had written the entire song himself.)

When *Graceland* came out in 1986, both the United Nations and the African National Congress placed Simon on their blacklist of musicians who had defied their boycotts, and the controversy surrounding its making coincided with American culture's 1980s preoccupation with multiculturalism and political correctness. Was Simon just "appropriating" African music for his own gain in the same way that white musicians had been borrowing/stealing from African American blues and R&B since the beginnings of rock 'n' roll? Had Simon, by recording in South Africa, defied the letter or the spirit of the cultural boycott imposed by the UN and the ANC, in the process hurting the anti-apartheid cause, or had he in fact, through his music, helped spread awareness not only of the beauty of black South African culture but also of the dire political and economic plight of South African blacks? Such questions swirled around the world tour that followed in the wake of the album's massive success, with protestors coming to venues where Simon and his players performed and calling him an apartheid sympathizer, a dupe of the South African government, and much worse. Simon held a number of press conferences trying to stem the tide of criticism and clarify his position. Of course he opposed apartheid, he insisted: that was so obvious that to tell his audience such a thing would sound like preaching. No, he didn't believe he had defied the cultural boycott; he believed that the music they were making was not only unifying people but also calling attention to the injustice in South Africa; in fact, hefty proceeds from the tour went to a charity called Children of Apartheid (as well as other charities).[2] Though the American leg of the tour was attended mostly by white audiences, the international segments of the tour were true transcultural celebrations, with most reviewers noting the extraordinary spectacle of huge mixed-race audiences joyfully grooving to music that until then had been the province of either African audiences alone or a tiny group of Western fans. By the end of the tour, the UN, convinced that Simon's efforts in the main contributed to racial comity, took him off their blacklist; the ANC, less forgiving, waited until 1992.

Though Simon in general was never entirely comfortable playing live, the Graceland tour invigorated him so much that when it was over, he soon set about contacting Brazilian and West African musicians about laying down tracks for a new album. *The Rhythm of the Saints*, a kind of South American sequel to *Graceland*, was recorded in a similar fashion, with Simon and Halee going to Rio de Janeiro and recording basic rhythm tracks with local musicians, then returning to New York to forge the tracks into fully developed songs with a mixture of South American and American session players. The result was not as buoyant, melodically lush, or as immediately accessible as *Graceland*, but if the reviews weren't quite as ecstatic, they were highly respectful, sales were more than honorable (it reached #4, eventually selling 2 million copies in the United States), and, in songs like "The Obvious Child," "Born at the Right Time," and "Further to Fly," contributed some classic music to the Simon canon.

His days of miracle and wonder continued when Simon, performing on an episode of "Saturday Night Live" in 1990, met Edie Brickell, the lead singer and songwriter for the band Edie Brickell and the New Bohemians, who were enjoying a hit with "What I Know" at the time. The two fell in love and eventually married in May of 1992. (It's Simon's only marriage to stand the test of time: they've been together for over two decades, and have three children.) Yet the frenetic pace with which Simon had been living, recording, and performing since February 1985 hardly fell off after Simon concluded the Born at the Right Time tour in 1992—a tour that included another Concert in the Park, this one Garfunkel-less, featuring a solo Simon backed by African and South American musicians performed before 750,000 fans. (The concert was later released as a double CD.) In 1993, a two-CD best-of boxed-set package, *Songwriter: 1964-1993*, was released, and Simon toured in support of it, eventually bringing on his old partner and transitioning the tour into a full-fledged Simon and Garfunkel tour. And then there was his brash decision to write and stage a Broadway musical.

The idea for the musical actually came to him back in 1988, when Simon became fascinated with the story of Salvador Agron, a young Puerto Rican immigrant who joined a gang in Brooklyn back in the late 1950s and who, along with a fellow gang member, killed two white boys during a rumble. The story was a sensation in the New York media at the time—Agron was dubbed the Capeman because he was wearing a cape at the time of the murders—and Simon vividly recalled following the story in the papers and TV at the time. After his conviction for the murders, Agron's death sentence—at sixteen, he was one of the youngest persons ever to be condemned to death—was commuted to life imprisonment: Eleanor Roosevelt, the former First Lady, pleaded on his behalf, arguing that Agron's violent and impoverished upbringing made it impossible for him to develop a moral compass. Agron spent nearly twenty years in prison, and apparently rehabilitated himself: grossly unrepentant at the time of his crimes, he eventually became a born-again Christian and even obtained a bachelor's degree (in sociology and philosophy, no less) from the State University of New York. When he was released in 1979, he worked with gangs and spoke out against gang violence for several years before succumbing to pneumonia and dying in 1986. Simon saw Agron's odyssey as a morally fraught and very American story about immigration, gang culture, racism, crime, and redemption that, on stage, would complicate and enrich

Broadway's usual ideological simplicities. And the musical possibilities, he figured, were endlessly intriguing: there was first of all the doo-wop music popular in New York in 1959, which Simon knew so well from his own 1950s recordings. And there was the Latin American music that had fascinated him since "El Condor Pasa" in the 1960s and that he had returned to while making *The Rhythm of the Saints*.

Only the ensuing musical turned out to be one of Broadway's biggest disasters. Though Simon was a complete novice to the Broadway musical form, at first he insisted on complete artistic control, setting himself up for the kind of failure that dogged him when he tried to handle all the reins to his film flop, *One-Trick Pony*. Though he enlisted his friend Derek Wolcott, the Nobel Prize–winning poet from the island of Saint Lucia in the West Indies, to help lend authenticity to the lyrics and to the story (or "book") of a Puerto Rican boy immigrating to America, Simon resisted the advice of longtime Broadway professionals and made any number of egregious mistakes that seriously raised production costs (including the hiring and firing of three different directors) and delayed the opening of the play. It didn't help that Simon was rather condescending to the Broadway musical scene: "[Simon] made no secret of his general disdain for the Broadway musical form," the *New York Times* wrote as the play was about to close. This songwriter with absolutely no prior experience working on the stage "said he also hoped his work would reinvigorate and even reinvent the form, bringing a more contemporary and sophisticated pop sensibility to Broadway."[3] When the play finally opened in January 1998, it was eviscerated by the critics, closed after a paltry sixty-eight performances, and reportedly lost $11 million, much of it Simon's own money. His days of miracle and wonder were over.

GRACELAND (1986)

What stunned long-time fans and first-time listeners when *Graceland* initially came out wasn't just the instrumentation—the chugging accordions (played in South African, Latin, and zydeco styles), basslines slithering like underwater snakes, drums that boomed louder than the simulated cannon from "The Boxer," guitar parts so glittery they were the aural equivalent of diamonds on the soles of your shoes, the hilariously loopy pennywhistle solo on "You Can Call Me Al," the saxophone parts that sounded like the bursting of a laugh. It wasn't just the raucous background vocals of "I Know What I Know" or the polyrhythmic clatter of African and Latino percussion so precise and inventive that it seemed to embed itself in the part of the brain that demanded, "DANCE!" And it wasn't merely the overall ebullience of the sound, a sound that found a way to transform—one's tempted, for once, to use the critically abused word *transcend*—the melancholy of Paul Simon's voice and worldview into exuberant musical celebration. It was finally the lyrics that were a breakthrough—song lyrics that, far from the tightly wrought narrative or thematic structures that he was known for, emerged from a freewheeling, associative, and almost subconscious songwriting process where he was less interested in "planting" ideas that he had previously come up with than in discovering ideas *while* he was writing. In a 1990 interview, he said, "I'm interested in what . . . I *find*, as opposed . . . to what I'm planting. I like to be the audience too. I like to *discover* what it is that's interesting to me. I like to discover it rather than plot it out."[4] The new lyrics emerged as confidently poetic, sweet and wittily tailored to Simon's voice, their frankly New York–centric urbanity so strikingly incongruous with the "roots" music that inspired it that it made a new kind of sense: "world music" as a true overlaying of American lyrical concerns over African instrumentation. And those lyrics were all delivered in an offhand conversational style that wrung all manner of ironies, ambiguities, and tenderness out of the words. All these things together set the seal to the album's bold originality.

The album's opener, "The Boy in the Bubble" is to my mind one of Simon's five greatest achievements as a songwriter. Beginning with a sweet, even timid accordion riff that soon gets augmented by big, echoing drums, a bumpy groove of a bass line, and later by synthesized guitar and keyboards, it immediately announces itself (and the album as a whole) as a cross-cultural hybrid: indigenous South African rhythms mingled with first-world high-tech synthesizers, and lyrics that take stabs at defining nothing less than the postmodern zeitgeist. If "American Tune" were a state of the union address, "The Boy in the Bubble" would target the state of the planet, befitting a new world connected by a wired mass media culture and transformed by high technology and multinational economic arrangements of the greatest intricacy. It's hard to think of a song by any pop artist that has its audacious reach, formal fascination, or insight into, frankly, the mysterious, uncanny way it felt to be alive in the mid-1980s: "The way the camera follows us in slo-mo," indeed.

The lyrics don't develop linearly, and tell no coherent story, but that very fact speaks not only to Simon's new method of writing but to his formal awareness of the chaotic conditions of the planet he was attempting to capture in song. Veering from a description of a terrorist bombing in the opening stanza to vague, disconnected allusions to "a loose affiliation of millionaires and billionaires," to musicians zooming up the pop charts, the song is drawn together, nonetheless, by the evocative, polysemic refrain "these are the days of miracle and wonder." *Miracle* and *wonder*, to most ears, connote good things, but Simon uses the words to suggest something more multivalently awe-inspiring. True, cross-species heart transplants ("the baby with the baboon heart") and medical procedures that put a "boy in a bubble"—inside a completely antiseptic environment to protect him from deadly toxins or allergens— are indeed wondrous "miracles" ("medical is magical") that stun us even as we immediately draw them into the realm of the normal and the expected. But so are "lasers in the jungle" that bring high-tech killing machines into third-world environments, or the growing ubiquity of "cameras that follow us in slo-mo." Those cameras not only were violating our sense of privacy but also creating an entire simulacral realm of second-order reality that—as postmodern theorists like Jean Baudrillard and Fredric Jameson, or novelists like Don DeLillo (in *White Noise*) were suggesting in the mid-1980s—we were, more and more, confusing with material reality. Life, as it was beginning to be revealed through mass media to the wired-in observer in the 1980s, was wondrous in a way that mixed the sublime and the dislocative: "staccato signals of constant information" flooding us with so much data—banal, mysterious, and awesome—that we can't help but feel frightened by its capacity to make one feel both powerful and powerless at the same time.

But maybe the song's keenest lines are these: "The way we look to a distant constellation / As it's dying in the corner of the sky." There are a number of ways to read this couplet, among them these two: (1) these are days of miracle and wonder because we can look *at* a constellation thousands of light years away knowing that it's dying (because we're equipped with miraculous astronomical equipment that tells us that), thus giving us a sublime sense of the gigantic dimensions of the universe and our tiny place in it; and (2) these are days of miracle and wonder because our scientific prowess has given us the power to imagine the vast dimensions of the universe, and thus to imagine how a distant constellation—perhaps beings on a planet somewhere in that constellation—might look *at us*, how amazing, disturbing, and literally incredible this planet and its human inhabitants must look to truly alien eyes. "The Boy in the Bubble" has a bigger vision than any song Simon wrote up to this time, and points toward the overt concerns with spiritual vastness, empty space, eternity, mortality, and immortality that will animate so much of his late work.

Just as we are catching our breath at the visionary fascinations of "Bubble," Simon slides demurely into "Graceland," a song every bit as strong as the album opener, but in so different a way—listen to Demola Adepoju's tender pedal steel guitar and Ray Phiri's filigreed electric guitar, as well as to Simon's open-hearted vocal—that the album's vision begins to deepen beyond the cool, objective universal panorama of "The Boy in the Bubble." Using the same rhythm section from "Bubble" but adding Adepoju and Phiri to the mix, Simon and his band create a mood that's simultaneously danceable and meditative, weary and hopeful, befuddled and joyful, broad-canvas spiritual and small-scale autobiographical. The song is about a man who drives to Elvis Presley's Graceland mansion with his son after a grueling breakup with a woman, and Simon has confirmed its autobiographical roots. After a recording session in New Orleans, Simon and his son drove back to New York City, taking a route that first led them along the Mississippi river (which, in a knockout simile, was "shining like a National guitar") and then east "through the cradle of the civil war" to Memphis, Tennessee, home of the Presley mansion. In the song, the speaker recalls the romantic breakup (that would be with Fisher, of course) as he's driving, and the stanza that begins "She comes back to tell me she's gone" is one of Simon's finest moments on record. That the woman has ironically "come back" to tell him she's leaving him leads to an irritable, slightly comic aside—"as if I didn't know that"—but then he recalls the emptiness of his bed and "the way she brushed her hair from her forehead," and the irritation gives way to an acute sense of loneliness and loss. But even better is the way he describes love's disappearance:

> Losing love
> Is like a window in your heart
> Everybody sees you're blown apart
> Everybody sees the wind blow

The image of lovers with hearts like shattered windows, the wind whistling through broken glass for all to see, is classically and simply poetic, immediately graspable but somehow mysterious at the same time, and it's worthy of Lorca or Garcia Marquez. No wonder, then, that the speaker wants to go to Graceland, whose symbolic name is equally grand and simple: he wants to find a land of grace; he wants the same shot of redemption that the character in "You Can Call Me Al" wants, whereby he can end the "falling, flying, or tumbling in turmoil" and the ghostly memories that he's experienced ever since his breakup. That the song ends on an optimistic note—that the speaker at song's conclusion says "I've a reason to believe / We all will be received / In Graceland"—carries an almost ecstatic charge. Simon, hardly known for large-scale affirmations in a career of mostly bleak lyrical observations, has managed—through the warm bedrock of the music, his compassionate vocal, the splendid imagery—to convincingly evoke radiance, and the light from the song spreads generously over the rest of the album.

"I Know What I Know" follows, a song whose music, originally recorded by General M. D. Shirinda and the Gaza Sisters on their own album, was re-recorded by the band, now with Simon's musical and lyrical contributions. Featuring the loudest, splashiest drums Simon had to that point ever committed to record, two lead guitars playing deliciously over one another, and background vocals that, slightly abrasive and discordant, take a Westerner's ears a little getting used to, the music is uncompromisingly South African, unlike the album's two openers, whose rhythms easily blend into the rhythms of Johnny Cash–like country ("Bubble") or American melodic pop ("Graceland"). What is most striking about the song, however, are the satirically urbane lyrics, which jar so strangely with the indigenous South African music that it takes a few listenings before the originality of the conception comes through. The lyrics detail a man at what appears to be a glittery party (in New York or L.A.) filled with people of shallow sophistication—the man asks a woman if she was recently awarded a Fulbright; the woman asks him if she knows him from "the cinematographer's party"—who are afraid to "blow against the wind" of cultural fashion. The song's speaker, though, recognizes the shallowness for what it is, and grounds himself in the awareness that, as he tells himself, "we come and we go"—that is, we are born and we die—"That's a thing that I keep / In the back of my head." The music and lyrics of "Gumboots" are similarly incongruous, if not as successful: the music, performed by the Boyoyo boys and other musicians, is a boisterous mélange of danceable rhythms, fleet accordion riffs, and an explosion of a sax solo, while the lyrics—nimbly uttered by Simon in his best charmingly ironic mode—give us a light-hearted but inconclusive little tale about a New Yorker in a cab "rearranging my position" about a friend who has suffered a breakdown.

Side 1 of the album—the CD revolution that would make the concept of "sides" obsolete was only then gathering steam—concludes with the astonishing "Diamonds on the Soles of Her Shoes," a cooperative venture featuring Ray Phiri's group Stimela, and co-written by Joseph Shambalala of Ladysmith Black Mambazo, a South African *a cappella* group whose performance on the record lends the album its most original moments. The song, first performed for a "Saturday Night Live" audience months before the album's release, created a welter of Monday morning water-cooler talk that gave the upcoming album great advance publicity, and rightly so. The lyrics are nothing to write home (or a critical analysis) about: it's a frothy rich-girl-poor-boy tale whose only real distinctiveness comes when Simon sings, "And I could say Oo oo oo / And everybody here would know / What I was talking about," because it's frankly true: while the lyrics don't spell out what he's talking about, the music is so buoyant and happy-making that we give our assent anyway: sure, we say, I know what you're talking about; you're talking about joy. Ladysmith Black Mambazo's background vocals—grainy baritones sung in the *isicathamiya* style and uttered in their native Zulu—sound ancient and contemporary at the same time, afflicted with a history of suffering but infectiously in love with redemptive music-making. Combine that with Simon's fluid, jaunty melody and a vocal delivery so innocently un-ironized that it all sounds like a fairy tale, and the song becomes another Simon classic.

The album's quality hardly declines on side 2, which starts off with the album's sole hit single, "You Can Call Me Al," which reached #23 on the American charts. (It was released twice: the first release failed to garner radio airplay, but after the album took off on its own, it was re-released, the second time with a droll video featuring the then-hot Chevy Chase. It's a measure of the album's terrific word-of-mouth and overall consistency that it was able to sell so humongously without the benefit of multiple hit singles.) The song's initially propelled by a simple eight-note synthesizer riff that, as the music builds, gets enhanced by a delirious bass line (including a short, slaphappy solo in the song's mid-dle) and then a raucous horn section that doubles the keyboard riff and powers the song into overdrive. Our protagonist here is a comically confused, middle-aged, overweight sad-sack in crisis (much like Fat Charlie the Archangel in "Crazy Love, Vol. II," or if you forget about the weight problem and take the character seriously, the speaker of "Graceland"). He complains of how hard his life is, more or less equates "redemption" with getting himself "a photo opportunity," and fanta-sizes, like some reverse Walter Mitty, about entering some cartoon graveyard, digging for bones, and being chased by hounds. What he needs, he realizes, is a partner, and bargains with some off-screen wom-an to be her "long lost pal" if she'll agree to be his "bodyguard." (The names "Betty" and "Al" come from an inside joke between Simon and his first wife, who once attended a party of the famous composer Pierre Boulez, who kept referring to Paul as "Al" and Peg as "Betty" during the event.) In the second verse, the man, still lonesome and bodyguard-less, finds himself in a strange city, without wife and family, or role model either (the role model's "ducked down some alleyway / With some roly-poly little bat-faced girl"[!]) and evidently mixed up in some obscure mess that makes him need a bodyguard even more. Of course, the music is so spirited and fun that we know that this will have a happy ending, which we get in the third verse, in which the man now finds himself in the Third World, a foreigner unable to understand the lan-guage, but finally able to take in the extraordinary array of life around him—not just the orphanages and "cattle in the marketplace" but also the "angels in the architecture / Spinning in infinity" until he has his own epiphany and seems released of his confusion. Simon has said the third verse is really about his own experience arriving in Johannesburg to record in February 1985, but the "man" of verse 3 seamlessly blends with the sad-sack in the first two, and the "Hallelujah!" at the end is the joyful expression not just of a character who's emerged from a midlife crisis but also of a singer, Simon himself, who's found his way out of his own—by rediscovering the source of the things that have driven him since he was a boy, the "roots of rhythm": music itself.

Which, it turns out, is the theme of the song that follows, "Under African Skies." Expertly sung by Simon and Linda Ronstadt in gorgeous duet—the timing and harmonizing of the syllable-heavy lines "Give her the wings to fly through harmony / And she won't bother you no more" can't have been easy to capture—the song is overlaid with winsome guitars by Ray Phiri, American avant-pop instrumentalist Adrian Belew, and Simon. The lyrics compare the African musical roots of one "Joseph" (Shabalala, presumably, of Ladysmith Black Mambazo) with those of Ronstadt, who grew up in Tucson, Arizona, and make the point that wherever one grows up, the "roots of rhythm" are the same: music is the universal language. But there's an additional and more interesting observation hidden in the refrain, which seems to be about neither Shabalala nor Ronstadt but about Simon himself, who "After the dream of falling and calling your name out"—another allusion, it seems, to his divorce from Fisher—has rediscovered "the roots of rhythm," that is, music's fundamental power. That's why the song "is the story of how we begin to remember": it's a record of Simon's own rehabilitation while making *Graceland*, his own rediscovery of what causes "the powerful pulse of love in the vein"—not romantic love, but the love of music.

"Homeless" takes the album's biggest risk—it's a song co-written by Simon and Shabalala, in both the English and Zulu tongues, and sung entirely *a cappella* by Simon and Ladysmith Black Mambazo. Simon began with the lines "Homeless, homeless / Moonlight sleeping on midnight lake" and had Shabalala and his band play with it. Shabalala translated and arranged these languid apolitical lyrics for his singers, but then added a few of his own, sung both in English and Zulu:

> Strong wind destroy our home
> Many dead, tonight it could be you

After the song's appearance, some black South Africans artists, including Hugh Masekela and Miriam Makeba (the exiled couple who were perhaps black South Africa's most respected musicians at the time and who toured with Simon on the *Graceland* trek) "spoke emphatically as the song of their own anthem," with the image of a great wind destroying "our home" aptly summing up the disastrous effects of apartheid in their homeland.[5] In the yearning sad weight of its choral voices

("somebody cry why why why?") with the group's distinctive vocal effects, and with the overtly political lyrics, "Homeless" is the album's
outlier, though it has the effect of anchoring the album in the conditions of apartheid, and bringing to the surface what most of the rest of
the album allows to simmer subliminally.

"Crazy Love, Vol. II," the album's final song created with African
musicians, is more vintage Simon. With Ray Phiri's sparkling guitar
swirling all over the track and Simon's vulnerable-bemused voice telling
us the tale of Fat Charlie the Archangel (listen for Simon's masterfully
comic take on the pseudo-melancholy line, "Sad as a lonely little *wrink-*
led balloon"), who has found himself numbed to the core by a failure
over a love affair and is now seeking a divorce. The song eludes the
snares of sentimentality by virtue of Simon's ironic rendering of the
vocal, and frankly by the generous offering of the refrain's melody,
which is big and simple and extraordinarily satisfying. The line "I don't
want no part of your crazy love," repeated (with slight variations) twenty
times in the song, is plausibly readable as a knock at Fisher, but even if
it isn't, it's wonderfully cathartic anyway, providing the kind of release
that rock music was born to provide.

The album's closing numbers—"That Was Your Mother," recorded
in Crowley, Louisiana, with Good Rockin' Dopsie and the Twisters, and
"All Around the World, or the Myth of Fingerprints," recorded in Los
Angeles with rockers Los Lobos—round out *Graceland*'s world music
tour, adding Caribbean-flavored zydeco and Los Lobos's hybridic mixture of 1950s rock 'n' roll with traditional Mexican music to the table.
"That Was Your Mother" is a good-natured, energetic workout of zyde-
co-influenced rock 'n' roll, with a toss-off lyric about a man telling his
son about the roots of his parents' relationship—dad falling in love with
a girl "pretty as a prayerbook" and understanding that "if that's my
prayerbook/ Lord let us pray!" It's minor Simon, but it keeps the good
vibes of the album going. The closer with Los Lobos is better, with Los
Lobos's rhythm section riding a deep R&B groove and lyrics suggesting
that the "myth of fingerprints"—the idea that all fingerprints are absolutely unique, and by extension, that all humans are as well—is just that,
a myth, and that "I've seen them and man / They're all the same."
Simon himself has tried to make the case that this is another angle on
the album's themes of universalism,[6] but the lyric ends obscurely, with
the myth of fingerprints being the reason "we all must live alone." This

is one place where Simon's new devotion to the virtues of nuanced ambiguity does him no favors. In any case, the song is better known as the locus of a battle between Simon and Los Lobos, some members of which accused Simon of stealing their music and never giving them song credit.[7]

It does no injustice to Simon's career to say that *Graceland* is his Kilimanjaro—there are plenty of surrounding peaks (*Bridge Over Troubled Water, Paul Simon, Rhythm of the Saints, Surprise, So Beautiful or So What*) to ensure it doesn't utterly dominate the landscape. That it's his greatest album is Simon's own judgment on the matter as well—he asserts as much in "Under African Skies," the documentary that's included on the twenty-fifth anniversary edition of the *Graceland* CD release. Besides the usual virtues of his solo work—the lyrical penetration, the melodic invention, the meticulous production values, the voice mixing melancholy and irony in exquisite fashion—*Graceland* adds, finally and simply, the elation of music-making: going to Africa helped him rediscover his love of music after years of personal and career struggle, and that love instilled in him a creative urgency that continued with *The Rhythm of the Saints.*

THE RHYTHM OF THE SAINTS (1990)

The most common reaction to *The Rhythm of the Saints*—a current that ran through almost all the contemporary reviews, and has more or less become received opinion since—is that "it suffers by comparison" to *Graceland.*[8] And that's true, as far as it goes, though it suffers mostly by virtue of its intense seriousness and relative lack of pop sense. By 1990, four years after *Graceland* erupted onto charts worldwide, opening the floodgates not just to a re-appreciation of Paul Simon's music but to a deluge of African and African-based world-beat releases in the United States, the American public was eager for another of Simon's globe-trotting musical excursions. Prepared for a new bout of cross-cultural exuberance—the ebullient *frisson* that would doubtless ensue when Simon combined his syncretic talents with the lavish sensuality of Brazilian and West African music-makers—listeners to *The Rhythm of the Saints* were met by something quite unexpected: musical elation reined tightly in by a somberness and a difficult, elliptical philosophic/

religious reflection that tamps down the music's joy even as it soberly explores the territory that *Graceland* announced as Simon's own: the desire for redemption, a search for meaning that looks beyond the worldly to something unabashedly spiritual—the transcendent. This album doubles down on *Graceland*'s ginger embrace of spiritual possibility ("I believe we all will be received in Graceland"); the "spirit voices" are calling in *The Rhythm of the Saints*, and Simon is, sometimes desperately, longing to hear them. Yet the album merely perches on the edge of a spiritual precipice: Simon takes seriously the leap into faith that's adumbrated in *Graceland*, but he's not at all sure that he can, or ought to, jump. (He'll stand on that edge, weaving and wavering, the rest of his career.)

Perhaps because it's carrying such heavy baggage, *Rhythm of the Saints* lacks *Graceland*'s sweet humor, its light-footed ironies, the friendly way it insinuates itself into a listener's consciousness. *Rhythm*'s rhythms, in a way, say it all: they are harsher, at times grating: the percussion, complex and fascinating as it is, often feels less a celebration of life than an agitated background to anxious soul-searching. And while the album is filled with some of the most melodically beautiful moments in Simon's canon—"the open palm of desire" lines in "Further to Fly"; the gentle sway of the chorus of "Born at the Right Time"; the penultimate verse of "The Cool, Cool River"—Simon often buries them in the third or fourth minute of a song carried not by melody but by sharply percussive rhythms. Of the original release's ten songs, only three—"The Obvious Child," "Born at the Right Time," and "Spirit Voices"—burst out of their forehead-creased speculations into anything like *Graceland*'s hope or celebration, and even in those three songs the hope is tenuous or ambiguous. The rest of them frankly and unapologetically *brood*: on the Chernobyl nuclear disaster ("Can't Run But"); on a "speeding planet" that "burns" and whose hungry millions and ecologically "injured" shorelines are neglected by those addicted to profit by any means ("The Cool, Cool River," "The Coast"); on a Western culture whose reliance on science and technological know-how bury the fragile intimations of faith-based knowledge ("Proof"); and on a ubiquitous "anger" in the world that "moves like a fist through traffic" to cause all manner of political and social pain ("The Cool, Cool River").

Not for any of this must we mourn nor murmur, though: the album's relative dearth of simple pop pleasures is made up for by its grown-up, if frequently obscure, meditations, starting with its opener, "The Obvious Child." The backbone of the song—and really of the album in general—is supplied by the drums, here played by Brazilian legends Grupo Cultural Olodum, who in "The Obvious Child" provide a West African– and Caribbean-inflected Brazilian rhythm called *samba reggae*, which combines those two musical forms with a few others indigenous to South America, like merengue and salsa. The drums come on unaccompanied for sixteen seconds of intense pounding before the song proper kicks in. Simon's vocal starts off no-nonsense: it's the voice of a middle-aged man who's been around and clearly doesn't "expect to be treated like a fool no more." The speaker's trying to get to the heart of matters, and certain things are becoming "obvious" to him: lies aren't always simply lies, for instance—he has learned to account for nuance, the subtle contingencies of circumstance. And then, more boldly, there's this: "the sky" is *not* "just the sky"; the sky seems to promise a realm of the *beyond* that he can't name but which he nonetheless feels sure exists (he's so sure, in fact, that he claims it's "obvious"). The closest he comes to characterizing this realm is to note that the "cross is in the ballpark." This is a difficult image to conjure: it first calls up, perhaps, a Christian revival meeting held at a baseball stadium. But Simon's on to something different: using "in the ballpark" as a metaphor, the speaker suggests that, for him, redemption ("the cross") is in the realm of possibility ("in the ballpark"). It's a marvelous colloquial pairing of two concepts not normally associated with each other, and the result is a fresh rendering of the notion of the hope for salvation.

The speaker's resolve that "the cross is in the ballpark" comes, it turns out, as the result of a meditation on time's passage—one of Simon's enduring themes. The verses tell the story of a man who remembers a time—now long gone—when he was in love and he could say, "These songs are true / These days are ours" (probably an allusion to Simon's own 1960s, either with Kathy Chitty or with Peggy Harper). The fruit of his love was a son, Sonny, who himself grew up, married, and moved away. After a short interlude where the speaker sits in a room, seemingly all day long, watching the effects of the sun's rise and fall on the room's light—more meditation on the mystery of time's movement—he continues the chronicle of his son's life, with the speaker imagining the grown-up and married Sonny now feeling trapped in his life, and reminiscing on his past just the way his father, the song's speaker, is doing in the song. Sonny sifts through his high school year-book and, in the song's most affecting lines, marvels about the fate of his classmates: "Some have died / Some have fled from themselves / Or struggled from here to get there." The melancholy here is acute: with the drums turned way down in the mix, Simon's sorrowful voice evokes the sad wonder of time's passing as powerfully as it did in "Slip Sliding Away." Only in the final verse, with loud drums returning to the fore-ground and the speaker's willful voice intent on bullying through life no matter what, does the song regain its early momentum, with its final (and, I'd argue, desperate) insistence on the possibility of the cross's redemption. Yes, the cross is in the ballpark, Simon suggests: it *must* be, or else time's passage toward death is just too hard to contemplate.

"Can't Run But," which follows, percolates tensely to the startlingly original percussion by the Brazilian group Uakti (who play instruments partly of their own invention) as well as additional instruments like the talking drum, chicote (a whip made from animal hide that is lashed on objects to make sounds) and triangles and cassinets. The densely packed rhythms, heated but restrained, are unsettling, as is the central riff, the same series of notes that are played simultaneously by two instruments but in different keys. The lyrics reinforce the unease: the song is about the speaker's desire to avoid a wide array of disturbing events (a nuclear meltdown, a bad dream, the failure of art in the face of commerce) even though he fully recognizes he can't run from them—he can only "walk much faster than this." The avoidance is pointless, however. The world is closing in: "A winding river / Gets wound around a heart . . . / Tighter and tighter," and even if the "waters part" (suggesting some sort of deliverance), no Canaan awaits on the other side of the riverbank—just a suffering blues band exploited by the music business. The lyrics aren't quite focused—they're in fact pretty scattershot, but the music clearly creates a mood of high anxiety, appre-hension, even claustrophobic dread: the longing for redemption, for "waters parting" to reveal the promise of salvation, is rudely cut off. If "The Obvious Child" hasn't sufficiently clued the reader to the fact that *The Rhythm of the Saints* is no optimistic *Graceland* sequel, "Can't Run But" confirms it.

"The Coast" takes the nonlinear, impressionistic image-gathering of "Can't Run But" and extends it over a larger, and frankly more confus-ing, canvas. Introducing the shimmering guitar of Vincent Nguini, whose graceful presence on *Rhythm* is almost as decisive as Ray Phiri's on *Graceland*, the song also brings back Ladysmith Black Mambazo for some subtle background vocals, and throws an American horn section into the mix, anchoring it all in churning, burning percussion. This time, the lyrics take an almost confoundedly jagged course, beginning with a family of musicians who spend the night before a funeral in a village church bedecked with "the Rose of Jericho and Bougainvillea." There's another verse about the startling divide between the first world (a trip to the abundant markets in Washington) and third world (a place "where the evening meal / Is negotiable if there is one"). The funeral scene and meditation on hunger are unified by the refrain, "This is a lonely life / Sorrows everywhere you turn," sung in Simon's by-now-perfected vulnerable voice. But this is immediately followed by another, deeper and coarser, voice—evidently that of a craven music executive, who encourages the singer to appropriate the very sentiment we've just heard (about the lonely life) in order to increase his sales, since "when you think about it / That is worth some money." (Incidentally, this aesthetic move—introducing a sincere voice only to cancel it immediately with an ironic comment on it—is a hallmark of the postmodern, which tends to cast suspicion on all forms of sincerity without quite denying their pull. Simon, as conflicted as any popular artist could be about the contending forces of sincere artistic expression vs. the desire for success [which is more than happy to exploit that sincerity for commercial purposes] touches here on the lines from "Can't Run But": "The music suffers / The music business thrives." In fact, the seriousness of *Rhythm*, its refusal to capitulate to the normal commercial strategies—there are few hummable melodies, few radio-friendly refrains, little in the way of hooks—might be reflected in these lyrics, and might be Simon's reaction to the mega-success, and renewed commercial pressure, that he experienced with *Graceland*.)

But the song's knotted meanings hardly stop here. Starting with the fourth stanza, the lyrics shift course entirely, as does the melody line. (It's possible that Simon, as he often does, sewed two different songs into one, and the seams are showing.) In any event, we're met with lines that are perhaps the most obscure of Simon's career. Who is the speaker trying to "prove" his love to? When he says, "If I have money / If I have children," what is he referring to? What are we to make of the repeated and evocative refrain—"Summer skies and stars are falling /

All along the injured coast"? That image is chock full of ambiguities, if not outright confusion: summer skies suggest openness and beauty; an injured coast suggests environmental degradation. And what about those falling stars—are they beautiful moments on a summer night, a metaphor for nature's attempt to heal the injured coast, or suggestive of some larger "fall"? It's impossible to tell, and Simon's vocal tone doesn't clarify his meaning. I doubt Simon knows what he means here—this is one of the moments on the album where his desire to write intuitively and not care to make too much sense (perhaps he'd been heeding the advice of David Byrne in his Talking Heads film, *Stop Making Sense*) inhibits rather than liberates the meaning of his language. Simon's flirtation with elliptical meaning reaches a height on the *Rhythm* album, and nowhere more on the musically beautiful but lyrically baffling "The Coast."

"Proof," like "The Coast," presents images that seem almost randomly juxtaposed, but it's held together by a surer sense of its own theme. "Proof" presents two ways of looking at the world: one, based on the standard of "proof," is pragmatic and scientific; the other, which the singer labels as "faith," is intuitive, spiritual, emotional. The "faith" parts of the song are calm and smoothly melodic, evoking love, trust, and an open "sky flecked with signs of hope," while the "proof" sections (the chorus) are harsh, metallic, urbanly agitated, and in the lyrics suggest anger and craziness, and insist not on trust between souls but on some objective standard of "proof" that requires neither trust nor intimacy. Simon sets "faith" and "proof" against each other, and has no illusions about which one is currently winning out in the world: "Faith is an island in the setting sun / Proof is the bottom line for everyone." It's a dark observation clearly at odds with the speaker's desire for the opposite, and it reinforces the idea that the album's search for "spirit voices" is a desperate one.

"Further to Fly," track 5 on this album of ten songs (on the original release), is, to me, *Rhythm*'s centerpiece, one of Simon's greatest songs, a middle-aged meditation that combines Simon's penchant for melodically wandering recitative-like verses with some of his most beautiful melodic passages. It also perfectly captures Simon's melancholy search on the album: fully immersed in the suffering involved with the search for transcendence, it's fully committed to the journey nonetheless. Utilizing a broad array of instrumentation combining Brazilian touches like bongos, water bowls, talking drums, and *chakeire*, West African background vocals, and Western synthesizers and a horn section, the song is a gorgeous amalgam of traditions every bit as musically rich as what Simon achieved on *Graceland*. On top of polyrhythms melded together into a measured syncopated beat, the song's speaker begins wistfully, invoking a "time / When you'll be tired / As tired as a dream that wants to die"—clearly a recognizable state to a large segment of Simon's longtime fan base, the now forty- and fifty-somethings who struggled for decades to maintain faith in the dreams of their 1960s youth, not to mention just the faith to keep going in a world where one is no longer young. Immediately, however, he reminds the subject of the song that as tired as one is, there is "further to fly"—life isn't over, the struggle never ends. Stirred to passion again, perhaps, by conversation with a woman whose beautiful hair is a "spinning darkness," the speaker has to admit that maybe the conversation is "going nowhere." He stalks through the world worried about losing his loved ones, losing his memory, watching his children grow up and leaving, or even "thinking / Am I crazy." As old and tired as he is, however, he recognizes—in one of the most beautifully sung lines in all his work, that "the open palm of desire / Wants everything / It wants everything": the life force still streams within him. Simon sounds here a little like Saul Bellow's middle-aged millionaire Eugene Henderson (in *Henderson the Rain King*), who runs around an airport tarmac yelling "I want! I want! I want!" Simon's tone isn't comically frenzied, as Bellow's is; it's arguably more moving, though: the calm, almost childlike vulnerability of Simon's voice perfectly balances desire and sadness, as if he is hopelessly tied to a force that will subject him to endless rounds of happiness and grief, beauty and disappointment, love and loneliness. "The open palm of desire"— an image again as simple and striking as something out of Lorca, or perhaps Wallace Stevens—is like an image out of a dream, haunting one in and out of sleep. Luckily, as the song proceeds, the connotations of this desire tilt positive: it's the "strength to push like spring" or the "strength to let you go" (perhaps a reference, again, to Carrie Fisher, the subject of the song that follows). In any case, at song's end, the open palm of desire is accepted by the singer: he links it up with "The Rose of Jericho," a plant that in some Catholic rituals is associated with Christ's birth and therefore with redemption.

"She Moves On" is Simon's last paean to Carrie Fisher—she's written that the song is about her, claiming that he wrote it after a trip the couple had taken to the Amazon river after their divorce was final.[9] Simon has been more circumspect, saying only that "that song is close to my heart. Too close to the heart."[10] It's a song that rocks recklessly back and forth in time, from the end of a relationship to its beginnings and middles, back to its beginning, then to its end and aftermath. If one were to rearrange the song's narrative to read chronologically, it would start with the speaker feeling the "bite" of loneliness "whenever you believe that / You'll be lost and love will find you." From there, the singer chronicles the beginning of a new love with a mercurial woman who "fights a fever [and] . . . burns in bed" and who wonders, bewitchingly, if the emotions she feels for him are "as near to love as love will ever be." Ensnared by her mystery, he hears her siren song (sung now by four female background singers): "You have underestimated my power / As you shortly will discover." Whereupon the speaker "falls to his knees," fearful that in his hopeless devotion to her he will be "abandoned, forsaken," and unable even to find his voice again. Then, of course, the relationship ends, and after a suitable period of mourning, the speaker finds that "I feel good" and "blessed" that he's managed to escape her. Not only has she moved on, but so has he. The decision to jumble the relationship's chronology is a good one. It allows Simon to begin the song with him watching the woman's plane "lift" when she leaves him, then lets us enter his mind as he examines the wreckage of their relationship in a jumble of memories before returning at song's conclusion to watching the plane, and her, move on.

"Born at the Right Time," the most commercially accessible, conventionally structured, and emotionally soothing song on the album—the one song here that would have fit nicely on *Graceland*—was released as a single but failed to chart, an indication that Simon's music, though still tremendously popular, was no longer speaking to top 40 audiences. The song, which adds guitarist J. J. Cale to Simon's large corps of *Rhythm* musicians, is an embarrassment of melodic riches—both verse and refrain are breezily hummable. The song is, quite simply, about the startling beauty of childhood innocence. Invoking long-treasured religious allusions to Moses and Jesus as children, "Born" gives us a picture of a newborn as a pure unsullied soul who not only has never been subject to loneliness, lies, fear, or the denial of his or her needs, but also is somehow blessed by being "born at the right time." In the second and third verses, the speaker talks about how he and his cosmopolitan businessman, "traveling people" who dine in expensive restaurants and spend their "Euro-dollars / All the way from Washington to Tokyo," are taken aback by the babies they see in the airports: "They follow me with open eyes / Their uninvited guest." The speaker realizes that, as comfortable as he and his buddies are to the transient ways of the jet-set class (one might think here of George Clooney's character in the film *Up in the Air*, or James Axton in Don DeLillo's novel *The Names*), he knows that the world belongs to the innocent: as powerful an operator as he might be in the world, he is in fact the child's guest, and not a particularly welcome one at that. And though the world is overpopulated ("The planet groans / Every time it registers another birth"), hope lies with the promise of children who grow up unspoiled, unhurt, and, well, lucky—"born at the right time." The song's optimism sticks out among the tortuous meditations that fill out most of the rest of the album: it nods—ever so lightly, with a *soupcon* of comic irony, even—in the direction of salvation and redemption. The song is a Wallace Stevens–like fable, a kind of "supreme fiction"—a work of art that seduces us with its vision, a vision that impels aesthetic if not spiritual assent.

"The Cool, Cool River" is another of *Rhythm*'s ambitious songs that, like "The Coast," tantalizes us with the possibilities of elliptical insight but that, on deeper inspection, stumbles once again into obscurity. Like "Proof," it juxtaposes two opposing powers—an "anger" that pervades the world of politics as well as daily life and that Simon images as a "cool, cool river," and another, gentler power of hope that "believe[s] in the future" and that sends its "battered dreams to heaven." The anger is associated with music that is insistent, rushed, vocally exact, but cold; the hope is backed by music that is gentler and more soothing, Simon's vocals softer and sweeter. There are intriguing moments here: when Simon sings about the "rage of love" turning inward into "prayers of devotion" that are "the memories of God," one would very much like to know what he means. The repeated refrain "Song dogs barking at the break of dawn / Lightning pushes the edge of the thunderstorm" is similarly fascinating, and unfortunately just as opaque. Another example of Simon's experiment with cryptic lyrics simply not getting across to the listener.

"Spirit Voices" recounts the journey of a speaker who "sailed up a wide river"—presumably Brazil's Amazon—to a jungle village where he attends the healing ceremony of a sick little girl whom he calls "Heaven's only daughter." The details—walking by moonlight to the *brujo's* (or witchdoctor's) door, seating himself next to women nursing their babies, a "lime-green lizard scuttle[ing] down the cabin door"—are richly expressive, and both the percussive rhythms and the melody lines are easy and calming. "All of these spirit voices rule the night," the speaker sings reassuringly, and when, as part of the ritual, he agrees to drink what might be a slightly spiked "cup of herbal tea," he suddenly hears what the voices are saying. This portion of the lyrics, written and sung by famed Portuguese singer-songwriter Milton Nascimento, are light as air—befitting spirit voices—and exhort the listener to have "heart" and "passion," and to "trust in the power of tomorrow." It's the one song on the album that fully embraces the unseen world unapologetically, somehow managing to escape the world of "proof" and of spiritual doubt that pervades most of *Rhythm*.

The concluding title song is the most richly rhythmic track on the record. Gliding on a thick cushion of groove—mostly supplied by the percussion group Uakti—the song is, in some ways, as lyrically knotty and cryptic as "The Coast." The lyrics read like the prayer of a man struggling to communicate to a god the speaker doesn't know if he can believe in (shades of "Some Folks' Lives Roll Easy"). The gods he is speaking to are Olodumare, the creator god, and Babalu-aye, "the lord of the earth" of the Yoruba religion, a religion practiced extensively in Nigeria and other West African countries. (The speaker's background isn't clear, but given the allusions to drugs and his attempts to "glide away from a razor or a knife," he may be an African drug runner.) But he wonders if the gods, "smiling in heaven," are indifferent to him ("Do my prayers remain unanswered?"), and so, in the refrain, he decides to "reach in the darkness" in order to confront his problems. To "reach in the darkness" is, in a way, the whole album's desperate lunge at the transcendent. The song, and the album as a whole, recounts story after story of attempts to enter the world of the spiritual. These attempts are most often frustrated, but glimmering hints of momentary release and redemption abound, not least in the music itself. Yes, "sometimes even music / Cannot substitute for tears" ("The Cool, Cool River"), but sometimes it can: there is saintliness in the rhythms of these songs, mysteries of love, compassion, succor, transcendent beauty, and maybe glimpses into the beyond that Simon and his musicians infuse into their playing and singing, and that can hardly be described in words. So for all of the recondite lyrics of *The Rhythm of the Saints*, the music's meaning comes through powerfully: here is Paul Simon longing for God, reaching into the darkness to find Him, and finding only the flesh of his own grasping hands.

SONGS FROM "THE CAPEMAN" (1997), THE CAPEMAN (ORIGINAL BROADWAY CAST RECORDING, 2008)

The music for Simon's white elephant of a musical comes down to us in two forms. One is *The Capeman*, the official Broadway cast recording—songs performed by the talented original cast, which includes Marc Anthony, Ruben Blades, and Ednita Nazario, and which features two full hours of music, much of it solid evocations of traditional Caribbean folk, 1950s New York doo-wop, contemporary Broadway pop, and rich admixtures of all three. Though hardly the breakthrough Broadway musical Simon intended, it displays an enormous amount of hard work, craft, and dedication. The other is a single-CD selection of tunes from the musical, sung mostly by Simon himself, titled *Songs from "The Capeman."* Simon, on this solo album released in 1997, excised almost all of the story's expository material, the short snippets of libretto that served to keep the narrative moving, as well as a number of the larger showpieces, presumably because they don't translate well to a voice like Simon's. Among the virtues of the original cast recording is that it does what Simon's *Songs from "The Capeman"* doesn't—it programs the songs in chronological order, thus allowing the listener who hasn't seen the show (which is almost all of us, since the play closed so rapidly and has never been revived in its original form) to follow the plot. And it appears the arc of Salvador Agron's story was as important to Simon as was the opportunity to investigate new musical styles and mount a Broadway play.

The Salvador (aka Sal) of *The Capeman*—the book and lyrics were written by Simon and Caribbean poet Derek Wolcott—is born in the poor town of Mayaguez, Puerto Rico, as the only son of Esmerelda, an impoverished and divorced mother working in a convent. Sal, from the beginning a temperamental boy subject to tantrums, is mistreated by the nuns—he's beaten badly for wetting his bed—and his mother quits her job as a result. In despair, she uses all her savings to consult a "santero," who prophesizes that Salvador will one day commit a murder, which terrifies the mother and leaves her susceptible to a preacher who marries her and takes his new family to New York. However, Sal's stepfather beats him as well, and soon the marriage is over—Sal is left fatherless again. As he grows up in a Puerto Rican immigrant neighborhood in Brooklyn, he's seduced into the street life by one Tony Hernandez, who pulls him into the notorious gang the Vampires. The early Brooklyn songs evoke a world not unlike *West Side Story*, with its alternating songs about street violence and romantic escape, though *The Capeman*'s language is considerably more blunt and realistic. Everything changes when Sal and Tony run into two Irish American gang members, and end up killing them. When Salvador is captured (wearing his cape), he shows no remorse: "I don't care if I burn; my mother could watch me," he says, and in a real TV interview included on the original cast recording, appears so emotionally numb as to be sociopathic. The story then follows Salvador as he goes to trial, where he's convicted and sentenced, at the age of sixteen, to death row, a sentence later commuted to life imprisonment. Sal is sent to some of the most notorious prisons in America (Sing Sing and Attica among them). During his twenty years of jail time, Sal rather miraculously rehabilitates himself— he called it his "rehumanization"—studying for a college degree, becoming a born-again Christian, and publishing some of his autobiographical writings. He gains a pen pal in "Wahzinak," an American Indian woman who reads some of his prison writings and falls in love with him. We also follow the suffering of his mother Esmerelda, as she attempts to deal with her own guilt and her loneliness living in America after her son's imprisonment. Twenty years pass, and Salvador is finally released on parole. He returns to his neighborhood to confront the local aftermath of his crimes (the song titled "You Fucked Up My Life" gives a taste of how he's received by his old friends) and in "Sal's Last Song" (on the soundtrack but not on Simon's solo album) confesses to his mother that he has no excuses for what he'd done: "I and I alone must bear the blame for the madness that was done," he admits. It was not some fate announced by the santero, not some prophecy he was to fulfill, not the poverty, not the shabby treatment of his stepfather, not the lure of the streets. He alone was responsible for his life and what he'd done with it. His mother, dreaming of this moment, tells him in relief: "It is repentance that makes good from evil," thereby sealing the narrative as a story of redemption.

Salvador Agron's story must have appealed to Simon in many ways for him to have devoted at least a half-decade of his professional life to it. The fact that the murder, the trial, and the media uproar occurred when Simon was himself a teenager suggests that the story affected him deeply when he was young, and that when Agron died in 1986, Simon's buried memories returned and offered themselves as stirring raw material for a new musical project. A story of a murderer's redemption, especially one who's a poor immigrant—"a person of color," as one of the characters puts it, who is dealt a terrible hand in his adopted country—certainly appealed to Simon's liberal sympathies, though the tone of political correctness and special pleading weakens the book. (Only one song, for instance—the rather interminable "Can I Forgive Him?"—is devoted to considering the feelings of the victims' mothers.) The chance to co-write the lyrics with Derek Wolcott, who was awarded the Nobel Prize in Literature while the two were working together, also must have been a big lure. Finally, the opportunity for Simon to return to his 1950s music roots—to explore doo-wop and the Latin-inflected music that had inspired him in his younger days—certainly must have been a big factor in Simon's decision to throw himself into such an enormous project. But the sum of all these motivations, not to mention the immense investment of time and energy, didn't pay off theatrically—or musically.

Simon's *Songs from "The Capeman"* cherry-picks most of the musical's best songs, but even among his thirteen selections, it's hard to get excited about many of them. True, "Satin Summer Nights," with its inspired doo-wop arrangement, Spanish guitar solo, and Marc Anthony's sweet vocal performance, is a delight, an expert evocation of both the innocent romanticism of 1950s New York immigrant communities and the brutally violent impulses festering underneath. "Born in Puerto Rico," the musical's opening statement and summary of Agron's story, is suffused with Simon's patented melodic melancholy, and Simon's moving vocal performance feels personally impelled (in a way that the rest of the album doesn't). "Vampires," with its stalking piano riff, haunting trumpet, and Simon's aggressive street vocals, helps us understand the pressures Sal felt to join a gang. And "Adios Hermanos," the song Sal sings as he heads off to court for his sentencing, is an expert piece of Broadway songwriting, effectively combining detailed recitative with memorable melodies. But much of the rest of the album is labored, easily forgettable, misguided. Esmerelda's two songs, as well as "Trailways Bus," are curiously bereft of melodic interest; "Time Is an Ocean," stuffed with ideas about prison and oppression, feels preachy and way too unsubtle for a Paul Simon composition. And the others—"Bernadette," "Quality," the two parts of "Killer Wants to Go to College"— sound very much like the filler they are.

Simon was defiant about making *The Capeman* to his exact specifications, and initially demanded total creative control over the material and the production. That the whole project, once complete, went so quickly up in flames suggests that Simon's (deserved) self-confidence tilted into (unwarranted) arrogance: he was unable to accept that he was even more over his head with *The Capeman* than he was with *One-Trick Pony*, and could not work effectively with those who might have helped him rescue the project. The deeper the production fell into disarray, it seems, the more Simon asserted himself, attempting to correct what he wasn't experienced enough to fix. In any event, the critical verdict on the play—the *New York Times* critic wrote that "the show registers as one solemn, helplessly confused drone. It's like watching a mortally wounded animal. You're only sorry that it has to suffer and that there's nothing you can do about it"—doomed the play from the beginning, and within weeks passed into history as one of Broadway's more ignominious enterprises. [11]

It was Simon's second major failure since he'd become a star. But by 1998, Simon, a pop music veteran of thirty years standing, was able to weather his botched Broadway venture much better than he did his failures of the early 1980s. His days of miracle and wonder may have been over, but it helped immeasurably that he was now happily married to Edie Brickell, with whom he was raising a family. Escaping Broadway, he was able to ensconce himself in the compensations of wife and children, reassess his career, and emerge in the new century with a trilogy of strong personal albums about love, God, and death that have put a seal on his status as one of America's great and enduring songwriters.

6

THINKING ABOUT GOD

1998–2014

Sit down, shut up
Think about God
And wait for the hour of my rescue
—"Everything about It Is a Love Song"

Consider Paul Simon circa 1980, deeply depressed, suffering a crippling episode of writer's block, and limping away from his first major career failure, *One-Trick Pony*. Compare him to the artist who survived the commercial debacle of *The Capeman* in 1998: this is the difference between a man panicked by the first flush of audience rejection and someone possessing mature confidence burnished by four decades of riding the ebbs and flows of fame. When *The Capeman* closed after only sixty-eight performances in late March of 1988, Simon didn't huddle up into despair or fly cross-country seeking out miracle therapists. He simply went home—to his wife, Edie Brickell, and their children, the third of whom was born a month after his musical shuttered its doors—and soon enough, got back to work. In the new century, Simon felt no need to conquer the pop world again—it was by then, of course, unconquerable by the likes of Simon, dominated as it was by boy bands like N'Sync, the hip hop of Eminem and Jay-Z , and grunge's aftermath, and Simon's sensibility had no truck with such trends. This allowed him to focus on developing his own musical interests, and to investigate further the pressing themes of his sixties and seventies: the strangeness and sublimity of life lived when considered from the prospect of death and eternity. Like countless late-life artists before him, Simon was now considering existence *sub species aeternitatus*—that is, under the aspect of eternity—and it suffused much of the music he was now making.

So he had much more on his mind than career failure. Batting away media reports that he had "withdrawn" after *The Capeman* closed, Simon told one interviewer:

> Here's the frustration. . . . When you get your information from the media, it's not right. The play closed in the early spring, a month [later] my son was born. It wasn't withdrawal, it was parenting. By the following fall I began to work on finding this band [for *You're the One*] so the withdrawal, if the implication is that I withdrew in a wounded way, is not true at all. I went into life instead of art and then in due course, as it usually does, some artistic impulse grabbed me and I went back to work to find out what that was.[1]

"In due course," Simon not only got a new band together—headed up by guitarist Vincent Nguini, who was so vital to the sound of *The Rhythm of the Saints*—but also found time for a joint tour with his old 1960s rival, Bob Dylan. Dylan, who had embarked on a touring schedule so relentless that people started calling it the Never-Ending Tour (which, it turned out, stretched well into the new century), was still riding high from *his* late-career renaissance (the one begun by the outstanding 1995 album *Time Out of Mind*) and asked Simon to come along on over thirty American dates. Offering themselves as co-headliners and switching off as opening and closing acts each show—a decision that acknowledged their near-equal status in the pop pantheon—they each played generous solo sets, then paired up for a few songs together each night (these usually included "The Sound of Silence," a medley of Johnny Cash's "I Walk the Line" and Elvis's "Blue Moon of Kentucky," and Dylan's "Knockin' on Heaven's Door"). At the time, this appeared to be a final burying of the hatchet between the two men, though perhaps it wasn't, since in 2011, Simon, smarting from Dylan's rejection of his offer to sing on the *So Beautiful or So What* album, let his irritation show, telling an interviewer: "I usually come in second (to Dylan), and I don't like coming in second."[2] (Simon, in his seventies, may have his art directed at the heavens, but his competitive streak remains fully earth-bound.) The music Simon has made in the twenty-first century encompasses a significant amount of live performance (solo, with Dylan, and again with Garfunkel), as well as three albums' worth of new music—thirty-one songs of masterly craftsmanship, often surpassing beauty, and a late-life reckoning with spiritual matters that Simon has been honing into sharper and sharper focus. Anyone trying to deal with the question of Paul Simon's lasting contributions to American popular music will have to reckon not only with "Darling Lorraine," "How Can You Live in the Northeast?," "Wartime Prayers," and "Hurricane Eye" but also with searching investigations of spiritual intimation like "Everything about It Is a Love Song," "Outrageous," "I Don't Believe," and just about the entire *So Beautiful or So What* album.

His first album of the twenty-first century, *You're the One*, is a casually expert, restrained pull-back from the large-scale projects that had occupied Simon since *Graceland*. Organizing the songs around the quieter rhythms of voice and guitar—rather than drums, as had been the case with the last two solo albums—as well as modest arrangements and slightly more straightforward lyrics than those that hampered many listeners' appreciation of *The Rhythm of the Saints*, Simon easily reestablished his *bona fides* as a singer-songwriter. The album was received well, going gold in the United States (selling more than 500,000 copies), entering the U.S. and U.K. top 20, and nominated for an Album of the Year Grammy. Simon toured extensively in support of the album, with live (and in the case of "Hurricane Eye," terrifically vivid) versions of three of *You're the One*'s songs slipped onto the extended version of the *You're the One* CD.

Not long after returning to his home in New York City, radical Islamic terrorists hijacked two planes loaded with passengers and plunged them into the two towers of the World Trade Center on September 11th, 2001 (a third plane crashed into the Pentagon; a fourth crashed in an open field in Pennsylvania), altering the course of American foreign policy, not to mention its popular culture, for the next decade, and sending Simon on a songwriting path that would profoundly affect his next album, *Surprise*, released in 2006. But before he began work on the album, he coproduced Edie Brickell's new studio album, *Picture Perfect Morning*, released in 2004, and accepted, along with Garfunkel, a Grammy Lifetime Achievement Award for their work as a duo. The pair's performance at the Grammys was so graciously received that Simon and Garfunkel once again agreed to put aside their differences and tour together. Doubtless, some of the reasons were mercenary—Garfunkel hadn't had any real musical or film success in over two decades, and Simon, who hadn't had a hit album in more than a decade, didn't mind the renewed exposure to remind fans of *Graceland* (not to mention *Bridge Over Troubled Water*) that he was still alive and kicking. The tour, as S & G tours always are, was a big success: after a long North American trek, the tour was extended to Europe, and ended with a show at Rome's Colosseum before a reported six hundred thousand fans.

Surprise, released in 2006, was recorded and produced in collaboration with Brian Eno—the writer/producer/avant-garde sound-shaper who started out with Roxy Music in the early 1970s, made a string of experimental albums of popish avant-garde music (e.g., *Another Green World*, *Before and After Science*), and is probably best known for his explorations of "ambient music" and his production work with David Bowie, David Byrne, and U2. Simon and Eno shared a love of African rhythms (see Eno's album with Byrne, *My Life in the Bush of Ghosts*), but Eno's contribution to *Surprise* had less to do with rhythm than it did with subtle electronic studio effects that (post)modernized Simon's sound: ghostly keyboards, synthesizer loops, distorted guitars, the smooth sheen of advanced technology. The album features some of the strongest songs on a Simon album since *Graceland*, and I'd argue that, with its anguished meditations on America in the post-9/11 era and its sublime and sometimes very funny reflections on beauty and mortality, it's one of his best solo albums. Many critics heralded *Surprise* as a "comeback," and though it did well critically and commercially (it reached #14 on the U.S. charts and #4 in the U.K.), it seemed a little late in the day for such characterizations. After five decades, he wasn't making comebacks: he was just making strong Paul Simon music.

He did the usual solo tour for *Surprise*, came home to accept the Library of Congress's Gershwin Prize for Popular Song, bought a house in Connecticut after decades out on Long Island, continued to help raise his family, did a two-month world tour with Garfunkel in 2009, and began to compile material for his final album to date, *So Beautiful or So What*. Released in April 2011, the album gently melds the African and South American influences of his *Graceland/Rhythm* period with American folk idioms—throwing in some new stuff as well, like a sample of a black preacher's sermon and some Indian arrangements—all in the service of what we might expect from the now sixty-nine-year-old songwriter: more sweet, funny, savvy, and increasingly penetrating meditations on aging, death, and the possibilities of religious or spiritual transcendence. By turns fanciful, ironic, and dead serious, *So Beautiful or So What* is exquisite pop meditating on God: Simon's voice is still water-soft and smooth but possessed of more emotional coloring than ever; the arrangements are crafted and produced to a high gloss; the melodies complex but catchy—and it's all in the service of Simon's focused obsession with life's meaning, death, and the afterlife. The reviews of the album were some of the best of his career, and worldwide sales exceeded that of any of his albums since *The Rhythm of the Saints*.

YOU'RE THE ONE (2000)

The album opener, "That's Where I Belong," begins so quietly, with a gentle wash of synthesizer eventually overlayed with bamboo flute, vielle, vihuela, and Vincent Nguini's marvelous guitar—delicate as spring rain—that it's practically an announcement that Simon has downshifted from the mighty musical projects that had occupied him in the 1980s and 1990s. It's a straightforward, open-hearted, vulnerably sung love song devoted to two objects: one to music itself, the other to (one presumes) his wife, Edie Brickell. That this thrice-married man begins the album with a simple statement of faith in (his last, one again assumes) marriage is heartening: the two middle verses of the song, where the speaker notes his wife's smile, the sound of her singing (Edie, of course, is a singer), or "the way you turn / And catch me with your eye" are fetching bits of mature romantic pop, complete with a transportive bit of glossolalia—Simon's keening "ah-ee-ah-ee-ah-ah-ah"— that says more about where the speaker "belongs" than any lyric could. ("That's Where I Belong" is not, incidentally, Simon's first song about Brickell. That distinction goes to "Thelma," recorded in 1993 and first released on the career-summarizing box set *Songwriter*, and then included on the "expanded" CD version of *The Rhythm of the Saints*. "Thelma," heartening in its own right, is the product of a man bursting with the joy and anxiety of a great new passion. The speaker in "That's

Where I Belong" has weathered the highs and lows of new love; his primary emotion toward his wife is clearly a philosophic gratitude.) But the song is also about music and songwriting. The song begins:

> Somewhere in a burst of glory
> A sound becomes a song
> I'm bound to tell a story
> That's where I belong

Those lines can probably stand as Paul Simon's mission statement not just for the album but also (retrospectively) for his whole life since he strapped on a guitar. The speaker here recognizes himself as, *irreducibly*, a songwriter, "bound"—chained—to the lifelong (and for Simon torturous) task of writing music that interprets, mourns, and celebrates the life he lives. (Lord knows, he may be suggesting under his breath, he's no great shakes as a filmmaker or dramatist. Songwriting is all he's got.) What redeems the difficulty of such a life—and I think I believe him here—is not the money or the fame but the "burst of glory" that comes when "sound becomes a song." Simon adumbrated the glory of songwriting in "Song about the Moon" in the early 1980s, but "That's Where I Belong," with its ethereal sonic setting, gives support to a full spiritual reading to the word *glory* here. In preparing this album, Simon was sitting down, shutting up, and thinking about God, but when he got down to it, his medium for "thinking about God" was, and is, inevitably, music. It's a major theme that carries through much of the three albums that follow.

"Darling Lorraine," which follows, clocking in at 6:41, is the longest song in the Simon catalogue and earns every second of its length. One of Simon's most perfectly realized songs, it's a straight chronological narrative (rare since *Hearts and Bones*) about a long troubled relationship, from its origins in "the sin of impatience" to its end in wife Lorraine's death. The lyrics' ability to convey the sudden and perplexing emotional shifts that plague relationships—from hopeless longing for the lover to outright sickening rage and back again—is so precisely etched that the listener feels like she's in the middle of a John Cheever or Ann Beattie story. And the accompanying music is just as strong, cueing the listener to every shift of emotional nuance with impressive precision. The couple here, Frank and Lorraine, is as ordinary as pea soup. Frank, timid and risk-averse, seeks only comfort and safety but falls crazily in love with the "hot," "cool," "light," and "free" Lorraine, and somehow manages to snare her into marriage. But after "the usual married stuff," Lorraine feels trapped and announces that she's leaving him, whereupon the music rises to match Frank's panic and anger: "What—you don't love me anymore? . . . You're not the woman that I wed / You say you're depressed but you just like to stay in bed." Simon's rendition of Frank's outburst perfectly balances comedy and poignancy, capturing beautifully the man's alarm and dismay at losing the one thing in life that holds him together. (He's the twin of the speaker in "Slip-Sliding Away," who says that his "love is so overpowering that I'm afraid I will disappear.") But the nasty fight ends with them deciding to stick it out, and with Frank's saying (in Simon's plaintive vocal): "I loooonnng for your love." The arrangement returns then to its original verse melody and Simon's careful vulnerable vocal: Frank informs us that he's never made it financially, and that "if it had not been for Lorraine," he might have made a go at being a musician. (We recognize this for what it is, though: an increasingly unhappy husband dreaming of "what if?") But he's tugged back to her in the next verse, in which Lorraine makes pancakes for him on Christmas morning, and the couple watches "It's a Wonderful Life" on television. The music and vocal are so delicate here that it's almost a soporific, which is surely Simon's intention: what Frank wants out of his marriage is precisely this closed-in intimacy and sentimental comfort. (In this, we're reminded of the lovers in "I Do It for Your Love.") But of course, Lorraine doesn't: the music rises again and, sure enough, Frank and Lorraine are back in a fight, which ends with Frank yelling, "I'm sick to *death* of you, Lorraine." Then, as if to give Frank what one part of him desires, Lorraine becomes deathly ill. Frank, in renewed panic at losing her, tells her, "Your [labored] breathing is like an echo of our love," and tries to comfort her with extra blankets and sweets from the corner grocer. It's to no avail, however: she passes away with "the moon in the meadow" and "all the trees . . . filled with April rain." The song is a tiny masterpiece of domestic realism, expertly calibrating its emotional shadings so that Frank and Lorraine's serious/ludicrous marriage ultimately leaves us with a sense of wonder. If the song also leaves us with a feeling of loss and emptiness, it may be because Frank and Lorraine never lift their heads to contemplate something that might transcend their bittersweet love: it's resolutely earthbound.

"Old," another completely realized composition, is, along with *Surprise*'s hilarious "Outrageous," Simon's late-middle-aged take on aging (and renders altogether moot *Bookends*' sentimental take on getting old). It takes off from a 1950s-era strummed guitar riff that evidently reminded Simon of Buddy Holly so much that he begins the lyrics with a memory of listening to Buddy Holly when he was twelve. ("Old" is a good example of Simon's latter-day songwriting, in which lyrics are inspired by the sound of music that Simon is writing. He's no longer a "poet [first] and a one-man band." He "discovers" his themes from the music he's playing, rather than "planting" them ahead of time.) But the speaker can't stay in the past: soon enough, he's reminded that he's "getting old," which sets him off on a funny meditation on what's *really* old: Jesus Christ's birth, two thousand years ago, is old; "Wisdom is old, the Koran is old, the Bible is old"; and if that's not enough to give him some perspective on his own advancing years, how about this? "We estimate the universe at 13–14 billion [years]," and since the Lord conceived the universe, God had to be there even before *that*. So: "God is old / We're not old." Now, as an argument this is of course ridiculous, but that's part of the point: when the end starts to stare us in the face, we're likely to pull all sorts of rationalizations out of our hats. The arrangement, not just the teenage rocking rhythms and the swooping, silly guitar parts behind the "getting old" chorus, reinforces this. But there's more to the song than satire: as in "The Boy in the Bubble," Simon is expanding the time and space parameters of his music, the scope of his concerns broadening to embrace the sublime: the context of the speaker's life is now billions of years of time and light years worth of distance. We'll see more of this in "Hurricane Eye" from this album, "Another Galaxy" and "Once upon a Time There Was an Ocean" from *Surprise*, and "Love and Hard Times" and "Love Is Sacred Eternal Light" from *So Beautiful or So What*.

You're the One takes a bit of a dip after its superb opening triad. The title tune, its tight bass and drum rhythm reminiscent of the thrusting beat of "Late in the Evening," never quite lifts off, despite a smartly sung second verse and a lovely two-line digression where Simon, in a voice and quivering melody line that resembles a Middle Eastern prayer or perhaps a Jewish cantor, sings: "You are the air / Inside my chest." But the chorus is decidedly repetitive, even a tad dull, and the lyrics' "point"—that lovers, seeing their relationship from different points of view, blame each other when love changes, when they should realize that love's shape changes as much as "clouds and waves and flame"—is a bit banal for all the musical workup. "The Teacher," which follows, is perplexing. It has the feeling of an art song, hushed, carefully composed, and rather beautifully sung, and comes across as another of Simon's fables, like "Born at the Right Time" or "Pigs, Sheep, and Wolves" (from later on this album), only thematically it's as unfocused as "The Coast" or "The Cool, Cool River." Here, the speaker tells the story of a family who comes under the influence of a guru-like "teacher" who, taking advantage of their spiritual bafflement, enslaves them in his power so that by song's end they're pleading for him to "carry me home my teacher / Carry me home." That the preacher, mid-song, becomes monster-like, dividing himself in two, half of him eating forests and the other half "sucking all the moisture from the clouds," reads like an intrusion from a Ted Hughes poem, and the straight seriousness (almost self-seriousness) of the song flattens its impact: the lighter ironies that animate the rest of the album's songs about faith and spiritual search are nowhere in sight.

Things pick up on "Look at That," one of Simon's strongest "whimsy" songs in years. It's clearly the work of a man who has been living with little people in his house—children who still possess that innocent enthusiasm for learning ("Off to school we go!") not to mention an instinctual love and trust for parents that the speaker sees as redemptive and worthy of emulation, even though to "ask someone to love you / Takes a lot of nerve." The song's instrumentation, featuring airy bamboo flutes and Nguini's fleet-fingered guitar sprinkling bright-colored notes like fairy dust, lovingly complements (and in its way, engenders) the "com[ing] aware, com[ing] alive" that is the song's theme.

The sunniness of "Look at That" is slightly shadowed in the easygoing south-of-the-border simplicities of the resonant "Señorita with a Necklace of Tears," whose *faux-naif* speaker seems almost Candide-ish in his tolerant acceptance of life and his optimism that there's "nothing but good news." During the song's bridge, he admits, however, that if he "could play all his memories" on his guitar, the song he'd write would be called "Señorita with a Necklace of Tears." The tears would represent "every sin I'd committed," which suggests that music is not just catharsis but also confession and redemption. The crucial change here from "that's the way it is" to "that's the way it *was*" (his sins now being *past*) suggests that music is for him a form of spiritual cleansing, a theme that, of course, Simon has been courting since *Graceland*.

"Love" is a rare Simon misfire, a sincerely sung paean to love's saving graces that is probably as heartfelt a missive as he could have sung to his wife, but that, despite a lovely guitar figure, is bogged down in an uncertain melody line and a mushy chorus. (Simon must have a high opinion of it, however: he chose it as one of the two songs to represent *You're the One* for a best-of, *The Paul Simon Compilation*, released in 2002.) The animal fable "Pigs, Sheep, and Wolves," which follows, immediately dispels any whiff of soft sentiment, however, with a vocal performance of such slimy snark that it's as if he were channeling Randy Newman. Simon, freeing himself of a voice that too often limits itself to precisely the narrow solemnity of "Love," revels in the nastiness of this tale of a pig who kills a sheep and lets a wolf take the blame for it. Simon is a great character actor here, and even if the narrative doesn't amount to much, it's one of the funniest songs he ever recorded.

"Hurricane Eye" is probably the album's showcase—it's the other *You're the One* song on *The Paul Simon Collection*—and comes complete with a dense musical setting chock full of competing instrumental textures, changing time signatures, shifting tempos, and lyrics as evocative/elusive as anything on *The Rhythm of the Saints*. High-spirited, even jolly, about the tempests that await us even when we feel "peaceful" inside a "hurricane's eye," the song begins with the light-footed gallop of percussion and a gently picked banjo—an instrument that can't sound sad even if it tried—backed by a sweet mesh of acoustic guitars. Our speaker here contemplates the universe in astronomical terms (as is Simon's latter-day wont), specifically the "goldilocks" phenomenon, which tells us that the Earth, since "it's not too hot / Not too cold," is snugly set inside a band of space—93,000,000 miles from the sun—that provides conditions that are "just right" for the growth of living things. Which is to say: mankind is a weird and lucky product of the grand joke that is the Big Bang and Evolution, and here we are now, plopped down in history, "home in the land of the homeless." (This theme will get reiterated on *So Beautiful or So What*'s "Love Is Eternal Sacred Light.") This sets the speaker off on an energetically associative rant whose details feel plucked out of the collective unconscious ("the shadow of a horse," "faces painted black in sorrow and remorse," "crucifix and arrow," "the bridge of time") and tossed almost willy-nilly onto the lyric sheet. The effect is to portray an existence as chaotic as it is "homeless," which—my tenuous reading suggests—compels the speaker to "pray / With crazy angel voices / All night / Until it's a new day," knowing full well that whatever peace he finds in the world is temporary and illusory: the hurricane eye will pass and we will soon enough be tempest-tossed again. Halfway through the song, some rock guitar enters, the tempo picks up, and the percussion goes into a martial rhythm that suggests we're about to enter some kind of storm. What follows is the speaker's almost-taunting list of "redemptive" projects that one might take up to fight this storm: "You want to be a leader? . . . You want to be a missionary? . . . You want to be a writer?" Sure, he suggests, go out and "change the game" or save the world, but don't forget that the hurricane is always around the corner, and the only defense against it is, finally, giving oneself up to, and appealing to, the unseen forces of the universe, which is to say, prayer. "Hurricane Eye" is one of Simon's most sardonic songs, but it has the courage to take on its chaotic vision with conviction and a penetratingly comic irony.

Positioning "Quiet" as the album's closer is deceptive. The sound is calm but eerie, *resigned*—the instrumentation provided chiefly by a slightly funereal pump reed organ and a ninety-six-tone harp, as if the song were a soundtrack to a scene in a movie where an old man dreams of his passing out of life into death's dream kingdom. And indeed, the lyrics tell us of a speaker who is "heading for a time of quiet," "solitude," and "peace without illusions," "when the perfect circle / Marries all beginnings and conclusions." The vocal follows no apparent melody— Simon seems to be searching for a melody as he goes, mimicking the obscure journey the speaker is on as he approaches death, and Simon's purposeful attempt to write a song without a strong melody works to the song's advantage. Along the way, the speaker strips himself of the folly of ambition and the hunger for "the change inside the purse," which allows him finally to lie "by a lake of sacred water." The water is sacred, but the nature of the death he awaits is unclear, as is any afterlife. He is, like the character in "Everything about It Is a Love Song," "await[ing] the hour of my rescue." Still, the song has a sense of laying down one's arms, of ceasing the struggle, that the rest of the album strenuously rejects ("Darling Lorraine" and "Hurricane Eye," the two best songs, reject them most strenuously), which is why I suggest that its placement at the album's end is deceptive. *You're the One*, far from closing any-thing, opens the last stage of Simon's career. Far from wrapping any-thing up, it illuminates even more questions that "thinking about God" has been coaxing in him, and leads to the bold achievement of the next two albums.

SURPRISE (2006)

One of the biggest surprises on *Surprise*, even to long-time Paul Simon fans used to his promiscuous appropriation of musical styles, is the loud distorted electric guitar that opens and dominates the first track, "How Can You Live in the Northeast?" That guitar sound, which will get a bit of a workout on "Wartime Prayers," "I Don't Believe," and "That's Me" as well, is the sound of clean "classic" American rock, and is a stylized (some would say corporate) harnessing of the frustration and aggression at the base of early rock 'n' roll. Now, Simon's talent (vocally, lyrically, and musically) has never lent itself toward the expression of violent emotion: his blessing/curse has always been that he's a guy with a sin-cere, lucid voice who expresses long-considered, thoughtfully complex emotions. So the *stylization* of rock aggression is about all we can ex-pect from Simon. Still, "How Can You Live in the Northeast?" demands a sound that at least touches on the rage that comes with the contem-plation of terrorism and chaos—and that guitar is a pop signifier for it.

The more prominent aural surprise on *Surprise* is, of course, Brian Eno's "sonic landscapes," as the album liner notes put it. Eno's elec-tronic keyboards and synthesizers on *Surprise* transcend the usual ef-fects of computer-based synthesizers—which is, generally, to "cool out" the music's passion or give it a distanced, high-tech edge (though Eno can do that, too, if called on: listen to the stabs of percussive keyboard in "Once upon a Time There Was an Ocean"). His mastery of synthe-sized sound enables him to create warmly human aural effects that mirror and enhance the subtleties of Simon's own voice as well as the shimmering beauty of Vincent Nguini's guitar work, particularly on songs like "Everything about It Is a Love Song," "Wartime Prayers," and the "God will" ending of "Outrageous." *Surprise* nearly matches *Graceland* or *The Rhythm of the Saints* as a triumph of musical synthesis—only this time the combinations of musical tradition include the electronic pop avant-garde.

The topical occasion for "How Can You Live in the Northeast?" is, of course, 9/11, but its theme is a broken America divided by region and religion, ethnic tension, and a blue-state-red-state politics that turns our national discourse increasingly into a Tower of Babel. 1974's "American Tune" left us with the image of a "Statue of Liberty / Sailing away to sea" but with a speaker still committed to the work of restoring some of that lost American promise. But the central speaker of "Northeast," Simon's new-century American tune, is buried by a cross-current of accusative voices that, like talking heads on a cable news show, can't or refuse to understand one another. It's a song that, in the wake of 9/11 and a number of national disasters (among them the Mississippi river floods of 1993 and 2002), suggests that the very "multi-culturalism" Simon had been celebrating musically since *Graceland* has come at the price of a stable sense of American unity. "Weak as a winter sun, we enter life on earth," the speaker begins, but immediately, he notes, we're branded by "names and religion" which, while expressing our diversity, also (increasingly) ghettoize us. "How can you tattoo your body?," someone asks. Another counters: "Why do you cover your head?" Still another wonders, "How can you eat from a rice bowl? The holy man only breaks bread." At the end, the speaker calls for some kind of solidarity, reminding us that almost all of us come from immigrant stock, but the reminder comes across as ineffectual, buried in the din of fear and suspicion (powerfully evoked by Eno's synthesizers and that distorted guitar) gripping the country in the post-9/11 era.

"Everything about It Is a Love Song," like many of Paul McCartney's compositions, patches together a number of disparate musical and lyrical fragments. Unlike many of McCartney's songs, Simon creates a remarkable unity out of them, here beautifully illuminating, even mimicking, the creative process Simon undergoes when composing a song. Beginning with a description of a speaker-songwriter "locked in the struggle for the right combination of words in a melody line," he tells us that this struggle leads him into his imagination, which in turn leads him to "open the book of my vanishing memory." Filled with regrets, he vows to "sit down, shut up, think about God, and wait for the hour of my rescue." Note the progression: fiddling with songcraft opens the door to his imagination, which in turn leads to the vast troubling book of memo-

ry, and to spiritual speculation. (The circle will close at the end of the
song, when spiritual speculation leads back to . . . songwriting!) The
portion of the song where he turns those troubling pages of memory is
highly percussive, apprehensive, nerve-grating—thinking about his life
sub species aeternitatus is no picnic. When he emerges from the meditations, however, he's ready to "shoot a thought into the future, through
my lifetime. And beyond." And in that beyond, he finds himself "on the
ancient road in the song when the wires are hushed." It's a frustratingly
vague line, but it and some of the phrases that end the song ("Golden
clouds," "The earth is blue") suggest that he has come out of his speculations (with its thinking about God) in a blissful space, adoring the
earth ("Everything about it is a love song") and honoring it with the
song we have just heard. In "Everything," Simon describes not just his
process of songwriting, but also his own particular form of prayer. They
turn out to be, perhaps, the same thing.

"Outrageous," spurred by crackling drums and Simon's crunchy dis-
co-era guitar riffs, starts off as one of Simon's funniest-ever songs about
a crotchety old guy making a fool of himself trying to stay young, and
then opens out into a sweet musical balm, insisting that God's love is
constant when human love wears away. The nervy jitter of the guitars
sets the mood for the speaker, who begins the song by spitting out a
barrage of random outrages—the exploitation of the poor, the lousy
food in the public schools, even the outrageousness of his own com-
plaints about what's outrageous. And he's a tired, poor man, doing nine
hundred sit-ups a day to keep in shape for his lover, and "coloring my
hair the color of mud, mud, okay?" (The disgusted way Simon pro-
nounces "mud, okay?" is a tiny smattering of comic genius.) Of course,
his real concern isn't aging, but of losing the lover: his constant question
is "who's gonna love you when your looks are gone?" And there's no
answer until the guitars shift away from their earlier freneticism (and an
aggressive one-note solo that seems to drive the speaker deeper into his
fear) to breezy, evanescent picking (and Eno's loping keyboards),
whereupon the speaker seems to finally get it: "Who's going to love you
when your looks are gone? *God will.*" Of course, he can only understand this now that "my will [has been] broken by my pride and my
vanity": he's nobody special, "just an ordinary player in the key of C."
The acceptance of God's love comes from a giving up of ego, of ambition and pride. "Outrageous" does more thinking about God, and con-

nects to Simon's musings about pride, envy, and ego in "Quiet" from *You're the One* and "Wartime Prayers" from this album.

"Sure Don't Feel Like Love," minor if wicked Simon, is about the curse of "conscience," that self-judging part of us that is always telling us we're "wrong and wrong again." It's that voice that "feels like a threat / A voice in your head that you'd rather forget": it gives us no rest and it "sure don't feel like love." The speaker is harried by his conscience, and longs for a love—or at least the comfort food of "some chicken and a corn muffin" (!)—to relieve him of his guilt. The song's essentially comical, with a speaker who tries to slyly evade the promptings of conscience and even underplays his guilt ("I remember once in August 1993 / I was wrong"), but his very underplaying only emphasizes his enslavement to it.

With "Wartime Prayers," we're back to major Simon. It's *Surprise*'s strongest (and most tender) song, a philosophical meditation on the despair of terrorism, and on the "hunger for the voice of God" in those who experience it. In its large-hearted sympathies, it echoes Don De-Lillo's great essay on 9/11, "In the Ruins of the Future," and rivals Bruce Springsteen's "The Rising" as one of pop music's most thoughtful responses to the tragedy. Beginning with Simon's melody-less musings on the meaning of prayer during peacetime, he adds, "All that is changed now" that we are at war. (In 2002, the United States invaded Afghanistan, arguing that Afghanistan was the center of activity for Al-Qaeda, the terrorist group headed up by Osama Bin Laden who were responsible for the 9/11 attacks. In 2003, the United States invaded Iraq, with the George W. Bush administration arguing that Saddam Hussein's regime sponsored global terrorism and possessed weapons of mass destruction. Weapons of mass destruction, of course, were never found. Such facts may help explain "the lunatics and liars" lines from "Wartime Prayers": the "lunatics" include Bin Laden and his terrorist cohorts, the "liars" most likely referring to Bush; his vice president, Dick Cheney; and defense secretary Donald Rumsfeld, who beat the drums for war under false pretenses.) Whereas prayer in peacetime is personal—"appeals for love and love's release"—in wartime, even those who are secular find that "when the wounds are deep enough" the pain is so unbearable that "we wrap ourselves / In prayer." The song's secular speaker presents himself as a mere "halfway decent man," but also someone who, during wartime, is "trying to tap into some wisdom /

Even a little drop will do." The song is about despair so intense that the only relief for it is the decision to give oneself up to God. One of the things that give the song its enduring power is Simon's idea to bring in the Jessy Dixon Singers as backing gospel choir. This is the same group that supplied backing for the gospel portion of *Live Rhymin'*, and the results here are spine-tingling—the lure of giving oneself up to a greater power in prayer is powerfully evoked.

The back end of the album—its final six songs—aren't as strong, but suffer only by comparison: the first half of *Surprise* is as strong as the first side of *Graceland*. The second half of *Surprise* kicks off with a two-song mini-suite about "acts of kindness," with "Beautiful" running without pause into "I Don't Believe." "Beautiful," cheerful without descending into whimsy, is about a couple who keep adopting children from poverty- or war-ridden countries, bring them home to a world of go-karts, candy stands, and summertime waterslides, and find their children, and life with them, beautiful. The last child they adopt, from war-scarred Kosovo, "cried all night / Could not sleep" when they brought him home, and that's the only—and the only necessary—shadow in this otherwise sunny celebration of good will. The song's end runs right into the wittily titled "I Don't Believe," a song whose central line is not about disbelief at all: "I don't believe a heart can be filled to the brim then vanish like mist as though life were a whim." Which is to say, "I Don't Believe" is about someone who *does* believe: believes that life's riches (laughing children, their beautiful mother, a "clear summer evening as soft as a kiss," and crucially, "acts of kindness") aren't just pleasures to be savored, but evidence of something eternal surviving the temporal. For someone of this disposition, life *can't* be a whim. The very beauty and kindness he finds in the world argues for something greater. Of course, Simon being Simon, his speaker worries even this intimation: "Maybe the heart is part of the mist," he muses: maybe our powerful intimations of transcendence are only a temporary feeling, a trick we play to convince ourselves death isn't the end. Maybe, maybe, maybe. He can't resolve the issue: he can only say, "Maybe's the exit I'm looking for," that is, the *possibility* of transcendence is what he needs in order to escape despair. As if to reinforce how much that possibility sustains him, he reiterates, at song's end, how "acts of kindness . . . release the spirit with a whoop and a shout." "I Don't Believe" is one of Simon's clearest statements about the desire to believe in the transcendent, even if the speaker here can't make that leap of faith, and if it weren't for its weak, unmemorable melody, it would be one of Simon's major songs.

A second diptych follows, comprised of two songs about escaping a stifling life. The first, "Another Galaxy," fueled by the gentle pulse of Eno's synthesizers and a thick skein of Simon's overlapping guitars, is about a would-be bride who decides on the morning of her wedding, "in a chip in time," that she can't go through with it, and leaves for "another life, another galaxy." What's notable about this well-worn scenario is the equation of "life" with "galaxy": as in so many of Simon's twenty-first-century songs, his characters' lives are lived in the context of vast spaces and possibilities, including the "maybe" of transcendence.

"Once upon a Time There Was an Ocean" hints at some of the same possibilities. Here we have a character who could be the Frank from "Darling Lorraine," only one who had the gumption to leave his unhappy marriage before it was too late. He begins by telling us he was once "an ocean"—that is, someone who was fluid, who flowed with time and circumstance—but because of the "unstoppable" circumstances of a life devoted to a "dead-end job" and the usual "burdens and strife," he's hardened into a "mountain range," rock-solid and set in his ways. Whenever the speaker describes his dead-end "mountain" of a life, Eno's synthesizers are harsh and grating; when he remembers the freedom and possibilities of those times when he was "an ocean," the music is fluid and freeing. The speaker finally leaves his life behind and moves to the city, where he says, "I'm easy / I'm open—that's my gift": he's rediscovered the ocean in himself. This is where "Another Galaxy" left off—with the exhilaration (and fear) that comes with the rediscovery of possibility. But "Once upon a Time" digs deeper. The speaker receives a letter from home in "fragile and strange" handwriting—some family member, evidently, is dying. Though he had vowed that he would never go home again, of course he does, to a funeral, where "all the old hymns and family names came fluttering down as leaves of emotion." And there he realizes that "nothing's different, but everything's changed." It's a wonderfully multivalent line: on the one hand, the speaker realizes that at the funeral he's both a boy ensconced in familiar family tradition—nothing's changed—and a man alienated from it all—everything's changed. But the line also reminds us that one of the characteristics of an ocean is that it, too, is something that changes constantly and never changes—that it unceasingly churns and ebbs and flows while seeming to us as eternal as anything gets on Earth. The speaker has escaped his life as "mountain range," but he now has to deal with a fluidity he may not have been prepared for, the fluidity that comes from recognizing that death and life are part of the same process.

Though it's not the last song on the album—"Father and Daughter," Simon's lovely, disarmingly pretty tribute to his daughter is—"That's Me" is the real album closer. With its fluttery guitar figure laid over some of Eno's more obvious, almost comical synthesizer effects (at times he sounds like he's using an old-fashioned Moog), the song covers long-combed-over Simon material. We get the biography of a guy who feels like a "land-locked sailor searching for the emerald sea." Then, in a fourth verse that is easily the most moving part of the song, love happens to him—and "the future is beauty and sorrow." This is followed by the image of the guy "walking up the face of a mountain," meditating on the stars, the past, and death. "I'm in the valley of twilight," he says, and "now on the continental shelf"—that is, slowly walking out into the ocean, presumably toward eternity. "That's me," he keeps saying, and that's true: that's Paul Simon all right, same as he ever was, always examining the past, being stunned by love, climbing a mountain, considering eternity, and thinking about God. It's not a great song—Simon seems more interested in the textures of his guitar against Eno's synths and the deeply echoed drums—but it does wrap up the album in a tight thematic grip.

SO BEAUTIFUL OR SO WHAT (2011)

On *So Beautiful or So What*, released when Simon was closing in on seventy, the pressure to make some reckoning with existence—to gather the spiritual intimations that he has been recording in his music since *Graceland* into some kind of summary statement—appears to have been intense. There's more thinking about God on *So Beautiful or So What* than on any other Paul Simon album. God (or His angels) is a manifest presence on six of the album's ten songs (even getting speaking parts on two); and one of the four on which He isn't—"Amulet"—is a guitar instrumental and mere (if quite pretty) filler. Simon invokes God in a full range of attitudes, too: in a prefatory poem/liner note,

Simon writes about his songwriting process as one in which he has "to care like hell and not give a damn at the same time," so it's no surprise that the products of his God musings veer from flimsy comedy to outright serious theological meditation. Frequently He is prayed to; once He appears as a joker who invented the Universe because "I had eons to kill" ("Love Is Eternal Sacred Light"). Another time the Lord pays "a courtesy call on Earth" with Son Jesus, only to get restless and abandon mankind to an eternal dynamic of "love and hard times" ("Love and Hard Times"). Throughout the album, God is a slippery entity—half the time He's comically anthropomorphized; the other half His presence is felt because Simon's speakers experience in their lives "simple kindness" ("Love and Blessings," which reinvocates the "acts of kindness" on *Surprise*) or, more broadly speaking, love itself. As Elvis Costello reminds us in his insightful liner notes, three song titles begin with the word *love*, and in all of them what's being referred to isn't merely the personal emotion between lovers, but the emotion of love as a manifestation of the divine. "Love Is Eternal Sacred Light" is the title of one of those songs, and that about says it all. The feeling of love isn't just the transfer of intense affection between two people, but a sign of transcendental blessing: on this album, to experience love is to wonder if one is in God's presence. "God is love," goes the New Testament's perhaps simplest and richest line (from 1 John 4:8), and Simon, whose theological speculations have leaned Christian more than Judaic since his very early days, seems to take the possibility very seriously.

Musically, the album comes off as a kind of effortless grand synthesis. For all its greatness, *Graceland* (like *The Rhythm of the Saints*) trumpets, almost ostentatiously, its distinctive blend of world music traditions. Both albums are the work of a musician in the heat of almost boyish discovery: hey, they say, look at this music I found on the other side of the world! And look what I can do with it! *So Beautiful or So What*, by contrast, is the work of someone for whom the enthusiasm of musical discovery has been quietly harnessed and sublimated into seasoned, refined craft. The Indian instrumentation in "Dazzling Blue" (and those charming "vocal syllables of percussion") is slipped into the arrangement with subdued grace. The syrup of romantic strings on "Love and Hard Times" is so subtly poured it's hard to tell how satirical they are. Even the samplings on "Getting Ready for Christmas Day" and "Love and Blessings," the most obviously new technique Simon's

brought into his repertoire here, is elegantly handled. The album genuinely sounds like Simon had nothing to prove, even to the new record
company, Hear Music, which released it: the sound is relaxed,
thoroughly professional, the work of a virtuoso going about his business,
searching for the sound—"Is it be bop a lula / Or ooh papa do" ("The
Afterlife")—that will get God's ear.

"Getting Ready for Christmas Day" opens the album with a bit of
studio trickery—the sound of the opening guitar chord is studio-altered, *bent*, as it were, slid a few notes down the musical scale until it
lands on its feet and begins, along with the drums, churning out a beat
that's infectious and gospel-like. Vincent Nguini's choppy guitar chords
sound treated, a bit synthesized, much like the voice of Reverend J. M.
Gates's sermon about Christmas, snippets of which are inserted three
times into the song and doctored so that his phrasings (and the responses of the congregation) fit precisely into the song's uncoiled spring
of a rhythm track. It's a cunning bit of studio craft, seamless-sounding
unless one's paying very close attention. Lyrically, the song is just as
cunning. The speaker begins by talking about how, during the Christmas season, with all those presents to be bought, "I got money matters
weighing me down." But then the Reverend Gates intercedes with
some perspective. (The sermon is a real one, delivered in October 1941,
and sampled from a recording put out by the extraordinary archivists at
Document Records.) His sermon brusquely cuts through the materialism of the Christmas season by reminding his congregation that while
they're "getting ready for Christmas Day . . . the undertaker, he's getting ready for your body." (To reinforce this, he later adds, "I may be
layin' in some lonesome grave, getting ready for Christmas Day.") The
song weaves details about the speaker's soldier nephew spending
Christmas "on some mountain top in Pakistan" with images of pre-Civil-
Rights-era black Americans trying to evade the jailer and the cop: all
reminders that the material obsessions of Christmas are evasions of
real-life struggles, and that we need to heed the "power and the glory
and the story of the / Christmas Day." The story, of course, is the story
of salvation, of a baby, born at the right time, to save mankind from the
despair of his fallen and mortal state. The song's energy and wit, and an
ingenuous last verse ("If I could tell my Mom and Dad that the things
we never had / Never mattered we were always okay"), keep the song

from sounding pedantic: instead, it succeeds in achieving the spirit of a revival meeting, joyful and enthusiastic.

"The Afterlife," whose swaying rhythm sounds like it might come from the churn of an accordion but seems to be a product of Simon's studio-altered guitar, is one of Simon's loveliest late-career compositions, so light on its feet that it feels graced, lucked into by an artist—usually bound to complexity—coming upon a fairy tale of the most lucid simplicity. Here we've got a guy who dies and enters the afterlife only to realize it's very much like modern life—it's bureaucratic ("You got to fill out a form first / And then you wait in the line") and, as in life, "it seems like our fate / Is to suffer and wait / For the knowledge we seek." But, because this is a fairy tale, the speaker finally gets to meet "The Lord God . . . face-to-face," whereupon he feels like he's "swimming in an ocean of love." He wants to speak, but the only thing that comes out "Is a fragment of song." And what is that fragment? Either it's "be bop a lula" or "ooh Papa Doo." In either case, all he can communicate to God is the essence of rock 'n' roll music, those glossolalic sounds that limn the passionate core of what rock 'n' roll has always tried to express. "The Afterlife," in the end, is a rock 'n' roll fable: it says that what all rock 'n' roll is doing—during its whole history, from Little Richard on down—is trying to talk to God, and waiting, as the speaker does here, for God's response.

Of all the songs that seem inspired by Edie Brickell—"Thelma," "That's Where I Belong," "Love," "Love and Hard Times"—"Dazzling Blue" is the most sheerly beautiful, with sweetly satisfying melody lines for verse, bridge, *and* chorus (a rare trifecta for any songwriter), Indian instruments backing an instantly memorable guitar figure, and lyrical sentiment that's tenderly romantic yet credible and *earned*. Before he met her, the speaker says, he lived in a world where illness and possibly death threatened ("the CAT scan's eyes sees what the heart's concealing"), where distance separated lovers, and where "maybe love's an accident, or destiny is true." But when he finds this woman, the speaker knows that *this* love was "born beneath a star of dazzling blue": that is, no accident—pure destiny. He remembers the miracle of a summer walk along the cliffs off the Montauk Highway when the two lovers imagined a future together, and suddenly there they are, their dreams coming true, lying together in a marriage bed among a cache of roses, under the dazzling blue star that harbingered their happiness. The music is carried by the generosity of the melodies and harmony vocals so lush they could easily be suited for Simon and Garfunkel. "Dazzling Blue" may be the most romantic song Simon has written since "For Emily, Wherever I May Find Her," only the idealization of love here feels earned, the product of a man who's waited decades for his chance and can fully appreciate love's gifts. It's also a song whose personal feeling is so strong that it approaches the transcendental: though Simon isn't explicit, the suggestion here is that love born under a star of dazzling blue is love born under the watchful eye of God.

"Rewrite" has the tender comic pathos of short-story writer George Saunders or filmmaker Lasse Hallstrom. Featuring some impressive guitar work by Simon backed by West African percussion instruments and a kora (a twenty-one-stringed instrument that looks a little like a banjo and sounds a little like a harp), the instrumentation and vocal melody line are light and whimsical, which befit the song's subject. "Rewrite" is about a Vietnam Vet who "Hasn't got a brain cell left / since Vietnam"; he works (by day, and for free, evidently) at a car wash, and at night works on a screenplay that he dreams he can "turn . . . into cash." But he's stuck: the screenplay is evidently autobiographical, with scenes about a father breaking down and leaving his family, and he prays to God to help him rewrite it. What's funny is that he instantly feels he's being listened to: "Help me, help me / *Thank you*! / I had no idea / That you were there." Is the guy just deluded? Maybe. By the end, he changes the screenplay to include a scene where "the father saves the children / And holds them in his arms," but as silly as he seems, his belief isn't: it has the very childhood innocence that Jesus called on his adult followers to imitate. The portrait of this guy makes him seem both moving and dumb . . . so beautiful and so what.

"Love and Hard Times" and "Love Is Eternal Sacred Life," placed smack in the middle of the album, are the album's obvious thematic centerpieces, though they're not necessarily the best songs. "Love and Hard Times" is certainly stronger lyrically than musically. As with many of his late-period songs, Simon tries to get by without a strong melody, relying more on sound-atmosphere and subtle vocal effects to keep the listener attending to him. (Over the years, Simon may have gotten bored by pop melodies, feeling the hummability requirement as a restraint on his creativity. He may find he can't stay interested in writing certain songs unless he invents complex, "sophisticated" runs of vocal notes that stray far from the pop mainstream. I find most of his melody-eschewing songs less involving—perhaps because they seem self-involved—but, to invoke a title from *Surprise*, that's me.) The lyrics open with God and Christ coming down to earth one Sunday to check out His creation. The earth receives the Lord with blossoming trees and singing birds—the comic orchestral arrangement is like an ironized version of an old Disney movie celebrating "nature"—but God, saying, "people are slobs here," is eager to get going. He will "disappear," He says, leaving the world to "love and hard times." And that's what the rest of the song chronicles: God-abandoned lovers falling in love—again we hear that comic orchestral arrangement—suffering the hard times when "the rains come / the tears burned," when the heartbeat is "uneasy" or the lovers are "out of control," and finally yielding to a sort of desperate reconciliation—"your hand takes mine"—whereupon the speaker, in a paroxysm of relief, sighs over and over, "Thank God I found you." Simon sings that last line with unusual passion—he sounds like he means it—and it's moving, but it doesn't quite make up for the labored, meandering music that precedes it. But note the song's meaning: God comes, and God goes, leaving behind hard times but also the possibility of love to endure it. People then find love and thank God for providing it. Romantic love is evidence of God's existence.

"Love Is Eternal Sacred Light" picks up on this notion that the earthly emotion of love is God's gift to mankind, though this song's God is even more sardonically characterized than in the previous song—here, he comes on like a knowingly negligent father who can't get himself to pay his child support. In a low, gravelly voice, he admits he made the universe as a joke, and that those pesky humans are always praying to Him that He love them. His response? "Well you know I love all my children / And it tears me up when I leave." (Not much it doesn't, one wants to respond.) So, here's another God abandoning his children to love and hard times. In this song, however, the human speaker's response to abandonment isn't tentative, as it is in the previous song. It is to assert love's "eternal sacred" nature more than ever: the entire refrain, sung to a galloping beat that builds momentum as it goes, runs roughshod over all doubt. Does that mean that Simon's asserting that love is eternal sacred light, evidence of God's existence? Hardly. He seems to be saying only what love feels like to human beings, caught up as they are in life's manifold confusions. The title refrain is spoken by a speaker, and that voice carries no more weight than the happily deluded screenwriter of "Rewrite" or the desperate lovers in "Love and Hard Times."

After the pretty instrumental interlude of "Amulet"—Simon plays crisp and deeply echoed jazz acoustic guitar (and also, if one listens carefully, occasionally hums to the music, like a pop Glenn Gould)—the mood shifts, in "Questions for the Angels," from sardonic to sincere once again. Backed mostly by acoustic guitar and a few other instrumental touches, the song would sound at home on *Still Crazy after All These Years* (though it's recorded much better than anything from the 1970s albums), though its theme is all late-innings Simon. Here we have a homeless man walking from Manhattan across the Brooklyn Bridge asking "questions for the angels." Some of the questions are practical ("Where will I make my bed tonight?"), some intriguingly, poetically speculative ("If an empty train in a railroad station / Calls you to its destination / Can you choose another track?"). At first, the homeless speaker himself wonders, "Who believes in Angels?," and answers, "Fools do." But when the question comes around again in the next chorus, his answer has changed: "I do," and the album picks up another believer, this one much like the others: in desperate straits, searching, and willing to suspend cynicism and disbelief in the hopes that the "Maybe" of God's love (recall *Surprise*'s "I Don't Believe") is really there.

"Love and Blessings" sustains the sincere mood of theological search. With Simon overlaying at least three guitar parts himself (including a synthesized guitar) and bringing in his daughter Lulu to sing back-up, Simon hearkens back to the "acts of kindness" theme from *Surprise*. Here, the speaker sings about the blessings of love and prosperity that, in the past, "fell like rain on thirsty land." Then the refrain kicks in, in which Simon samples a 1938 recording in which a black vocal group, the Golden Gate Jubilee Quartet, sings "Bop-bop-a-whoa" over and over, each line interlineated by Simon adding a line himself, like "Ain't no time like a good time, Charlie." The mood here is one of nostalgic buoyancy, a time when music is really the great expression of human happiness and gratitude for being (as in "The Afterlife," "Bop-bop-a-whoa" is how we talk to God), and the music really does effectively convey a time of "love and blessings." But when Simon returns to the verse, he has the speaker tell us that the rain has stopped (climate change is hinted at), and that "Came the autumn, drained of color / Maple trees just a little bit duller," signifying that the time of love and blessings is over. In the song's coda, the speaker reminds us that "love and kindness" are "ours to hold but not to keep"—temporary treasures that are all the more precious for their fleetingness.

The album, and this study, concludes with the title tune, propelled by a danceable (if repetitive) "Nawlins"-inflected rockabilly groove that's likely to get live audiences on their feet (not always guaranteed at a Paul Simon concert). It's his most Dylanesque song in ages—that is, the kind of song that rides an electric guitar riff hard and deep and spits out a bunch of associated lyrical observations, all held together by a central theme. Simon's song, more than anything, is a commentary on how he approaches his own music: on the poem/liner note on the CD sleeve, Simon alludes to the fact that while a piece of music may be "a thing of beauty," he also realizes it's not quite necessary to the world— that is to say: "Who needs it?" (He touches here on exactly the title theme of Elvis Costello's album, *All This Useless Beauty*, which may help explain Costello's endorsement of the record.) In other words, he's wondering what any musician occasionally wonders about his own work: given all the trouble in the world, given all the trouble in my own life (much of it caused by my obsession with music!), so what if my music sometimes is beautiful? What is the point of useless beauty? And the only answer he gives in the poem/liner note, and in the song, is that the question is unanswerable, or that we must give two diametrically opposed answers. Music is simultaneously "so beautiful"—that is, undeniable and unquestionably precious—and "so what"—that is, pointless, idle decoration in a desecrated world—and music, like life itself, "is what you make of it." Go ahead and sing "Be-bop a lu la," "Ooh papa doo," or "Bop bop a whoa"—one can, if one chooses to, make those phrases nothing less than offerings to God and man, as they are in "The Afterlife" and "Love and Blessings." We can, similarly—if we choose to—see romantic love, and acts of kindness, as evidence of God's presence. Or not. It all depends on the "maybe" in "I Don't Believe," the psychic bargain one makes to either believe in some benign transcendent presence or not.

Paul Simon's twenty-first-century albums hone in more and more on that "maybe," dramatizing it over and over again with different characters and different settings, and never coming down on one side or the other. In his seventies, he remains perched on that "maybe," "so what's" desolation on one side, a "so beautiful" graceland on the other. It's the ultimate thematic tension of his greatest music. Long may he waver.

FURTHER READING

Brantley, Ben. "The Lure of Gang Violence to a Latin Beat." *New York Times*, January 30, 1998. Available online at www.nytimes.com/mem/theater/treview.html?_r=4& res=9A01EFDF143AF933A05752C0A96E958260&. Accessed February 8, 2014. The infamous *New York Times* theater review that helped seal the fate of *The Capeman* on Broadway.

Christgau, Robert. *Christgau's Record Guide: Rock Albums of the '70s*. New Haven and New York: Ticknor & Fields, 1981. The first of Christgau's go-to record guides, containing thousands of capsule reviews of records released in the 1970s. Essential rock writing.

———. "South African Romance." In *The Paul Simon Companion: Four Decades of Commentary*, edited by Stacey Luftig, 180–88. New York: Schirmer Books, 1997. One of the most thoughtful considerations of the controversy surrounding the *Graceland* album.

Cocks, Jay. "Songs of a Thinking Man." In *The Paul Simon Companion: Four Decades of Commentary*, edited by Stacey Luftig, 198–203. New York: Schirmer Books, 1997.

DeLillo, Don. "In The Ruins of the Future." *Harper's Magazine*, December 2001, 33-40. Great (and rapid) response to the extraordinary events of September 11, 2001, by one of America's most important writers. To be read while listening to "How Can You Live in the Northeast?" and "Wartime Prayers" from *Surprise*.

Eliot, Marc. *Paul Simon: A Life*. Hoboken, NJ: John Wiley & Sons, 2010. Biography that takes Simon's life up through 2009. Vividly written but badly in need of fact-checking. Contains decent discography, though.

Fisher, Carrie. *Wishful Drinking*. New York: Simon & Schuster, 2008. One of Fisher's memoirs, containing, among much snark, her thoughts on Simon's songs about her.

"Gershwin Prize for Popular Song." www.loc.gov/about/awardshonors/gershwin. Accessed January 4, 2013.

Gitlin, Todd. *The Sixties: Years of Hope, Days of Rage*. New York: Bantam, 1987. One of the best chronicles of the 1960s, written by one of its vital participants.

Humphries, Patrick. *Paul Simon: Still Crazy after All These Years*. New York: Doubleday, 1988. Reliable biography written in the wake of *Graceland*'s success.

Jackson, Laura. *Paul Simon: The Definitive Biography*. New York: Kensington, 2002. Decent if hardly definitive biography of the artist.

Kingston, Victoria. *Simon & Garfunkel: The Biography*. London: Sidgwick and Jackson, 1996. A biography that deals with the lives of both artists, before, during, and after their break-up.

Landau, Jon. "The Rolling Stone Interview with Paul Simon." In *The Paul Simon Companion: Four Decades of Commentary*, edited by Stacey Luftig, 79–107. New York: Schirmer

Books, 1997. One of the most insightful interviews with Simon, conducted just as Simon's solo career was taking off.

Luftig, Stacey, ed. *The Paul Simon Companion: Four Decades of Commentary* . New York: Schirmer Books, 1997. Strong collection of essays, interviews, and reviews of Simon's work.

Lyman, Rick. "After 'Capeman,' a Chill in a Thriving Broadway Season." *New York Times*, March 7, 1998. A post-mortem on *The Capeman's* failure by the paper of record.

Marcus, Greil. "Review of Bob Dylan's *Self-Portrait*." In *Rolling Stone Record Review*, 514–30. New York: Pocket Books, 1971. The most famous (and negative) Bob Dylan review ever written by perhaps the greatest writer on rock in America.

Martin, Dan. "I Don't Like to Be Second to Bob Dylan." *The Guardian*, May 12, 2011. Available online at www.theguardian.com/music/2011/may/12/paul-simon-bob-dylan. Accessed December 12, 2013.

Mitchell, Joni. "Free Man in Paris." *Court and Spark*. Asylum Records 7E-1001, 1974.

Morella, Joseph, and Patricia Barey. *Simon and Garfunkel: Old Friends—A Dual Biography*. New York: Birch Lane Books, 1991. Useful co-biography of Simon & Garfunkel, taking the pair through the late 1980s.

Reid, Graham. "Paul Simon Interviewed (2000): The Attraction of Opposites." *Elsewhere*. www.elsewhere.co.nz/absoluteelsewhere/463/paul-simon-interviewed-2000-the-attraction-of-opposites. Accessed August 8, 2013. An excellent interview by a British journalist/critic conducted at the time of the release of *You're the One*.

Rolling Stone. *The Rolling Stone Record Review*. New York: Pocket Books, 1971. An eye-opening (naïve, excitable, very 1960s) collection of early rock criticism from *Rolling Stone*.

Schwartz, Tony. "Playboy Interview: Paul Simon." *Playboy*, February 1984. Available online at http://bkc.mikovice.com/small%20black%20beetles/paul%20simon%20playboy%20interview.pdf. Accessed June 12, 2013. Long and fascinating interview with Simon conducted in the wake of *Hearts and Bones'* release. Contains some of Simon's most revealing comments about Garfunkel, his first marriage, and the depression that followed the failure of *One-Trick Pony*.

Simon, Paul. *One-Trick Pony*. New York: Knopf, 1980. Simon's underwhelming screenplay.

Zollo, Paul. *Songwriters on Songwriting*. 4th edition. Cambridge, MA: DaCapo Press, 2003. An extraordinary compilation of interviews with songwriters conducted by the indefatigable Zollo. Contains a comprehensive interview with a brilliant and sometimes-acerbic Simon.

FURTHER LISTENING

The albums listed below include all of Paul Simon's studio albums, with Art Garfunkel or on his own, as well as live albums, and most of the best-ofs and box sets. Simon's catalogue has been subjected to the usual record-company pillaging: there have been countless CD reissues and remasterings, often supplemented with bonus tracks, as well as anniversary editions, various compilations, and repackagings. (Almost all the bonus tracks are live or alternate versions of existing songs; there are very few new songs released as bonus tracks.) I've felt no need to be an absolute completist here: if a reissue includes truly significant new material, I've included information about it; if not, I haven't. I've included no single releases, or other artists' releases that included Simon as singer or guitarist.(Other artist's songs or albums I've mentioned in the text are, of course, easily found by an online search.) The albums listed here were all in print at the time of publication; needless to say, additional live or compilations collections may appear at any time, as might (we all hope) new Paul Simon studio material. Because this book is most interested in his songwriting, official studio recordings containing new material are noted with an asterisk (*).

PRE-1964 MATERIAL

Tom & Jerry Meet Tico & the Triumphs. Hallmark. 2012. One of many unauthorized collections of early material, this one is an English import, available for purchase online, and collects twenty tracks originally released on 45-RPM singles between 1957 and 1962, all written by the young Simon and performed by Paul Simon with and occasionally without

Art Garfunkel, and performing under the names Tom & Jerry, Jerry Landis, Tico & the Triumphs, and other pseudonyms. Well-crafted stuff by a teen go-getter.

SIMON & GARFUNKEL

°*Wednesday Morning, 3 A.M.* Columbia Records. 1964. Tepid debut featuring folk chestnuts, a Bob Dylan cover, and five original Simon compositions, including the first acoustic version of "The Sound of Silence."

°*Sounds of Silence.* Columbia Records. 1965. The breakthrough album, most of it quickly recorded folk-rock, featuring the electrified "The Sound of Silence" and "I Am a Rock," a cache of memorable melodies and some poor stabs at poetic heaviness.

°*Parsley, Sage, Rosemary, and Thyme.* Columbia Records. 1966. The first album that Simon could spend time writing and recording. Highlights include "Scarborough Fair/Canticle" and "Homeward Bound." Lowlight: that nadir of Simon-ish pretension, "The Dangling Conversation."

The Graduate (movie soundtrack). Columbia Records. 1968. Massive hit album featuring only a sliver of new Simon & Garfunkel music. Includes two versions of "The Sound of Silence," two snippets that would eventually become "Mrs. Robinson," and lots of movie mood music by Dave Grusin.

°*Bookends.* Columbia Records. 1968. Simon's first real statement record, written and produced in the wake of 1960s concept albums like *Sgt. Pepper*, which took more than a year to record. Includes the outstanding "America" on its side-long suite concerning aging and time, plus a definitive version of "Mrs. Robinson."

°*Bridge Over Troubled Water.* Columbia Records. 1970. Reissue by Sony Legacy in 2011 includes the DVD documentaries "Songs of America" and "The Harmony Game." Megaselling final studio album by the duo, featuring the title workhorse, plus "The Boxer," "El Condor Pasa," and "The Only Living Boy in New York." Pop songwriting and performance at a very high level.

Simon & Garfunkel's Greatest Hits (best-of). Columbia Records. 1972. For a few years, the best-selling album of all time. Contains all the undeniable hits, plus a live version of "For Emily, Whenever I Might Find Her."

The Concert in Central Park (live). Warner Bros. 1982. The live reunion album. Solid and tasteful but . . . you probably had to be there.

Old Friends (three-CD best-of box set). Columbia Records. 1997. A superbly put-together box set, containing all their best work, plus fifteen unreleased tracks, most of them live recordings of previously released songs. With its informative booklet, it's as definitive a Simon & Garfunkel document as we are likely to get.

Live 1969. Columbia Records. 2006. A live album recorded at various sites during the duo's fall 1969 tour, prior to the release of *Bridge Over Troubled Water*. Contains a Carnegie Hall performance of "Bridge," till then unheard by anyone in the hall. The audience response is worth the price of the album.

PAUL SIMON SOLO MATERIAL

°*The Paul Simon Songbook.* CBS International. 1965. Reissued by Columbia Records 2004. Reportedly recorded very quickly in an English studio, this guitar-and-voice-only album contains early versions of "I Am a Rock," "April Come She Will," and other songs that will appear on subsequent Simon & Garfunkel albums.

°*Paul Simon.* Columbia Records. 1972. The first real solo album. Stripped of the studio gloss of late Simon & Garfunkel, with emphasis on acoustic blues, and containing "Duncan,"

"Mother and Child Reunion," and "Peace Like a River," Simon's greatest unheralded song.

°*There Goes Rhymin' Simon*. Columbia Records. 1973. Album that continued Simon's commercial winning streak with the hits "Loves Me Like a Rock" and "Kodachrome," but most notable for Simon's mournful, beautifully melancholy state-of-the-union address, "American Tune."

Paul Simon in Concert: Live Rhymin'. Columbia Records. 1974. Solo Simon in concert, taking risks. Includes rousing gospel backup by the Jessy Dixon Singers and tender instrumental backup by the Peruvian folk group Urabamba. Album photo shows Simon with the worst haircut of his life.

°*Still Crazy after All These Years*. Columbia Records. 1975. The crowning achievement of Simon's early solo career, a Grammy magnet that spun off multiple hit singles, including the wish-you-could-get-it out-of-your-head "50 Ways to Leave Your Lover." Still, perhaps the saddest and most depressed album of his career, mostly about the dissolution of his first marriage.

Greatest Hits, etc. Columbia Records. 1977. A sensible best-of, with the sublime addition of the new "Slip-Sliding Away." Columbia Records' attempt to cash in before Simon exited the label.

°*One-Trick Pony*. Warner Brothers. 1980. A surprisingly wan, limp soundtrack of Simon's wan, limp film. "Late in the Evening," "Ace in the Hole," and "One-Trick Pony" supply a little life. CD reissue contains the sweet simulated 1960s protest song "Soft Parachutes."

°*Hearts and Bones*. Warner Brothers. 1983. His most personally embattled album, with Simon struggling with depression, Art Garfunkel, Carrie Fisher, modern recording techniques, and the shadow of his failed film. The results are uneven, but the highs—"Allergies," "Hearts and Bones," "Song about the Moon," "Rene and Georgette Magritte . . . ," and both versions of "Think Too Much"—are some of the highest of his career.

°*Graceland*. Warner Brothers. 1986. Twenty-fifth anniversary edition, including a DVD documentary titled *Under African Skies* and five alternate versions or demos of studio tracks. Released by Sony Legacy. 2012. The pinnacle of Simon's career, a minor miracle of modern pop containing the most joyful music of his life, an often-sublime mélange that uncovered "the roots of rhythm" that American pop and South African music share. A "world-music" classic, it also shows an advance in Simon's lyrics, utilizing a looser, more associative and subconscious exploration of Simon's long-considered themes.

°*The Rhythm of the Saints*. Warner Brothers. 1990. Reissued by Sony Legacy. 2004. Simon's second album-length foray into "world music," this time with Brazilian and West African musicians. Percussion heavy and more abstruse lyrically, it's an able but considerably more subdued follow-up to *Graceland*. "Born at the Right Time" and "Further to Fly" are highlights. The Sony reissue contains the first American release of "Thelma."

Paul Simon's Concert in the Park (live). Sony. 1991. Simon's vindication as a live solo performer. Extremely well recorded, it concentrates mostly on *Graceland* and *Rhythm* compositions, and features only five Simon & Garfunkel songs, four of which come as end-of-the-show nostalgia nuggets.

°*Songs from "The Capeman."* Warner Brothers. 1997. Simon released this solo album ahead of the Broadway opening of the musical. The first five songs are fairly strong, particularly "Born in Puerto Rico" and "Satin Summer Nights," but the last eight already suggest how much trouble the musical was in.

The Capeman (Broadway soundtrack). 1998. Available only as a download, this recording features all thirty-nine songs in the show that at least allows one to follow the plot. Expertly performed by a multinational set of musicians and sung by the original Broadway cast, it's still stuffed with too many songs that are labored or forgettable. Simon appears only on "Trailways Bus."

°*You're the One*. Warner Brothers. 2000. A modest "comeback" album whose arrangements are quieter and more streamlined than anything he'd done since *One-Trick Pony*. Contains "Darling Lorraine," one of his greatest songs, and "Hurricane Eye," one of his most ambitious.

The Paul Simon Collection: On My Way, Don't Know Where I'm Going (best-of). Warner Brothers. 2002. A single-CD best-of, necessarily skimpy: a sampler for the casual fan.

°*Surprise*. Warner Brothers. 2006. An aural surprise, this collaboration with rock avant-gardist Brian Eno contains Simon's most "modern" and electronically assisted music. Features his responses to 9/11 in "How Can You Live in the Northeast?" and "Wartime Prayers," and his great comic hymn to aging, "Outrageous."

The Essential Paul Simon (best-of). Sony. 2010. A two-CD set containing thirty-seven tracks, a sensible if predictable selection from his first solo album through *Surprise*.

Songwriter (best-of). Sony. 2002. A British release, this is also a two-CD best-of, thirty-two tracks this time, which mostly duplicates *The Essential Paul Simon* but includes four Simon & Garfunkel songs, two of them performed live, and one of them, "Bridge Over Troubled Water," performed in her classic version by Aretha Franklin.

°*So Beautiful or So What*. Hear Music. 2011. One of the great late-life albums ever recorded, this album comes off as the work of a casual master, particularly on "Dazzling Blue," "Rewrite," and "Getting Ready for Christmas Day."

Live in New York City (includes concert DVD). Hear Music. 2012. Recorded during his run at Webster Hall in 2011, this CD gives us twenty songs from all periods of his career. Still in quality voice, Simon pulls out some surprises—"The Only Living Boy in New York" and "That Was Your Mother"—as well as hits the highlights.

Over the Bridge of Time. Sony. 2013. Another skimpy single-CD best-of, six of whose twenty songs come from the Simon & Garfunkel era. Another Sony attempt to cash in on a younger audience. Skippable.

The Complete Albums Collection (fourteen-CD box set). Sony. 2013. Just what it says. Includes all solo studio albums, plus *Live Rhymin'*, *Paul Simon's Concert in the Park*, and *Songs from "The Capeman."*

NOTES

INTRODUCTION

1. Paul Zollo, *Songwriters on Songwriting*, 4th ed. (Cambridge, MA: Da-Capo Press, 2003), 115.

1. A KID FROM QUEENS

1. From Tony Schwartz, "Playboy Interview: Paul Simon," *Playboy*, February 1984, available online at http://bkc.mikovice.com/small%20black%20beetles/paul%20simon%20playboy%20interview.pdf (accessed June 12, 2013).

2. "Gershwin Prize for Popular Song," www.loc.gov/about/awardshonors/gershwin (accessed January 4, 2013).

3. We might add "remote Amazonian villages" to the list of places one might hear Simon's songs. Simon tells the story of a trip to the Amazon he took in 1989: "We stopped in this Indian village. It was bigger than just huts; it had houses. It had two streets in it. And we passed a store where two kids were playing the guitar, a boy and a girl. They were maybe late teens or early twenties. And I was with my son. And they sang "The Sound of Silence." In Spanish. And they didn't know who I was. So then we sang "The Sound of Silence." They said, "Oh, you know that, too?" I said, "Yeah, I know that, too." Zollo, 229.

4. Joseph Morella and Patricia Barey, *Simon and Garfunkel: Old Friends—A Dual Biography* (New York: Birch Lane Books, 1991), 5.

5. Schwartz, "Playboy Interview: Paul Simon."

6. Schwartz, "Playboy Interview: Paul Simon."

7. Marc Eliot, *Paul Simon: A Life* (Hoboken, NJ: John Wiley & Sons, 2010), 13.

8. Patrick Humphries, *Paul Simon: Still Crazy after All These Years* (New York: Doubleday, 1988), 21.

9. Morella and Barey, *Simon and Garfunkel*, 87.

10. In his Playboy interview, Simon reminisces about those early Tom & Jerry days: "During this time we were singing together, I made a solo record. And it made Artie very unhappy. He looked upon it as something of a betrayal. That sense of betrayal has remained with him. That solo record that I made at the age of 15 permanently colored our relationship. We were talking about it recently and I said, 'Artie, for Christ's sake, I was 15 years old! How can you carry that betrayal for 25 years? Even if I was wrong, I was just a 15-year-old kid who wanted to be Elvis Presley for one moment instead of being the Everly Brothers with you. Even if you were hurt, let's drop it.' But he won't. . . . He said, 'You're still the same guy.' And he thinks I am." Tony Schwartz, "Playboy Interview: Paul Simon."

11. Greil Marcus, "Review of Bob Dylan's *Self-Portrait*," in *Rolling Stone Record Review*, 514–30 (New York: Pocket Books, 1971).

12. Humphries, *Paul Simon*, 97.

13. Joni Mitchell, "Free Man in Paris," *Court and Spark*, Asylum Records 7E-1001, 1974.

14. Eliot, *Paul Simon*, 186.

15. Humphries, *Paul Simon*, 122.

16. Eliot, *Paul Simon*, 214.

2. THE STRUGGLE FOR ORIGINALITY

1. Humphries, 37–38.

2. Simon's early work, which was recorded under the names Tom & Jerry, Tico and the Triumphs, Jerry Landis, and Paul Kane, have been collected legitimately as well as by bootleggers over the years. An album titled *Tom & Jerry,* which gathered his first four singles together with two new songs, was actually recorded in 1959, but it wasn't released until 1967, after Simon & Garfunkel became stars. At the time, Simon, embarrassed by his early work, tried to suppress the release, to no avail. Since then, various collections have been released in Europe, and are easily accessible for purchase over the Web. The collection I have been listening to is titled *Tom & Jerry Meet Tico & the Triumphs*, which brings together twenty of Simon's songs on a single CD. A

complete discography of his pre–Simon & Garfunkel work is available in Marc Eliot's *Paul Simon: A Life* (Hoboken, NJ: John Wiley & Sons, 2010), 253–55.

3. Simon's liner notes are painfully awkward: self-mocking ("I start with the knowledge that everything I write will turn and laugh at me"), they aim for hard-headed cynicism, but achieve only risible affectation.

4. Schwartz, "Playboy Interview: Paul Simon."

5. There's plenty of argument about who actually made the LP the dominant artistic format for the release of pop music—one could make cases for everyone from Frank Sinatra (*September of My Years*, 1965) to Frank Zappa (*Freak Out!*, 1966), and I cite Dylan partially for convenience, partially because the best case—which would take too long to make here—can be made for him.

6. There is one more ironic twist for students of the T. S. Eliot–Paul Simon connection. As Eliot fans know from his great essay, "Tradition and the Individual Talent," Eliot believed that true poetry issued only from writers who effaced their personality when they wrote, who purified their personalities out of existence in the crucible of art's "tradition." For our purposes, the irony is that Paul Simon only liberated himself from Eliot's shadow when he finally took Eliot's advice—when he stopped thinking of his writing as pure personal expression, when he rid himself of his personality.

7. Morella and Barey, 104.

8. Long unavailable after its one and only airing on television in December 1969, *Songs of America* was finally released as part of the 2011 re-release of the *Bridge Over Troubled Water* CD, a package that also featured the original album as well as a new documentary on the making of the album titled *The Harmony Game*.

9. One listen to the performance of "Bridge" on *Simon & Garfunkel Live 1969* (a CD not released until 2008) confirms for any skeptical listener the initial impact of the song. The Carnegie Hall audience, which was hearing the song for the first time, listens respectfully as the song begins—Simon & Garfunkel's audiences tended to be almost comically solemn before their heroes, as if the duo were oracular—but at the end, as Garfunkel's vocal soars over the piano's final chords, the audience erupts as if stunned by what it had just heard, and as if they clearly knew they were witness to an important bit of pop history.

3. IN THE AGE'S MOST UNCERTAIN HOURS

1. The speech can be viewed on Youtube at www.youtube.com/
watch?v=kakFDUeoJKM. The full text of the speech can be accessed at http://
millercenter.org/scripps/archive/speeches/detail/3402.

2. Robert Christgau, *Christgau's Record Guide: Rock Albums of the '70s*
(New Haven and New York: Ticknor & Fields, 1981), 354.

3. In a 1972 interview, he explains: "Last summer we had a dog that was
run over and killed, and we loved this dog. It was the first death I had ever
experienced personally. Nobody in my family died that I felt that. But I felt this
loss—one minute there, the next minute gone, and then my first thought was,
'Oh man, what if that was Peggy? What if somebody like that died? Death,
what is it, I can't get it.'" Jon Landau, "The Rolling Stone Interview with Paul
Simon," in *The Paul Simon Companion: Four Decades of Commentary*, edited
by Stacey Luftig, 79–107 (New York: Schirmer Books, 1997). If the song
doesn't "get" death—how many songs do?—it certainly evokes the feeling of
not getting it.

4. That "Tenderness" is about his relationship with Peggy is clear enough
from this comment in a 1984 interview: "[Peggy] could be critical. At first, I
was attracted to it I liked it that somebody was critical, because I felt that I was
someone who was praised too much. And I thought, Finally, someone who's
honest. But I began not to like it." Schwartz, "Playboy Interview: Paul Simon."

4. MISTAKES ON TOP OF MISTAKES ON TOP OF MISTAKES

1. Paul Simon, from the *Graceland* DVD.
2. Paul Simon, *One-Trick Pony* (New York: Knopf, 1980), 30
3. Eliot, 169.
4. Schwartz, "Playboy Interview: Paul Simon."
5. Eliot, *Paul Simon*, 179.

5. DAYS OF MIRACLE AND WONDER

1. Humphries, 120.
2. The controversy about the album and tour is usefully chronicled in
Humphries, *Paul Simon*, 120–46, as well as in part three of Stacey Luftig, *The
Paul Simon Companion: Four Decades of Commentary* (New York: Schirmer
Books, 1997), 149–88, which gathers several essays and articles about *Grace-*

land. Particularly penetrating is Robert Christgau's piece ("South African Romance," 180–88). Also useful in this respect are the interviews and discussions
contained in the documentary DVD titled *Under African Skies*, available in the
twenty-fifth-anniversary edition of *Graceland*.

3. Rick Lyman, "After 'Capeman,' a Chill in a Thriving Broadway Season,"
New York Times, March 7, 1998.

4. Zollo, 95.

5. Humphries, *Paul Simon*, 128.

6. Humphries, *Paul Simon*, 129.

7. Eliot, 191fn.

8. www.popmatters.com/review/152039-paul-simon-80s-remasters (accessed January 24, 2014).

9. Carrie Fisher, *Wishful Drinking* (New York: Simon & Schuster, 2008).

10. Jay Cocks, "Songs of a Thinking Man," Luftig, 198–203.

11. Ben Brantley, "The Lure of Gang Violence to a Latin Beat," *New York
Times*, January 30, 1998, available online at www.nytimes.com/mem/theater/
treview.html?_r=4&res=9A01EFDF143AF933A05752C0A96E958260& (accessed February 8, 2014).

6. THINKING ABOUT GOD

1. Graham Reid, "Paul Simon Interviewed (2000): The Attraction of Opposites," *Elsewhere*, www.elsewhere.co.nz/absoluteelsewhere/463/paul-simon-
interviewed-2000-the-attraction-of-opposites (accessed August 8, 2013).

2. Dan Martin, "I Don't Like to Be Second to Bob Dylan," *The Guardian*,
May 12, 2011, available online at www.theguardian.com/music/2011/may/12/
paul-simon-bob-dylan (accessed December 12, 2013).

INDEX

ABOUT THE AUTHOR

Cornel Bonca is a professor of English and comparative literature at California State University, Fullerton, where he teaches the contemporary novel, creative writing, and courses in rock 'n' roll history. His cultural journalism, fiction, and literary criticism have appeared in two dozen publications, including *Salon*, the *New York Observer*, the *Los Angeles Review of Books*, and *Modern Language Studies*, where he's written on David Foster Wallace, Bruce Springsteen, Don DeLillo, 9/11, the beat poets, Philip Roth, and the band The Airborne Toxic Event. He lives in Costa Mesa, California, with his wife and three children.